Feminism

& Ecology

Feminism & Ecology

Mary Mellor

NEW YORK UNIVERSITY PRESS
Washington Square, New York

Published in 1997 by Polity Press, U.K.

First published in the U.S.A. in 1997 by
NEW YORK UNIVERSITY PRESS
Washington Square
New York, N.Y.   10003

CIP data available from the Library of Congress

ISBN 0-8147-5600-X (hardcover)
ISBN 0-8147-5601-8 (paperback)

Printed in Great Britain

Contents

Preface

The aims of this book are to explore the relationship between feminism and ecology and identify the radical potential of feminist and ecological thought. Feminism and ecology are brought together in the ecofeminist assertion that women's subordination and ecological degradation are linked. This claim is examined through an exploration of political activism around women and the environment and the development of ecofeminist thought, together with responses to it from other radical, feminist and green perspectives.

In arguing for the radical potential of a link between feminism and ecology I do not claim that women are somehow essentially closer to 'nature', but rather that it is not possible to understand the ecologically destructive consequences of dominant trends in human development without understanding their gendered nature. The central theme in this analysis is the materiality of human existence. Put simply, human beings as human animals have bodies which must be developed and nurtured. These bodies, in turn, are embedded in a natural environment. Social theories that do not take account of this essential feature of human existence are starting from the false premise that human actors are disembodied and disembedded. It is not surprising, therefore, that in practice these actors turn out to be white, male, mobile and relatively self-determining as a result of economic and social privilege. They represent those who are able to harness science and technology and the benefits of economic 'progress' by putting the burdens of human embodiment and embeddedness on to other peoples, other species and the planet. These burdens are borne by underprivileged women and other subordinated groups who carry out necessary body-maintaining work, and the earth, species and peoples who bear the destructive ecological consequences of high levels of production, consumption and mobility. Ecofeminism brings together the analysis of the ecological consequences of human 'progress' from the green movement, and the feminist critique of women's disproportionate responsibility for the costs and consequences of human embodiment, to show how relations of inequality within the human community are reflected in destructive relations between humanity and the non-human natural world. To focus on inequality based on sex/gender in this context is not to imply that an analysis starting from racism, class exploitation or colonialism would be any less important or relevant.

The development of a radical social theory based on a feminist and ecological framework is particularly vital given the success of the radical right and various critiques of 'modernism' in undermining theories based on the material or structural analysis of power and inequality. Radical theories have become associated with the 'sins' of white, male-dominated Marxist/social democratic statism in practice, and with theoretical frameworks that have been based on ungrounded and unwarranted assumptions of the direction of human progress. There is certainly substance to these criticisms, otherwise they would not have been so successful in silencing much radical theory and practice. However, I would argue that it is not necessary to go down the postmodernist or postsocialist road. Postmodernists may be right to say that the direction of human history cannot be predicted, and postsocialists may argue that traditional patterns of political solidarity no longer exist, but that does not mean that it is not possible to analyse the conditions of humanity as it presently exists or look for new bases of solidarity. In this book I argue that the feminist and ecology movements as brought together in ecofeminism offer grounds for optimism for both critical social analysis and the politics of social change.

Acknowledgement

I would like to acknowledge all the resources and all the people known and unknown who have sustained me and given me space and time to write this book.

1

Introduction

Ecofeminism is a movement that sees a connection between the exploitation and degradation of the natural world and the subordination and oppression of women. It emerged in the mid-1970s alongside second-wave feminism and the green movement. Ecofeminism brings together elements of the feminist and green movements, while at the same time offering a challenge to both. It takes from the green movement a concern about the impact of human activities on the non-human world and from feminism the view of humanity as gendered in ways that subordinate, exploit and oppress women.

The green movement starts from the basic tenet of ecology, that all living organisms must been seen in relation to their natural environment. Humanity must always be seen as embedded within local and global ecosystems. The ecosystem surrounding any living organism imposes boundary conditions upon it. Humanity's failure to respect the ecological limits of these bounding conditions has caused the present ecological crisis (McKibben 1990). Greens then divide on whether humanity can use its technological ingenuity to overcome or adapt to those bounding conditions (light green or shallow ecology) or whether it is necessary for humanity fundamentally to rethink its relationship to the natural world (dark green or deep ecology).

Ecofeminists tend to share the perspective of deeper greens that humanity is not just reliant on its physical environment, but that the natural world, including humanity, should be seen as an interconnected and interdependent whole. This raises fundamental questions about the socio-cultural human world in relation to the non-human natural world, including humanity's own physical existence. While ecofeminism shares with (light and dark) greens a concern about the ecological damage caused by contemporary socio-economic and military systems, it also challenges the failure of the ecology movement and its theorists to address adequately male domination and women's subordination. Although green thinkers and activists pay more attention to feminism than most other political perspectives, ecofeminists have argued that they fail to see the fundamental role of gender inequality in creating the ecological crisis. This failure results largely from male domination of green movements themselves (Salleh 1984; Doubiago 1989; Mellor 1992c; Seager 1993).

Ecofeminism's challenge to feminism lies in its assertion that to the extent that human societies are biologically sexed and/or socially gendered, men and women stand in a different relationship to the natural world. Human embeddedness in the environment is related directly to human embodiment. Ecological impacts and consequences are experienced through human bodies, in ill health, early death, congenital damage and impeded childhood development. Women disproportionately bear the consequences of those impacts within their own bodies (dioxin residues in breast milk, failed pregnancies) and in their work as nurturers and carers. Some ecofeminists have gone further and argued that women have a greater appreciation of humanity's relationship to the natural world, its embeddedness and embodiedness, through their own embodiment as female. This opens up the whole question of human society and culture in relation to bodies, biology and non-human nature. To argue that women as biologically sexed or socially gendered beings are connected with, or in some way represent, the natural world is seen as dangerous by many feminists. It undermines the struggle that they have waged against the way the identification of women with nature has been used to justify women's subordination. Women have been seen as limited and determined by their bodies and thereby excluded from playing an equal role in public life. To open up the question of women's association with 'nature', as well as positively to assert it, would seem to be a regressive move. The ecofeminist case for doing so will be a central theme of this book.

There has been a tendency to identify ecofeminism with an essentialist universalism. It is seen as positing a biologically based unity between women and the natural world that excludes men and unites all women through their essential life-giving, life-loving 'natures'. Critics argue that such a perspective is reactionary as it essentializes and naturalizes both women and nature. This presents a falsely universalized image of 'woman' that ignores differences and inequalities between women. Much of this criticism has been aimed at ecofeminism in the United States (and particularly its West Coast variant) which has been strongly identified with radical/cultural feminism and the feminist spirituality movement. However, ecofeminism has been greeted with deep suspicion in many quarters even where it draws on materialist or socialist feminism rather than cultural or spiritual feminism (Hekman 1990; Biehl 1991; Agarwal 1992; Evans 1993; Jackson 1995).

Ecofeminism's link with cultural and spiritual feminism and more radical approaches to ecology led much early ecofeminist literature, particularly in the United States, not to distinguish between academic and poetic/spiritual writings. Although many of the writers were academics, such a split was seen as reproducing the division within western culture that had allowed science and expert forms of knowledge to be distanced from ecological and social life. The introduction to one anthology describes how:

> [I]ts chorus of voices reflecting the variety of concerns flowing into ecofeminism, challenges the boundaries dividing such genres as the scholarly paper and the impassioned poetic essay. In so doing, it acknowledges poetic vision as a form of knowledge and as one of the important steps in the process of global transformation. (Diamond and Orenstein 1990: vii)

The poetic and impassioned style of writing did, however, fuel some of the criticisms of ecofeminism as essentialist and mystical. As ecofeminism has matured, its writings have become more academic, although no less impassioned, losing some of the poetic energy of the early work, but setting out a more clear theorization of the connection between a feminist and an ecological framework (Mellor 1992a; Plumwood 1993; Mies and Shiva 1993; Warren 1994). Although ecofeminism is a diverse movement with differences in emphasis, and particularly in rhetoric, I would argue that its logic as it has developed in the past twenty years has produced a distinct and very valuable theoretical perspective on the relationship between human society and its natural surroundings that has implications for both social theory and political practice.

Ecofeminism as a movement

The history of ecofeminism can be found in its writings and in the wide range of women's involvement in environmental issues and grassroots struggles around the world. The size and impact of ecofeminism as a movement depends upon how broadly it is defined. A very narrow definition would only embrace those women (and a very few men) who identify themselves explicitly as ecofeminists. Many of these are academics who are contributing to the growing literature on ecofeminism, seeking to establish it as a perspective as well as a movement. A wider definition would include all women who campaign on environmental issues or who bring together feminist and ecological concerns, whether in grassroots actions or more formal movements. The broader definition would include women's campaigns on environmental issues even where a specifically feminist or ecofeminist politics has not necessarily been expressed.

While ecofeminism as a distinct body of thought has been largely (but not exclusively) developed by feminists in the North, its emergence must be seen in the context of a wider involvement of women in struggles and campaigns concerned with the environment around the world. It is important that the North's domination of the published literature (of which this book is yet another example) should not distort the history of ecofeminism or give the impression that it is a unified movement. As with all perspectives and movements that emerge within a framework of social and economic inequalities, ecofeminism carries the danger of reproducing those inequalities within its own structure and development (Amos and Parmar 1984).

Global inequalities mean that while poor, exploited and marginalized women bear the brunt of the physical, economic and social impact of ecological degradation, and engage in direct struggles around their immediate environment, those privileged by class, nation and 'race' dominate and formulate the debate that 'names' and theorizes that movement. This is not to underestimate the contribution of those women who have abandoned their privilege to join in grassroots struggles – but privilege once gained is always available if only as cultural capital. For those without access to even the basics of existence there is no choice. The danger in the domination of the ecofeminist movement by a North perspective is that a distorted view of the ecological crisis and the position of women will emerge. Amos and Parmar's critique of the women's peace movement could as easily be applied to ecofeminism:

> Internationally, while Black and Third World Women are fighting daily battles for survival, for food, land and water, western white women's cries of anguish or concern about preserving the standards of life for their children and preserving the planet for future generations sound hollow. (1984: 17)

Saving the whale, the preservation of wilderness, recycling or green consumer campaigns pale into insignificance against the immediate need for clean water, food, sanitation and personal health (Sen and Grown 1987, Rao 1989). However, it would be equally wrong to see these as in opposition. Amos and Parmar do not argue for a rejection of peace campaigning, but for western feminists to see the political issues that affect them in an international context. They also argue against an exclusively feminist focus that does not take account of the economic and political context: 'A definition of patriarchal relations which looks only at the power of men over women without placing that in a wider political and economic framework has serious consequences for the way in which relationships within the Black community are viewed, (1984: 9). Angela Davis makes the equally important point that those concerned with immediate economic and political struggle should not neglect issues like the campaign against nuclear weapons: 'Peace, my sisters and brothers, is a Black folk's issue and it is a Black woman's issue. The failure to realize this might very well cost us our lives' (1990: 64). Both are valid arguments. Struggles around socio-economic inequality must take account of the ecological context, while the concerns of ecofeminists in the North and the struggles of women around environmental issues in the South must both be seen in an international politico-economic context.

Ecofeminism and feminisms

Most ecofeminists follow radical feminism in identifying patriarchy, and particularly western patriarchy, as the main source of global ecological destruction. The central dynamic of western patriarchy is seen as the division of society into hierarchical dualisms. Culture and society are divided from the natural world; science and expert knowledge displaces traditional folk knowledge. A valued public world is carved out of the complexities of human existence, much of which remains in a private, domestic world. Above all, male/men/the masculine is valued as against female/women/the feminine. However, the historical period in which patriarchy is seen to emerge ranges from 4000 BCE (Eisler 1990) to the Greek city-states (Ruether 1975) to the Scientific Revolution (Merchant 1983). Such a wide-ranging historical sweep leaves the question of the role of patriarchy in pre-industrial and non-western societies in some contention. Some feminists, particularly in the South, have argued that ecofeminism has encouraged a benign attitude toward non-western patriarchy (Agarwal 1992). It has also been claimed that ecofeminism's emphasis on patriarchy deflects attention from racism, imperialism and capitalism as agents in gender oppression and ecological destruction (Lorde 1980, Agarwal 1992). Mies et al. (1988), on the other hand, argue that women suffer disproportionately in social and ecological terms, where there are patterns of exploitation based on colonialism, racism or worker exploitation.

Although ecofeminist thinking draws heavily on radical feminism and the critique of patriarchy, ecofeminists vary in the way they see patriarchal relations structuring the relationship between women and the natural world. Those who come from a cultural or spiritual feminist background will tend to stress male domination *per se*, and even maleness itself, as the cause of ecologically destructive and socially oppressive behaviour. Those who come from a socialist feminist background see the division of power, and particularly of labour, between men and women as holding the key to unsustainable patterns of development (Mellor 1992a; Salleh 1994). The two groups also differ in the connections they see between women and the natural world. Those from a cultural and spiritual feminist background will tend to stress an elemental connection between women and 'nature', while those who take a more social constructionist view of gender relations will tend to stress the historical and contextual basis of that connection. However, as will become clear, the similarities between ecofeminists in terms of their basic analysis far outweighs these differences, which often reflect differences in rhetoric.

In relation to other perspectives within feminism, there are strands that are incompatible with an ecofeminist perspective. One example is the liberal feminist argument for equal opportunities within the present socio-economic system. The approach of ecofeminism is summed up by one of the founders of the movement, Ynestra King: 'what is the point of partaking equally in a system that is killing us all' (1990: 106). Ecofeminism also opposes Marxist and socialist feminisms that do not challenge the ecological, as well as the economic, contradictions of the capitalist mode of production. For ecofeminists, equality through economic growth and 'development' for women, and for working-class, racially and (neo)colonially oppressed peoples, is not ecologically possible (Mellor 1993; Mies and Shiva 1993). They share the green critique that economic growth is a dangerous illusion (Douthwaite 1992). The present level of ecological destruction caused by industrialism and 'development' has substantially benefited only around one-fifth of the world's population. Even within rich countries such as Britain or the United States, about a quarter to a third of the population, mostly women and children, are living in poverty. Whatever claims women have for equality with men, for ecofeminists it cannot be on the basis of consumption and production as promised by capitalism, or even a communistic redistribution of wealth on the present model of industrial production and mass consumption.

Ecofeminism is also incompatible with a radically social constructivist position, whether from a phenomenological, socialist/Marxist or postmodern perspective. By this, I mean a perspective that prioritizes human society/culture not only epistemologically, but ontologically. Although some ecofeminist philosophers have embraced a postmodern critique of western culture (Cheney 1989), and many ecofeminists argue that women's subordination and ecological devastation have social causes, the ecological basis of ecofeminist thinking demands a rejection of perspectives that accords all agency to human society and culture. Meanings may change with discourses, human knowledge or power relations may affect physical and social conditions of life, but the physical materiality of human life is real, however it is described or 'constructed'. For ecofeminism, the natural world of which humanity is a part has its own dynamic beyond human 'construction' or control.

Such a realist perspective is deeply problematic for those feminisms that have sought to reject a biological construction of sex difference in favour of a socially or culturally constructivist view of both sex and gender. However, a rejection of wholesale social or cultural constructivism does not mean a collapse into ecological or biological determinism. What it is both politically and theoretically vital to understand is the relationship between socially constructed relationships and physical realities, whether of embodiment or embeddedness. It is this interface that concerns ecofeminism, the connection between the biological and ecological processes surrounding human society and women's subordination and oppression. For ecofeminists, concern for the vitality of the ecology of the planet is directly related to concern for women's lives and experiences. The postmodern/poststructuralist domination of contemporary social theorizing is presenting a false choice between radical social constructivism and various forms of universalism and essentialism. In this book I want to argue that the logic of the ecofeminist position demands a radical materialist and realist analysis.

Weaving threads

Early images in ecofeminist literature are of weaving and spinning (Daly 1978; Henderson 1983; Diamond and Orenstein 1990) and the arguments in this book are equally interwoven. A book on ecofeminism(s), feminism(s) and ecologism(s) must necessarily be a tangle of ideas, an interweaving of many threads that will sometimes gather into untidy knots or trail out in numerous loose ends. A great deal of the confusion will be around the meaning of words. 'Nature', in particular, is a very problematic concept (Soper 1995). Sometimes it refers to a metaphysical idea of 'Nature', often taken to be a consciously knowing agent – the 'mind of nature'. At other times it refers to the physical world that is the 'object' of scientific study and material exploitation. Sometimes it is taken to be only that aspect of non-human nature that has not been contaminated by 'man' – nature as wilderness. At other times it is taken to be the whole planetary ecosystem which includes human beings. Although, as will become clear, I see humanity as part of an embracing natural world, as most of the debate concerns the divorce between hu(man)ity and nature, I will generally use nature to refer to the non-human natural world.

Reference to women's subordination and male dominance in society is also difficult without presupposing the basis of that domination in the words used. Reference to male, men, masculine, or female, women, feminine can imply an essentialist approach either in terms of biological determinism (women's bodies make them think and act in particular ways) or universalism (all women share common experiences and responses) or appear to accept patriarchal definitions. Equally, concepts such as patriarchy, subordination and oppression demand an explanation of the relational dynamic involved. I will generally use male dominance to refer to the fact that all existing societies have a majority of men in the most powerful positions. I will also use the term 'patriarchy', as this is the concept used in many ecofeminist writings, although, as will become clear towards the end of this book, I am not happy with the term. I also would not wish the use of concepts such as male dominance and patriarchy to prejudge the theoretical explanation of that phenomenon. I do not intend the use of the word 'male' to imply biological determinism or to claim that all men are equally involved in the process of domination and all women are equally subjected to it. However, I do not adopt the position that male domination has no material or structural base and that there is not a substantive category of 'woman' to be addressed (Riley 1988; Butler 1990).

Another difficult area is the description of male–female inequality in terms of sex and/or gender. There has been much debate over these words (Oakley 1972; Gatens 1991a; Delphy 1993). The original division of the concepts was between that which related to biology (sex) and that which related to social characteristics (gender) (Oakley 1972), although it was quickly recognized that the two ideas could not easily be kept theoretically separate (Rubin 1974). Later writers have increasingly argued that sex, like gender, should be seen as socially constructed rather than biologically given (Delphy 1993; Butler 1990). As I have argued, from an ecofeminist perspective the latter approach is problematic, as it is not possible to see the body as (totally) socially constructed. I would follow Moira Gatens in seeing embodiment as a material and an historical phenomenon that cannot be 'degendered' through socialization or counter-socialization (1991b). It is true that there is no Archimedean point from which we can ascertain what of the body is natural as opposed to social. However, social constructions do not begin from a blank slate.

To say that human beings as reproductive mammals are embodied in sexed bodies does not imply anything about the sexual identity or sexual orientation of individual people, or even some unified and singular bodily form of the male and the female. Embodiment is a universal human condition, not a determining factor at the individual level. It is also important not to limit discussion to sex, sexuality and reproduction. Human embodiment covers all aspects of human biological needs and developments such as hunger, excretion, maturing and death. If the realities of human embodiment in its broadest context are not discussed, the ways in which the social consequences of embodiment have historically had different impacts for men and women will not be addressed. For this reason I will use the linked concept of sex/gender except where I am referring specifically to sexed bodies or to social relations that can be detached from human embodiment. It is also interesting to note with Donna Haraway that the sex/gender dilemma is one that is unique to the English language, and has undermined the ability of English-speakers to theorize the sexed body adequately:

> In the political and epistemological effort to remove women from the category of nature and to place them in culture as constructed and self-constructing social subjects in history, the concept of gender has tended to be quarantined from the infections of biological sex. Consequently, the ongoing constructions of what counts as sex or as female have been hard to theorize. (1991: 134)

The ecofeminist critique of modernity is also conceptually and linguistically problematic. Concepts like advanced, modern and developed all imply a positive value for western imperialist socio-economic structures. Pre-industrial, pre-modern and non-western all use the western socio-economic system as a referent. Third World implies that the 'western' system represents a 'First' World. Concepts like West and North posit a false geography of privilege. There are rich societies in the South (Australia, New Zealand) and in the East (Japan). Such a geographical divide also ignores the inequalities within societies. Not everyone in poor countries is poor or, in rich countries, rich. Following ecofeminist literature I will generally use the concept 'West' to represent European culture, and 'North' to represent the global capitalist economy and internationally dominant nation-states. Towards the end of this book I will develop what is, I hope, a more helpful way of addressing exploitative socio-economic and ecological relations.

The overall aim of this book is to explore the history and development of the various strands of ecofeminism and their relationship to elements of feminism(s) and ecologism(s). Ecofeminism, like the feminist and green movements, is one of the 'new' social movements that are increasingly being heralded as the source of a new politics, of a regenerated civil society for the twenty-first century (Wainwright 1994). The issues they raise are seen as formulating a radical critique of industrial capitalism (O'Connor 1988; O'Connor 1994) or forming the basis of a new radical movement (Merchant 1992). I will argue here, as I have argued elsewhere, that ecofeminism has a great deal to offer as a radical perspective, particularly as the basis for a reformulated socialism (Mellor 1992a, 1992b, 1993).

The next chapter looks at the emergence of social movements and perspectives that link women and the environment. It would not be right to subsume these all under the heading of 'ecofeminism', as they cover a broad range of environmental action in various parts of the world. Although ecofeminism has been very much dominated by the voices and political concerns of the North, the voices, struggles and experiences of the South are also central to its development. These struggles will be set in the international context of the development process and women's responses to it from around the globe. Women in grassroots movements, political movements and academia have taken their concerns about the impact of development on women and the environment to the heart of the international political system, although not necessarily from an explicitly eco-feminist perspective. The emergence and development of ecofeminism as a movement will be set alongside these actions and debates.

In the third chapter I will examine the theoretical debates within the ecofeminist movement, largely, but not exclusively, from the North. The central division is between those who see women's biology and/ or culture as creating a special and direct affinity between women and the natural world, and those who see this relationship as socially constructed, a debate to which I have alluded above. Despite the different origins and orientations of ecofeminist thought, core themes emerge that will be taken up in later chapters.

Chapters 4 and 5 will address ecofeminist thought in relation to feminist theory. The fourth chapter will look at the heart of ecofeminism, the relationship between woman and nature. This is where ecofeminism comes most into conflict with other feminisms, and I will examine where these differences lie, in particular in relation to woman/nature and the body/biology. To do this it has been necessary to return to earlier feminist texts and retrace these debates, as well as address more recent feminist thought. I will argue that criticisms of essentialism levelled at ecofeminism can be met if concepts such as embodiment and its relationship to sex/gender are looked at within a materialist framework. Ecofeminist analysis shows how sex/gender inequality has been used to create the destructive nature/socio-cultural divide. Ending sex/gender inequality is essential if that divide is to be closed.

In the fifth chapter I will look at ecofeminism in the light of recent debates about women and knowledge, the feminist critique of western epistemology in general, and science in particular. Ecofeminism shares the epistemological critique of western dualism and the knowledge base of modernity in science and technology with other radical perspectives, including postmodernism. However, by emphasizing women and women's experiences, ecofeminism implicitly or explicitly, adopts a standpoint perspective. The idea of a specific women's knowledge and culture has been particularly strong in spiritual ecofeminism (Spretnak 1982, 1990; Starhawk 1982, 1987, 1990) and is also represented in Vandana Shiva's argument for the importance of women's indigenous knowledge (1989). However, arguments for women's experience as the basis of a privileging knowledge is problematic, particularly from a postmodern perspective as recent debates within feminist epistemology have shown (Jaggar and Bordo 1989; Nicholson 1990; Alcoff and Potter 1993). I will hope to show that a materialist and realist ecofeminism can plot a route out of this theoretical quagmire.

The sixth chapter will look at the relationship between ecofeminism and green thinking, particularly deep ecology. While ecofeminists have used green thinking in combination with their feminism, green thinkers (who are mainly men) have been much more varied in their approach to feminist thought and to the place women have in their theories and visions of the 'good society'. In particular, there has been a long-running debate between ecofeminists and deep ecologists about the relative importance of androcentrism (male-centredness reflecting male domination over women and nature) as against anthropocentrism (human-centredness reflecting human domination over nature) in the breakdown of sustainable relations between human society and non-human nature. The central concept in deep ecology is biocentrism, or ecocentrism, that is, seeing nature or natural processes as more important than, or ontologically prior to, human interests or existence. Ecocentric thinkers see all other political perspectives, including ecofeminism, as human-centred and therefore as prioritizing human interests or claiming human ontological priority over the non-human natural world. I will argue that there is an ambivalence in the concept of ecocentrism in deep ecological thought which renders it potentially both idealist and dualist rather than materialist and holist. However, a materialist and holist conception of ecocentrism, I will argue, is helpful in framing a materialist ecofeminism.

In the seventh chapter I will look at ecofeminism in relation to ecoanarchism, ecosocialism and Marxism. In particular, I will look at the ideas of Murray Bookchin and the critique of ecofeminism that has been developed from his ecoanarchist perspective. In relation to Marxism, eco-Marxism and socialist feminism, I will return again to the issue of embodiment and the sexual/gender division of labour, and argue that although Marx can be criticized from an ecofeminist perspective, his historical materialist analysis, particularly in the *Economic and Philosophical Manuscripts*, is still relevant if reformulated on an ecofeminist basis.

The final chapter will bring all these ideas together and set out the framework of a realist and materialist ecofeminist analysis. I will not argue that ecofeminism is *the* solution, as this would mean adopting the reductionist position that sex/gender inequality is the basis of all other oppressions. However, I will argue that the insights of ecofeminism can inform a more comprehensive historical and materialist perspective that can explore the dialectical relationship between humanity and the natural world, as well as the dynamics of human society. With deep green thinkers I see humanity as part of a natural world that has its own dynamic beyond the control of embedded humanity. Despite all the postmodern denunciations of 'totalizing theories', I will argue that a structural understanding of human existence as embodied and embedded beings is necessary if the ecological crisis and women's subordination are to be addressed. However, within this understanding there can be no final 'truth' about the human condition. Nor would I assert a 'naturalism' in the sense of ecological determinism. 'Nature' has no will or destiny. The natural world in its totality has agency, but not consciousness. While humanity is embedded in the natural world, its interrelationship with its environment is an historical process. As conscious and socially constructive beings, humanity dialectically interrelates with non-human nature in different ways over time and across cultures. Neither humanity nor 'nature' are determinant; what is inescapable are the consequences of the dynamics between them.

The centrality of feminism to this perspective is that women can be seen as playing a socially constructed mediating role between hu(man)ity and non-human nature. However, relatively few women play this role purely as *women*, but as people caught in a matrix of oppressions that embrace many men as well. What ecofeminism reveals is a wider analysis of relationships of mediation as between 'society' and 'nature'. Such an analysis would embrace not only patriarchy/male-domination, but other socio-economic dominations, as well as the domination of nature. These structures of mediation are tangled in such a way that most people are exploiters and dominators in some contexts, and exploited and dominated in others. It is, therefore, the structures of mediation themselves, rather than particular societies, groups and individuals, that have produced the patterns of subordination, exploitation, oppression and exclusion that affect so many people, including the vast majority of women, and the non-human natural world.

Throughout this book I hope to show that ecofeminism, in its own spinning and weavings, together with those of other radical movements and perspectives, can produce a social and political analysis that will provide a basis for the solidaristic political action on a global scale that is so desperately needed.

2

Women and the Environment

Women's role in ecological struggles and debates since the nineteenth century, as with all women's social and political involvement, has been 'hidden from history' (Rowbotham 1973). Histories of ecology in the North credit the German Ernst Haeckel with naming the subject in 1873 (Bramwell 1989), while the contribution of his contemporary, the American ecologist and educationalist Ellen Swallow, is largely ignored, although she equally could be claimed to have founded the science of ecology (Clarke 1973; King 1983a). It is also interesting that while Haeckel chose a name based on the Greek *oikos* meaning household or dwelling, it was Ellen Swallow who showed the direct connection between daily domestic life and the environment (Hynes 1985).

In the early 1870s Ellen Swallow was the first woman student to be admitted to the Massachusetts Institute of Technology (MIT) and she stayed on to become its first woman instructor. She was multidisciplinary; a water chemist, industrial chemist, metallurgist, mineralogist, engineer and expert on food and nutrition. Her aim was to understand the environmental dynamics of industrialization and to provide the community, particularly women, with the expertise to monitor their own environment. She established a laboratory for women at MIT in 1876 and an interdisciplinary education programme. She lobbied government for a nutrition and pure food programme and did much to reduce hazards in industry. For Swallow the importance of educating women was that the home, even more than the workplace, was where primary resources such as nutrition, water, sewerage and air could be monitored. She argued that science should be placed in the hands of women so that 'the housekeeper should know when to be frightened' (ibid.: 292). Swallow's unique and far-sighted initiatives were not appreciated by a science establishment that was rapidly segmenting into distinct disciplines. Even less understood was her insistence on working with women. As a consequence, her pioneering multidisciplinary work with women has entered the history books as 'domestic science'.

Almost a hundred years later another woman scientist in the United States was one of the key figures in pioneering the green movement of the late twentieth century. Rachel Carson, a marine biologist and scientific journalist, published her warnings of the danger of pesticide and herbicide accumulation in 1962. In very much the way that Swallow envisaged, Carson was inspired to write her book *Silent Spring*, by the observations of a woman friend, who claimed that aerial spraying of DDT was killing songbirds and robins in her garden. Carson argued that herbicides and pesticides would accumulate through the food chain, so that chemicals spread on crops would poison the birds and animals (including humans) that fed on them directly or indirectly. The death of birds that had fed on chemical-laden plants and insects would result in the silent spring of the title. She pointed out that such chemicals never disappeared; instead they would build up in water and soil, often carried far away from the spraying site. Although Carson did not articulate an explicitly feminist or ecofeminist perspective, her critique of scientific approaches to the natural world presaged later ecofeminist critiques: 'as man proceeds toward his announced goal of the conquest of nature, he has written a depressing record of destruction, directed against not only the earth he inhabits but against the life that shares it with him' (Carson 1985: 83).

The government's and chemical industry's response to Carson's warnings was to mock her as an emotional fanatic, a spinster in galoshes who worried about birds. As Hynes points out, Carson's science arose from a love of nature that inspired her to write 'compelling, imagistic' poetic prose (1985: 296). Male-dominated science could not accept the idea that love and knowledge were compatible and mutually supportive (Rose 1994). However, Carson's work was not silenced, and its importance has been acknowledged on many occasions by the growing ecofeminist movement, particularly in the United States. Conferences were held to celebrate the twenty-fifth anniversary of the publication of *Silent Spring*, and a leading ecofeminist anthology was dedicated to the memory of Carson as a 'remarkable and modest woman' who thought that loving the natural world was essential to understanding it (Diamond and Orenstein 1990).

Another early critic of western technology, particularly in the field of development, was Barbara Ward, a British-born academic. Ward evoked the image of 'spaceship earth' in 1966 and was an early critic of the adverse effects on the South of the modernizing push towards worldwide economic development. Pointing to the interdependence of the world's peoples, she argued that economic changes needed to be morally justified and should show how change could be managed in such a way as to conserve the natural environment at a planetary level. Barbara Ward's work had a major impact at the international level, inspiring the United Nations to hold a conference on Human Settlements and to development of the UN Environment Programme. The UN commitment not only reflected the work of Ward, who, with René Dubos, published the influential *Only One Earth* in 1972, but was also a response to the growing alarm about the limits to economic growth that were indicated by computer projections on issues such as natural resource reserves and pollution as well as the highly contentious area of population (Meadows et al. 1972; Sen 1994).

While women such as Rachel Carson and Barbara Ward were putting ecological questions on to the national and international agenda, certainly in the North, women across the globe were doing what Ellen Swallow had envisaged one hundred years before. They were expressing concern about the ecological degradation within their own communities. Ecology, a word derived from the Greek for household, was coming 'close to home' (Shiva 1994a).

Grassroots struggles

The grassroots environmental movement expands our sense not only of what is possible, but of what is necessary. It is a movement that is fuelled by persistence, resistance, stubbornness, passion and outrage. Around the world, it is the story of 'hysterical housewives' taking on 'men of reason' – in the multitude of guises in which they each appear. (Seager 1993: 280)

In the past twenty years, grassroots campaigning around the ownership, control and use of the environment has taken on the 'men of reason' from the Amazon basin to the Himalayas, and from Kenya to the United States (Epstein 1993). In the South, feminist critics of the 'steam-roller' of technological modernization and global capitalism drew attention to the threat to both women and the environment from so-called 'development'. They showed how women were experiencing particular hardship, as commercial farming, logging and mining invaded their traditional way of life and they were drawn into highly exploitative and health-threatening forms of production (Mitter 1986; Mies 1986; Sen and Grown 1987; Shiva 1989).

In the North, the ecological dangers of industrialism and militarism became increasingly apparent and were highlighted through the campaigns of the peace and environmental movements, as well as through grassroots struggles. The peace movements in Europe and North America expanded rapidly in response to the NATO decision in 1979 to site cruise missiles in Europe. There was widespread concern not only about the immediate danger to human life from nuclear weapons and nuclear fallout, but also about the danger that atmospheric dust would cause a 'nuclear winter'. The developing ecofeminist movement in the North had its roots in both the feminist and the peace movements. Ecofeminism in the United States was also galvanized in the late 1970s by the near disaster at the nuclear power station at Three Mile Island and the threat to health from toxic waste discovered at Love Canal, Niagara Falls, New York State.

It is hard to say why particular examples of grassroots struggle become symbolic of a social movement when there are many examples of similar campaigns elsewhere (Merchant 1992; Ekins 1992; Seager 1993). However, certain struggles seem to illuminate issues and concerns that lie at the heart of those campaigns and the way in which women's relationship to the natural world has been both revealed and constructed through them. This is particularly true of the Chipko movement in the villages of the Himalayas, the Green Belt movement in Kenya and the Love Canal campaign in the United States. Shiva argues that '[e]nvironmental movements like the Chipko have become historical landmarks because they have been fuelled by the ecological insights and political and moral strengths of women' (1989: 67).

The Chipko movement

The forest is our mother's home, we will defend it with all our might. Women of the village of Reni in the Garhwal mountains of the Himalayan Range. (Anand 1983: 182)

The Chipko movement of the Garhwal Himalayas is probably the best recorded of the struggles that have come to symbolize the relationship between women and the environment (Anand 1983;

Dankelman and Davidson 1988; Shiva 1989; Jain 1991). Chipko (meaning 'hugging' in Hindi) gained worldwide publicity in the mid-1970s through the action of Himalayan villagers (mainly women) hugging trees to prevent them from being felled. The movement had some success in getting the Indian government to support a moratorium on tree-felling and pay attention to the need for broad-leaved indigenous trees to prevent soil erosion and support the subsistence economies of local villages. Chipko activists argued that commercial pine or eucalyptus plantations provided work for some villagers (mainly men), but did not meet the needs of women who were almost all involved in cultivation and relied on trees for fuel and fodder for animals (Shiva 1989; Jain 1991).

Despite the impression sometimes given that the Chipko movement emerged as the spontaneous action of women preserving trees (Sontheimer 1991; Ekins 1992), the movement has a much more complex political base. Its inspirational example was not the outcome of women's immediate physical and spiritual identification with the forest, but, rather, it grew out of a 'mosaic of many events and multiple actors' involving the long and purposeful struggle of politically committed followers of Gandhi in the region (Shiva 1989: 67–77). Shiva also argues that the origins of hugging as a means of protest goes back three hundred years to when a group led by a woman sacrificed their lives to protect a grove of sacred trees (ibid.: 67).

The exact date of the re-emergence of tree-hugging is difficult to discern. Anand dates it as 1974 in the village of Reni (1983: 182); Jain gives the date as 1973 and credits male co-operative workers with the re-invention of hugging as a means of protest (1991: 168); Shiva dates it rather later, when women became more central to the protests. Whatever the exact date, the origins of the Chipko movement lay in Gandhian organizations in the Garhwal region of Uttar Pradesh state in the Indian Himalayas. Mira Behn, a follower of Gandhi, had settled in the Himalayas in the 1940s and begun to study the ecology of the region. Other women, like Sarala Behn and Bimala Behn, started ashrams for the education of hill-women, bringing together the traditional relationship of hill people to their environment, the political and spiritual teachings of Gandhi, and the very immediate material needs of local women.

A second Gandhian link was to a co-operative founded in 1960, which, originally, employed men in construction work, but which from 1964 sought to develop forest industries such as sap-gathering and wood products. The co-operative found great difficulty in getting access to trees and was alarmed in April 1973 when the government gave a private contractor permission to fell in the village of Gopeshwar. According to Jain (1991), a 100-strong protest prevented the cutting of the trees. A few months later, in June 1973, the co-operative workers supported another protest in a village 80 kilometres away, by joining hands around the threatened part of the forest.

Although in the early stages of the Chipko movement village men and women united against commercial forest development, their interests soon began to conflict. For Vandana Shiva this was the crucial stage in the movement. While the men were interested in gaining access to the forest for local village commercial development, the women wished to preserve the forest for their traditional subsistence needs and to guard against soil erosion. Shiva also sees the origins of women's opposition to cash-generating development in their struggles against male alcoholism in the 1960s. She argues that the decisive moment came in the village of Adwani when the headman's wife led the women to embrace the trees of the forest in opposition to her own husband who was the local contractor. It was at this point that the Chipko movement became 'ecological *and* feminist' (Shiva 1989: 76; italics in the original).

Shiva, who was trained as a nuclear physicist, was inspired by the actions of the women in the Chipko movement to abandon her original career and set up a Foundation for Science, Technology and Natural Resource Policy. She has campaigned worldwide not only for forest protection, but for recognition of the role of women in the wider defence of local environments on which they depend for firewood, forage and water. Her ecofeminism is based on the observation that for poor rural women of the South, their link with the natural world is the reality of their daily lives; all struggle is ecological struggle (Shiva 1989). In terms of this wider agenda Joni Seager argues that the Chipko movement 'now symbolizes Third World resistance to misdirected "international development" . . . [and] has come to symbolize a struggle for autonomy from the stranglehold that Western reductionist science has come to have on resource management' (1993: 266–7).

These struggles have highlighted the importance of the political role of women, which has begun to be recognized more widely in India itself, particularly in the peasant movements (Omvedt 1989). In Maharashtra state all-women village councils began to emerge in the 1990s, adopting for their campaign the slogan '*hirvi dharti, stri shakti, manav mukti*' (green earth, women's power, human liberation) (Omvedt 1994: 106).

Kenyan Green Belt movement

The Kenyan Green Belt movement has also provided inspiration for the wider ecofeminist movement. Again, the movement was not a spontaneous action on the part of women, but thousands of them were inspired in 1977 by the initiative of Anatomy Professor, Wangari Maathai, to launch a rural tree-planting programme. The first trees were planted on 5 June, World Environment Day. The Green Belt movement was always perceived as a women's programme and was organized through the National Council of Women. Its aim was to solve the fuel problem in rural areas, as well as preventing creeping desertification and soil erosion, by surrounding each village with a 'green belt' of at least a thousand trees. The movement provided the trees and a small sum to employ a local person to tend them.

Women responded readily, and hundreds of local women's tree-planting groups were set up. By the mid-1980s six hundred tree nurseries had been set up employing between two and three thousand women, and over a million trees have now been planted. Green belt schemes are also being established in twelve other African countries (Seager 1993; Ekins 1992; Merchant 1992). The global linkages of women's ideas and struggles is illustrated by the fact that Wangari Maathai cited Barbara Ward as a source of her inspiration (Jones and Maathai 1983). Maathai's initiative is also echoed in the United States by the work of Rachel Bagby in greening inner-city environments (Bagby 1990). Bagby has turned approximately five acres of derelict city land in a Black neighbourhood into garden plots and founded the Philadelphia Community Rehabilitation Corporation. Like Maathai, her aim is to combine a greening programme with wider aims of providing employment and education. A high political profile and involvement in radical struggle is not without its dangers, however. Wangari Maathai has been placed under house arrest in Kenya and was attacked and severely injured in the early 1990s.

Love Canal, United States

In the North, the campaign over toxic waste at Love Canal has had something of the same symbolic importance as the Chipko or Kenyan Green Belt movement in the South. It coincided with the nuclear accident at Three Mile Island power station in 1979 and heightened sensitivity to the inherent danger in industrial and high technology production. The experience of the residents of Love Canal has come to represent the fears of people in industrial societies about the hidden dangers that surround them.

Love Canal is a blue-collar neighbourhood of about twelve hundred homes in the suburb of Niagara Falls, New York State. In 1978 one of the residents, Lois Gibbs, became concerned about the health of her neighbourhood when her son became epileptic and her daughter developed a rare blood disease. She then found that among her neighbours there was an unusually high proportion of miscarriages, stillbirths and birth defects. She believed that the problems were connected with the fact that the estate was built next to a dump of more than twenty thousand tons of toxic waste. It was eventually revealed that the estate had been built near the site of a mile-long trench, fifteen yards wide and from ten to forty feet deep. It had been dug originally in the 1890s as a grandiose scheme for a canal at around the time when Ellen Swallow was campaigning for an integrated approach to environmental issues. The abandoned canal trench was used for many years as a chemical dump, and when it was full it had been covered over and designated for building land. A school had been built right over the site (Hynes 1985). The chemicals had also leached into underground streams and were spreading into adjacent land, as had been anticipated by both Ellen Swallow and Rachel Carson.

When the state authorities refused to believe her claim that the health problems of her neighbourhood and the toxic waste dump were connected, Lois Gibbs led a two-year struggle for relocation. However, it was not until women had vandalized a construction site, burned an effigy of the mayor and been arrested in a blockade that government officials began to take notice. Even then Lois Gibbs found that her evidence of the ill health of her own family and those around her was not taken seriously until she got a scientist to put her 'housewife data' into 'pi-squared and all that junk' (Seager 1993: 265).

Women in other local campaigns also found themselves accused of being 'hysterical housewives' when they tried to raise issues about the dumping of waste. As one Black woman from the southern United States put it: 'You're exactly right, I am hysterical. When it comes to matters of life and death, especially mine and my family's, I get hysterical' (Newman 1994: 58). Involvement in grassroots struggles are politicizing increasing numbers of women. Seager calculates that, worldwide, women form 60–80 per cent of the membership of environmental organizations, although this is not always evident from the leadership profile (1993: 263–4). She also notes that most women who become involved in grassroots movements have not been active before and often have to run the gauntlet of accusations of ignorance and hysteria not only from 'experts' and officials, but from their own male relatives.

Lois Gibbs falls into just this pattern. She recalls that she 'grew up in a blue collar community, it was very patriotic . . . I believed in government' (quoted Krauss 1993: 111). Gibbs 'wanted to have six children and be a homemaker. I moved into Love Canal, and I bought the American dream . . . I never thought of myself as an activist or an organiser. I was a housewife, a mother, but all of a sudden it was my family, my children, my neighbours' (Gibbs 1993: ix). Drawing on her experience of women in grassroots campaigns, she also notes the tensions that can arise in families where men feel that their role as protectors of the family is threatened:

> In many families, the woman who becomes active is seen as a threat to the 'strong' male. He feels that he is losing control over 'his woman' and might feel that he is being outdone or 'outshined' by his mate, a problem that is exhibited if she is successful . . . Pressure begins to build on her as she tries to balance her commitment to the cause with the conflicting demands that come out of her (male) mate's emotional needs. (quoted in Seager 1993: 275)

Gibbs's experience at Love Canal and her disillusionment with the democratic process led to her setting up in 1981 a national network, the Citizens' Clearinghouse for Hazardous Waste (CCHW), which has supported over four thousand local community campaigns against toxic waste.

What is so special about women?

If it is true that women have a 'special' relationship to the natural world, and a special awareness of environmental hazards, does this apply equally to all women? And can it only be said of women? While women-based grassroots and activist campaigns are emerging across the world on many issues, not all explicitly make connections between women and the environment. Also, there is a large number of grassroots campaigns concerned with environmental issues that are not women-based (Ekins 1992; Merchant 1992). Whereas ecofeminist literature tends to stress women's involvement in grassroots environmental campaigns, green writers, who are predominantly male, tend to see these as indigenous or 'local' campaigns.

In the United States, for example, growing awareness of the dangers of toxic waste has led to widespread concern about the siting of waste dumps in poor, Black and Hispanic neighbourhoods and on Native American lands. The United States has to dispose of the equivalent of 2,500 pounds of hazardous waste for every man, woman and child each year. One large dump that takes waste from forty-six US states is sited at Emelle, Alabama where 70 per cent of the population is African-American and almost all live below the official poverty line (Seager 1993: 274). This situation has led to a growing environmental justice movement, bringing together working-class, Black, Native American and other local communities in protest against the siting of toxic waste dumps and dangerous factories in poor neighbourhoods (Bullard 1990, 1993; Hofrichter 1993; Newman 1994). Nuclear contamination is also a problem. Winona LaDuke, co-Chair of the Indigenous Women's Network, which brings together Native American and Pacific Island women, reports that fifteen of the eighteen US nuclear storage sites are on Native American land, where also – mainly in Shoshone territory – all nuclear tests were carried out (LaDuke 1993: 99). Contaminated test sites have now been designated by the US government as 'National Sacrifice Zones' – a concept that obscures the fact that it is Native American nations that have been sacrificed.

When women play a major role in these movements, do they do so as women, or as poor, Black, Hispanic or Native American people? Even if women are over-represented among the poor, and disproportionately take part in grassroots struggles, particularly around communities, does this mean gender should be prioritized above class and racism? In the US anti-toxic social justice campaigns, even where women are at the forefront, their political identification is usually in terms of 'race' rather than gender (Epstein 1993). Bina Agarwal and Cecile Jackson have also expressed concern that an overemphasis on women's involvement in struggles such as the Chipko movement will give a false impression of a specifically *feminist* commitment, rather than women's involvement in peasant movements generally (Agarwal 1992; Jackson 1995). Agarwal is also concerned that an overemphasis on grassroots movements combined with a critique of western economic systems will ignore class and property relations within societies such as India. Rather than stressing a direct woman–nature relationship Agarwal argues that: 'the link between women and the environment can be seen as structured by a given gender and class (caste/race) organisation of production, reproduction and distribution' (1991, quoted in Braidotti et al. 1994: 100). For this reason Agarwal prefers the term 'feminist environmentalism' to ecofeminism.

Braidotti et al. join Jackson and Agarwal in being concerned that an uncritical celebration of grassroots movements would deflect attention from the inequality and oppressiveness, particularly towards women, in traditional communities. They criticize 'the tendency to idealize everything local and traditional while glossing over indigenous structures of exploitation and domination that were in place before the advent of development' (1994: 112).

An overemphasis on women may also obscure the fact that it is possible for women in more privileged communities to insulate themselves from toxic and other environmental hazards, at least in the short run. Local NIMBY (not in my backyard) campaigning by better off communities may not lead to NIABY (not in anybody's backyard) but a displacement of dangerous activities into poorer areas. Seager is also concerned that better-off women may deflect their concern into green consumerism, an activity that can easily be manipulated by shrewd marketing. If effective, green consumerism could lead to a new divide between the 'haves' and 'have nots' in terms of the environmental privilege of being safe from hazards in the home (1993: 262). Such concerns raise the central question of differences between women in relation to environmental hazards and environmental campaigning.

Seager, echoing Swallow, argues that women do have a key role *as women* in grassroots campaigning because they are often the first to become aware that something is wrong:

> Women worldwide, are often the first to notice environmental degradation. Women are the first to notice when the water they cook with and bathe the children in smells peculiar: they are the first to know when the supply of water starts to dry up. Women are the first to know when the children come home with stories of mysterious barrels dumped in the creek: they are the first to know when children develop mysterious ailments. (1993: 272)

What is common to women's grassroots campaigns, North and South, is women's vulnerability to environmental problems and their lack of access to the centres of decision-making which cause them. While women are disproportionately represented in poor and vulnerable communities, men are disproportionately represented in positions of power and influence. This means that women (and many men) bear the consequences of government, military, industrial and commercial decisions without being in a position to influence them. Their response is always 'end-of-pipe', they are not in a position to know or influence what goes into the pipe in the first place.

When greens call upon people to think globally but act locally they often overlook the fact that it is women who *live* locally (Mellor 1992c) – they have little choice but to think locally. They live near the waste dump, the poisoned well or the factory belching smoke. It is women who have to walk miles for water or fuel if local resources are depleted, whose mobility is threatened by roads and traffic, whose children cannot play safely. It is women who nurse the young, the old and the sick when they suffer from environmental pollution or depletion. This point has been made by women from the North and the South at national and international conferences, forums and seminars (Merchant 1992; Women's Environmental Network 1989; Shiva 1994).

There are, however, some differences in the environmental issues that face women in the North and the South. In non-industrial societies problems revolve around access to clean water and other resources as well as issues of poverty and health (Asian and Pacific Women's Resource Collection Network 1989). In the North problems are not always so immediate or so visible. As Wangari Maathai has pointed out, while the women of the South are struggling against visible problems such as desertification and soil erosion, 'at the global level we are fighting an invisible enemy' (Jones and Maathai 1983: 114). In the South immediate survival needs are paramount, but in the North ecological damage is more hidden. It lurks in the air and the ground and, although its effects can be felt, particularly in health problems such as the rapid increase in asthma, the cause is difficult to prove and the sense of risk is therefore more diffuse (Beck 1992). Campaigns have to assemble scientific and other forms of evidence that are often difficult to obtain or subject to official or commercial secrecy. However, campaigns once launched can be remarkably effective, as in the case of the British Women's Environmental Network (WEN) campaign against the use of chlorine bleach in disposable nappies and other paper products, arguing that it led to dioxin residues in human bodies and particularly women's breast milk (Costello et al. 1989).

What is increasingly common to women's involvement in environmental campaigning is that it is being built into a coherent critique of the present model of development based upon scientific knowledge, industrial technology and the capitalist market economy. Campaigns around the environment are being brought together with campaigns around women's rights, health and economic well-being.

Women, environment and development

Economic development, that magic formula, devised sincerely to move poor nations out of poverty, has become women's worst enemy. Roads bring machine-made ersatz goods, take away young girls and food and traditional art and culture; technologies replace women, leaving families even further impoverished. Manufacturing cuts into natural resources (especially trees), pushing fuel and fodder resources further away, bringing home-destroying floods or life-destroying drought, and adding all the time to women's work burdens. (Devaki Jain, founder member of Development Alternatives with Women for a New Era (DAWN) 1984; quoted in Pietilä and Vickers 1990: 35)

Grassroots movements in the South around the impact of environmental factors on women are closely associated with a wider movement concerned with women's economic and social position within the 'development process' (Kabeer 1994). Evidence of the impact of the development process on both women and the environment emerged throughout the 1970s and 1980s. It is in the critique of development that the connection between women's experiences and the environmental crisis has been most clearly demonstrated.

The idea of 'development' was launched by US President Harry Truman in his inaugural speech in January 1949. More correctly, he launched the concept of 'underdevelopment'. The United States was seen as the apex of a 'ladder' of progress involving industrialism and the commodification of provisioning. Whole societies would move, over time, from subsistence, non-commodified rural life to increasingly urbanized, technologically sophisticated forms of production based on waged work. The road to progress led from fishing and farming to fashion and Fordism. In the 1950s the United Nations, on the initiative of the US, set up a Development Programme to fund and support this process through international structures such as the World Bank. Behind the concept of development was an assumption that the western way of life was superior to the 'backward' ways of non-western societies. The development process also spread into agriculture, where the 'green revolution' promised to end problems of hunger and poverty through biologically engineered species of staple crops developed by laboratories in the North. Western science, like the western way of life and the capitalist industrial economic system, was seen as inherently superior to indigenous farming practice and knowledge.

As Sachs has argued, following the development process has been a disaster for most non-western countries: 'the aspiration of catching up has ended in a blunder of planetary proportions' (1993: 5). By the 1980s the GNP of two-thirds of humanity was 15 per cent of the world total, while the industrial nations, with 20 per cent of the world's population, scooped 80 per cent. This was also reflected in consumption patterns, as the industrialized nations absorbed most of the world's resources. After dramatic initial increases in crop yields, the green revolution also faltered, as high demand for pesticides, fertilizers and water brought increasing economic and environmental strains (Shiva 1989). Nations that had been encouraged to borrow huge sums of money on the promise of eventual economic returns found themselves having to turn more and more of their resources into cash to pay ever-increasing debts. According to Chee Yoke Ling, of Malaysian Friends of the Earth, by the late 1980s 40 per cent of fertile land in the South was being used to grow non-food cash crops for export (WEN 1989).

As the global market economy and the development process started to make inroads into traditional communities, women's economic position became increasing insecure (Afshar 1985; Sen and Grown 1987; Mies 1986). Within traditional communities women's access to resources was often secured by usufruct, i.e. rights to use common or family land and resources without individual ownership. As commercial agriculture, mining and forestry began to overrun local village economies, women and the environment began to suffer (Afshar 1985; Sen and Grown 1987; Dankelman and Davidson 1988; Shiva 1989; Sontheimer, 1991). Lack of access to land, through the loss of common and family land to private ownership, led to women becoming increasingly impoverished and vulnerable. As most of them were responsible for providing a substantial part (if not the majority) of family food through subsistence farming, they found themselves working on increasingly marginal and infertile land. Where logging and damming removed nearby sources of water and wood, they found themselves, as the major collectors of fuel and water, walking longer distances each day (Dankelman and Davidson 1988). Men were increasingly being attracted, or forced by economic circumstances, to take waged work, often a good distance away, leaving the women to fend for the family in increasingly impoverished conditions. Economic necessity was also forcing women into waged work at very low rates of pay, often in dangerous conditions (Mies 1986; Mitter 1986). Given the patriarchal structure of both traditional society and the incoming development systems, they had no voice to express their concerns.

Campaigns over the impact of development on the environment and women emerged in the early 1970s. A major opportunity was created by the designation of 1975 as International Women's Year and the launch of the United Nations Decade for the Advancement of Women in Mexico. At the beginning of the decade the main focus of protest was the lack of women's involvement in development programmes. By the end of the decade the whole concept of development was being questioned. In 1975 the main criticism was that development had failed women by making totally false assumptions about their role in agricultural systems and in rural society generally. Development programmes had been based on the assumptions underlying the western industrial model of the sexual/gender division of labour – that men do the main productive work, while women stay at home. As Haleh Afshar remarked: 'male extension workers often carry an ideological image of households with male heads, the man tilling the land and the woman rocking the cradle and keeping the home fires burning' (1985: xiii). This was not the case for most women in the South or for poorer women in the North.

In 1970 Ester Boserup had published a pioneering piece of research that showed that women in sub-Saharan Africa were responsible for a vast proportion of agricultural work. She also showed how development processes not only did not aid women, but often made their lives more difficult. As men were pulled into the formal economy, women were left behind in the subsistence sector (Boserup 1970). Other examples began to emerge. National statistics for Egypt in 1970 showed women as forming only 3.6 per cent of the agricultural labour force, while interviews with women showed that 55–70 per cent of them were involved in agricultural production (Pietilä and Vickers 1990: 14). In 1972 census figures for Peru showed that women made up 2.6 per cent of the rural labour force, whereas 86 per cent of them were actually involved in agriculture (ibid.: 15). What had been revealed was the extent of women's unpaid subsistence work (Waring 1989), as well as an under-reporting of their waged work. Any development programme that did not take account of this massive amount of work was destined to fail women and the environment.

Dankelman and Davidson describe the typical day of a woman agricultural worker in India:

> She rises at 4 a.m. She cleans the house, washes the clothes, prepares the meal for her husband and children and leaves for the field at 8 a.m. She works there until 6 p.m., in the meanwhile nursing the small children she took with her. On her way back she collects fuelwood, and if necessary, drinking water. She cooks the evening meal, cares for the children and

tends the animals. At 10 p.m. she goes to bed. On such a day she might earn two rupees. (1988: 3)

Failure to understand the economic position of women also led to their being seen as the perpetrators of ecological damage. As women farmers were forced on to marginal land and women generally were forced to use the dwindling resources of trees and water, it appeared that it was they, rather than logging, damming and land enclosure, who were responsible for the environmental crisis.

In 1972 voices from the South emerged on to the international stage at the United Nations conference held in Stockholm on the human environment. This was one of the conferences inspired by the work of Barbara Ward, among others. A pattern emerged that was to carry right through the United Nations initiatives on environment and development, culminating in the Rio 'Earth Summit' in June 1992. The government-led discussions in the formal debates were met by the voices of non-governmental organizations (NGOs) giving an alternative, often grassroots version, of the impact on local environments and communities of the development process (Braidotti et al. 1994). One of the groups represented in 1972 was the Chipko movement, committed to preserving the natural forests of the Himalayas. As we have seen, this movement gradually became more closely identified with women's relationship to the natural environment and has been an inspiration for many ecofeminists (Shiva 1989; Merchant 1992; Seager 1993).

The pattern of involvement of women and other groups from the South in NGO meetings – held in parallel to UN debates – continued. While the formal governmental meeting of the 1975 UN Decade for Women conference in Mexico was attended by 1,200 delegates, there were 4,000 people at the parallel NGO conference. In the mid-decade meeting in Copenhagen in 1980 there were 7,000 people, and it has been claimed that 16,000 attended the 1985 NGO forums at the end-of-decade conference in Nairobi (Ostergaard 1992: 5). Estimates for the 1995 UN Women's conference in Beijing range from 25,000 to 40,000 despite the attempts of the Chinese government to minimize NGO impact on the formal conference (*Guardian* 19 September 1995).

Alternatives to development

Environmental concerns and women's concerns were not brought together immediately. At the 1975 UN Decade for Women conference in Mexico, and at conferences such as the International Women's Workshop held in Bangkok in 1979 or the Women and the New International Order held in The Netherlands in 1982, the main focus was on women's economic position. It was demanded that their economic needs be taken into account and that their voices be heard in the development process. This kind of campaigning has come to be known as Women in Development (WID). The basic argument of WID is that current development policies fail to recognize gender relations within households and the fundamental roles that women play in informal, rural and market economies (Harcourt 1994: 3). During the 1980s the WID arguments were taken on board by development agencies, as a result of which the WID approach has been criticized for endorsing the development process (Kabeer 1994, Harcourt 1994, Braidotti et al. 1994). In particular, the approach has been criticized for carrying the 'historical baggage' of the assumption of the superiority of the development process, and the inferiority of those who are going to be 'helped' and encouraged to participate (Apffel-Marglin and Simon 1994: 26).

By the 1980s the whole notion of development was beginning to be questioned. The 1982 conference in The Netherlands had concluded:

> Now we need another development both in the North and the South. Therefore, we need to recognize the views and interests of women and to create opportunities for their full participation at all levels of the society. Then the development would not any more take place only on economic terms, but also on human terms. (Pietilä and Vickers 1990: 90)

In the same way that the work of Ester Boserup and other women was very influential in highlighting the problem of women's lack of involvement in the development process in 1975, another set of evidence was assembled for the 1985 UN Decade for Women meeting in Nairobi. A group of twenty-two activists, researchers and policy-makers from Africa, Asia and Latin America met in Bangalore, India in 1984 to prepare an independent report on the position of women in the South. The group called themselves DAWN (Development Alternatives with Women for a New Era). The report which they presented, *Development Crises and Alternative Visions*, was published two years later (Sen and Grown 1987).

DAWN's survey of women's position at the end of the UN Decade for Women, was that women's position had considerably worsened: '[W]ith few exceptions, women's relative access to economic resources, income, and employment has worsened, their burdens of work have increased, and their relative and even absolute health, nutritional, and educational status has declined' (ibid.: 16). The crises that they saw in development were impoverishment, food insecurity and non-availability, financial and monetary 'disarray', environmental degradation and demographic pressure. The latter problem was becoming increasingly marked for women in the South. As concern about the environment had been raised in the North, the finger had been pointed at the growing population of the South. This, of course, ignored the fact that population figures in the North had only just stabilized after more than a century of rapid growth and dispersal through colonization (Hynes 1993).

In the late 1960s and early 1970s books were being written with titles such as *The Population Bomb* (Erlich 1972). The United States had also tied its development programme to population control. Highly authoritarian measures were being taken to impose population control on women in the South, who were also being given forms of birth control that were banned in the North or were experimental. Birth control became one of the most important arms of the struggle by women in the South against the imposed 'solutions' from the North. By the Cairo summit on population in 1994 some progress had been made, and it was agreed that encouraging women's economic and social progress (and particularly education) was the most effective way of promoting birth control. However, this still does not address the problem of how women in patriarchal cultures are going to give effect to their empowerment. Nor does it engage with the problem of the education of men in the need to take their share of the responsibility for birth control (Sen 1994). Hynes has questioned whether the Cairo approach has not in fact hijacked the issue of women's rights and avoided a more profound questioning of power relations: '[E]n route to Cairo, a woman's rights agenda has been a rhetorical means for a populationist end – a reduction of the poorest people on Earth – without a structural change in analysis' (1993: 47). The implication that population is the crucial problem for the sustainability of human life also avoided the political problems of tackling the question of over-consumption in population-stable countries (Mellor 1992a: 101 f.).

These issues were raised in the DAWN report which concluded that women's 'bodies have become a pawn in the struggles among states, religions, male heads of households, and private corporations' (Sen and Grown 1987: 49). They called for women to have the right to control their own fertility and for recognition that the so-called population problem was largely the result of poverty and lack of resources. It was not that people had outstripped the 'carrying capacity' of the land, as Malthusians such as Garrett Hardin had suggested (1968), it was that the land had been removed from the people.

The interaction of gender and class in the context of colonialism was a central theme of the DAWN report. All three contributed to women's experience of impoverishment, exploitation, sexual violence and political and social marginalization. Capitalism, colonialism, militarism, and fundamentalism were all male-dominated structures that oppressed women. Central to DAWN's analysis was women's role in the provision of basic needs as the basis of reproduction in human societies: 'by reproduction we mean the process by which human beings meet their basic needs and survive from one day to the next' (Sen and Grown 1987: 50). Women's social and economic marginalization, and the environmental crisis brought on by the development process, were undermining the basic means of survival for poor women.

DAWN brought environmental and economic issues together by highlighting the food–fuel–water crisis that women were facing. Commercial development had failed to take account of the interdependence of ecosystems. Loss of fertile land, damming of water courses and tree-felling all contributed to the crisis of survival. As the main providers of food, fuel and water, women were finding it harder and harder to sustain their families and themselves. They were often the last to eat, and their food intake was not necessarily enough to sustain their increasing burden of work (ibid: 58). DAWN argued that, as women were at the centre of the food–fuel–water crisis, a coherent and integrated policy to meet that crisis would need to have women, particularly those who were poor and landless, at its centre.

The importance of the DAWN approach was that it did not seek to argue for women to be included in the development process. It challenged the whole notion of development itself. Instead, a vision was presented of:

> a world where inequality based on class, gender and race is absent from every country ... where basic needs become basic rights and where poverty and all forms of violence are eliminated. Each person will have the opportunity to develop her or his full potential and creativity, and women's values of nurturance and solidarity will characterize human relationships ... child care will be shared by men and women ... means of destruction will be diverted to ... relieve oppression ... technological revolution will eliminate disease and hunger ... women['s] safe control of fertility ... participatory democratic processes, where women share in determining priorities and making decisions. (ibid.: 80–1)

Although focusing on environmental issues, DAWN did not fully incorporate a 'woman and environment' perspective until 1992, when it produced a document called *Environment and Development: Grass Roots Women's Perspective* (Braidotti et al. 1994: 101) However, the DAWN analysis did link the crisis of the environment with women's needs and question the development process.

The DAWN report was debated at seminars and conferences across the world before it was presented at the 1985 Nairobi conference at a forum on 'Women and the Environmental Crisis'. In all, over two thousand women debated the report at various different meetings (ibid: 11). The 1985 conference gave a much higher profile to women and the environment than the 1975 Mexico conference had done, with other well-known activists such as Vandana Shiva and Wangari Maathai playing a major role. Ecofeminism as a perspective had become increasingly important in the groundswell of activity around women and the environment. Campaigns and conferences linking women, the environment and development increasingly brought together grassroots activists from North and South, as well as researchers, academics, radical development and environment campaigners and political activists. Following a conference in Managua, Nicaragua in June 1989, a 'women's declaration' was issued:

> Women from around the world, meeting in the IV Biennial Congress on the 'Fate and Hope of the Earth' recognise that the global crisis of misused 'models of development' has brought us to the brink of disaster. This is seen in the abominable social, economic, political and cultural conditions which are particularly prevalent in the Third World. Women suffer most from these conditions.

An international seminar on 'Women, Environment and Development' was also called by WEN in London in March 1989. The keynote speaker, Vandana Shiva, argued that women were not marginalized in the development process by accident. They were, in fact, bearing the cost of development, as was the environment:

> The hidden costs related to the loss of visibility, the loss of the perception that women as producers sustain society throughout the world. The costs also of being robbed of the material base that makes production of sustenance possible; the forest, the soil, the genetic resources. (WEN 1989: 5)

The seminar also challenged the idea that growth could bring equality. This was not ecologically sustainable. Chee Yoke Ling of Malaysia called for the women's liberation movement to recognize the dilemma of the destructive force of technology and embrace 'minimalism'.

Workshops presented evidence from around the world on the relationship between women, the environment, development and grassroots responses. These ranged from village organizations in India, Zimbabwe, Sudan and Ghana, to campaigns about pesticides in Nicaragua and Malaysia, and women's involvement in radical political movements in Brazil (WEN 1989). The seminar called for a reconceptualization and redefinition of development to mean 'a process of change which safeguards the natural environment, enables women's self-empowerment, and balances social and economic needs' (ibid: 4). Evidence of the environmental problems women were facing and the grassroots solutions they were finding were also collected and published by Dankelman and Davidson (1988) and Sontheimer (1991). Dankelman and Davidson claimed that there were six thousand women's groups in Africa alone that were involved in various 'conserving' activities (1988: 177). Sontheimer also argued in her introduction that:

> [T]he predominant theme that emerges from a reading of the literature is not of women as victims of ecological crises, but rather the extraordinary ability of women to organize themselves to fight ecological destruction and carry out actions that both improve their lives and make a significant contribution to local community development. (1991: prelims)

Zed Press and Earthscan Publications in London have provided a particularly important channel for voices from the South, even if they have been filtered through concerned activists. As Dankelman and Davidson point out in the preface to their book published by Earthscan:

> It has not been possible, in this book, to convey adequately the drudgery and the suffering so many Third World women must face in their daily struggle to survive and care for their families. Nor have we done justice to the extraordinary resilience and energy these women display in impoverished and sometimes dangerous environments. Northern women, writing about life in the South, can do little more than try to give some voice to the voiceless. (1988: prelims)

There was not, however, a universal shift within feminist thinking about development. A study on gender and development, prepared for the European Union and published in 1992, makes no mention of environmental issues whatsoever, and advocates that all bilateral and multilateral development aid should incorporate a WID perspective (Ostergaard 1992). However, in 1993 the WID forum, part of the Society for International Development (one of the oldest NGOs formed in the early 1960s), called a round-table conference in The Hague to discuss 'Women, Environment and Alternatives to Development'. It was proposed that WID should become WED – Women, Environment and Development – and the main papers from the conference were published in a book *Perspectives on Sustainable Development* (Harcourt 1994). The conference concluded that 'development theory and practice founded on Western biases and assumptions, excludes both women and nature from its understanding of development and, in so doing, has contributed to the current economic and ecological crisis' (ibid.: 3).

While the WED approach has challenged the idea of women as 'victims' and pointed instead to their strengths and resilience at the grass roots, some concerns have been expressed. Braidotti et al. (1994) have noted a tendency to treat all women in the South as having the same experience and potential, as well as to romanticize their situation, which diverts attention from the power structures that surround and construct the situations in which many women find themselves. Having ceased to be seen as victims, women are coming to be seen as the solution: 'The prevailing image of women as agents fighting the effects of the global ecological crisis casts them as *the* answer to the crisis: women as privileged knowers of natural processes, resourceful and "naturally" suited to provide the "alternative" (Häusler 1994: 149; italics in the original). Braidotti et al. (1994) express similar reservations. From a postmodern perspective they argue that a new totalizing image of the valiant 'Third World Woman' is being presented that deflects attention from divisions between women. Such an image may also obscure the gap between the WED movement, largely made up of activists, academics and researchers, and the grassroots base. Braidotti et al. even question how extensive the grassroots base actually is. From a structuralist perspective Bina Agarwal calls for a transformative struggle around the woman–nature relationship rather than a celebration of it (1992).

Despite these criticisms, the WED process brought together important issues that directly challenged the international programme of development sponsored by the industrialized nations and the United Nations. The UN, like most development organizations, did not welcome the very critical turn that the women and environment campaigns were taking, but was persuaded rather belatedly to recognize this growing movement – in 1991 it called for a specific women's input to the 1992 Rio 'Earth Summit'. Two conferences were hurriedly called in Miami in 1991. The first, the 'Global Assembly of Women for a Healthy Planet', brought more than 200 women from all over the world, who presented their experiences of managing and protecting the environment to 500 invited delegates from development organizations. The second conference called 1,500 women together from eighty-three countries to prepare a Women's Action Agenda for the 'Earth Summit'. Braidotti et al. argue that the Miami conferences represent a 'major breakthrough' because 'for the first time ever women across political/geographical, class, race, professional and institutional divides came up with a critique of development and a collective position on the environmental crisis, arrived at in a participatory and democratic process' (1994: 103). In parallel to the Summit itself, in June 1992, the Brazilian Women's Coalition organized a women's conference, Planeta Femea, at the NGO forum in Rio de Janeiro. The result of these meetings was an input to Agenda 21 of the Earth Summit resolutions, in which the position of women was addressed, specifically in Chapter 24, where the need for the active involvement of women in economic and political decision-making was acknowledged. The relative lack of importance of women, however, can be shown by the fact that a calculation of the costs of implementing Agenda 21 was $600 billion for the whole programme, but only $40 million for programmes relating to women.

Sabine Häusler has described the outcome of the Rio Summit as 'a failure of global proportions' (1994: 146) and it has been generally categorized by green activists as an expensive failure (Sachs 1993). Even the process of bringing NGOs together in a semi-formal way was problematic. It meant that Amazonian indigenous peoples were rubbing shoulders with representatives of multinationals. Even so, any publicity given to the NGO forum presented it as made up of 'hopeless idealists, exotic Indians and groups of emotional women' (Häusler 1994: 148). Even the Planeta Femea group was not without its problems. The remarkable unity among all the delegates concerning women and the environment had led to a lack of sensitivity to divisions and inequalities between women. The problem of racism and lack of representation was raised by Brazilian women of colour (ibid: 150).

Häusler argues that the unity of the NGO delegates also enabled them to be co-opted by the UNCED process. Some notional acknowledgement of women in UN texts has meant that a policy that is effectively 'business as usual' has been made more acceptable (ibid: 151). Finger has made a similar point about the involvement of NGOs generally, whereby they are seen as giving tacit approval to what eventually become very watered-down policies (1993: 36). He particularly sees this process at work in the preparation of the 1987 World Commission on Environment and Development Report, *Our Common Future*, better known as the Brundtland Report. This Report envisaged the possibility of 'sustainable development', defined as 'development which meets the needs of the present generation without compromising the ability of future generations to meet their own needs' (1987: 43–4). The Brundtland Report did not specifically focus on the relationship between women and the environment and did not challenge the overall aim of 'development'. It did acknowledge the role of women in farming in a section on 'neglect of the small producer' (ibid: 124–5). Sustainable development has become a mainstream concept that tends to mean 'business as usual' or, according to the World Bank in 1992: 'sustainable development is development that lasts' (quoted in Sachs 1993: 10).

Women's voices are still not being heard even in pressure groups around the UN. A document issued in 1991 by the United Nations Environment Programme, together with the World Wide Fund for Nature and the World Conservation Union, entitled *Caring for the Earth: A Strategy for Sustainable Living*, makes no reference to women whatsoever. It calls for support from 'non-governmental organizations and professional groups; religious leaders and educators; business people, farmers and fisherfolk' (IUCN/UNEP/WWF 1991: 19). Even discussion of 'green belt' tree-planting only refers to 'volunteers, especially children' (ibid: 12). Häusler argues that women are now likely to become the targets for further policies of sustainable development and population programmes, and concludes: 'The past experience of such development projects has shown that they put more strain on already overworked rural women without necessarily leading to much-needed wider legal and political changes' (1994: 151). However, despite these criticisms, the Earth Summit and the Planeta Femea did provide the basis for the creation of a global network of campaigners and activists.

In the 1990s campaigns concerning women and the environment have continued to focus on the development process, in particular the growth of bio-technology (Abramovitz 1994). DAWN has recently called for a platform based on women and the environment, alternative economic systems and campaigns against reproductive engineering. Concerns about the latter have been raised by organizations such as FINRRAGE (Feminist International Network of Resistance to Reproductive and Genetic Engineering), launched in 1985 in Vellinge,

Sweden. In India the specific problem of using reproductive technology for sex determination has led to the formation of a Forum Against Sex Determination and Sex Preselection Group (1994). The Asian and Pacific Women's Resource Centre has also researched and reported on women's health and environmental issues more generally (1989, 1992).

These issues are of central concern to Mies and Shiva, whose challenge to western economic and technological 'maldevelopment' has led them to advocate a 'subsistence perspective' (1993: 297). By this they mean a needs-based economy which starts from the unpaid subsistence work of women and peasant peoples that attempts wherever possible to avoid the commodified market economy. They also condemn the new technologies of reproductive and genetic engineering outright: 'We can no longer argue about whether reproductive or genetic technology as such is good or bad; the very basic principles of this technology have to be criticized no less than its methods' (ibid.: 175). Mies condemns the new technologies as racist, sexist and ultimately fascist (ibid: 176) and Shiva has long been concerned about the threat to biodiversity of the new technologies: 'Biotechnology . . . makes it possible to colonise and control that which is autonomous free and self-regenerative . . . the seed, women's bodies as sites of regenerative power are, in the eyes of capitalist patriarchy, among the last colonies' (Shiva 1994: 129).

Abramovitz defines biodiversity as 'the sum of genes, species and ecosystems co-existing on Earth at any point in time (1994: 198). She draws together chilling evidence of the loss of species even in 'man-made' forms. For example, 96 per cent of vegetable varieties listed by the US Department of Agriculture in 1903 are now extinct. In Indonesia 1,500 local rice varieties have become extinct in the last fifteen years (ibid.: 199–200). Even where there is genetic diversity, commercial firms are increasingly wanting to 'colonize' and patent them in the 'Biodiversity–Biotechnology–Biobusiness link' (Weizsacker 1993: 121). Shiva argues that biodiversity and cultural diversity go hand in hand: 'Diversity is the characteristic of nature and the basis of ecological stability. Diverse ecosystems give rise to diverse life forms and to diverse cultures. The co-evolution of cultures, life forms and habitats has conserved the biological diversity on this planet' (1993: 65). Central to Shiva's critique is the role of women in maintaining diversity, particularly of knowledge (1989). Abramovitz has also argued for recognition of 'the vital role women play in understanding and managing the living diversity of their surroundings, and the importance of that diversity to sustaining women and the families they support' (1994: 198). There is, however, quite a leap between identifying women's central role as agents of environmental sustainability and the creation of a movement that embraces those ideas.

The emergence of ecofeminism

Women's involvement in grassroots struggles and global campaigns to do with the environment cannot be automatically claimed as evidence of the existence of an ecofeminist movement. As I have pointed out, claims for the size and importance of the movement depend upon whether the narrower notion of those who identify themselves as ecofeminists is taken, or a wider inclusive view that embraces all women involved in grassroots environmental movements even if they do not explicitly embrace a feminist or ecofeminist perspective (Lahar 1991). As Joni Seager has noted:

> Women who take the lead in community organizing are not necessarily feminists, nor are they necessarily aware of, or interested in, feminist analyses of power, culture, sexuality, structure. In fact, many women who are in the midst of a struggle against a daily-life threat express the view that feminist questioning is diversionary. (1993: 237)

Grassroots activists, as we have seen, were often people who had not previously been politically involved or committed, although the experience of campaigning was usually a deeply politicizing one. The women who did create ecofeminism as a movement on the other hand, often had a long history of activism in other feminist, peace or political movements. Many were also from academia, which opens the movement to accusations of being the preserve of middle-class white academics. This is the dilemma for many radical movements in an unequal society. Without inequality there would not be radical movements, but those with the most cultural capital to support the movements are often relatively privileged themselves.

Ecofeminism as a movement and as a perspective seemed to emerge spontaneously in several parts of the world in the mid 1970s – in France, Germany, the United States, Sicily, Japan, Venezuela, Australia and Finland (Kuletz 1992; Salleh et al. 1991). In the United States the new grassroots organizations and the early proponents of ecofeminism were brought together at 'Women and Life on Earth: A Conference on Ecofeminism in the Eighties', called in response to the nuclear crisis at Three Mile Island in 1979. One of the speakers was

Lois Gibbs, who pointed to the importance of women's politicization in grassroots action: 'The women of Love Canal are no longer at home tending their homes and gardens . . . women who at one time looked down at people picketing, being arrested and acting somewhat radical are now doing those very things' (quoted in Merchant 1992: 193). The conference, held in March 1980 in Amherst, Massachusetts, was organized by the writer Grace Paley and a leading ecofeminist Ynestra King, among others, both of whom had a long history of activism (Spretnak 1990).

Ynestra King, an academic, feminist and peace activist, saw the aim of the conference as being the exploration of the connections between militarism, feminism, healing and ecology (1983a: 9). The six hundred women who attended were united by both hope and fear, 'a fear for life and the awesome powers of destruction arrayed against it and out of hope – a hope for women's power to resist and create' (ibid.: 9). The resistance was against violence ' the violence against women in all its forms – rape, battering, economic exploitation and intimidation . . . the racist violence against indigenous peoples . . . the violence against the earth (ibid: 11). Opening the proceedings, King put the relationship between ecology and feminism firmly on the agenda:

> We're here to say the word ECOLOGY and announce that for us as feminists it's a political word – that it stands against the economics of the destroyers and the pathology of racist hatred. It's a way of being, which understands that there are connections between all living things and that indeed we women are the fact and flesh of connectedness. (quoted in Caldecott and Leland 1983: 6)

The Amherst conference laid the foundation for the Women's Pentagon Actions in November 1980 and 1981 when women surrounded the Pentagon peacefully for two days on each occasion. A 'Statement of Unity' adopted by the organizers of the action sets out clearly the connections that were being made: 'We are gathering at the Pentagon on November 16th because we fear for our lives. We fear for the life of this planet, our Earth, and the life of the children who are our human future' (Leland and Caldecott 1983: 15). The Pentagon action was in response to the decision to escalate the Cold War by the deployment of cruise missiles at sites throughout Europe. In Britain peace and anti-nuclear activists in Carmarthen, Wales followed the example of Scandinavian peace women who had walked from Copenhagen to Paris in protest. Demonstrators (including some men) from Cardiff marched to the cruise missile site at Greenham Common under the banner 'Women for Life on Earth Peace March 1981'. This led to the establishment of the (eventually) women-only peace camp at Greenham Common (Roseneil 1995). From the evidence, it might appear that the march was the spontaneous decision of a group of women and men in Wales, if not of one woman, Ann Pettit, who first suggested the idea. However, as Jill Liddington has pointed out, it grew out of a long history of peace and anti-nuclear campaigning that meant that there was 'a long road to Greenham' both for the marchers and for the women's peace movement as a whole (1989).

Although the primary motivation for the Greenham protest was anti-nuclear and anti-militarism, the experience of living on the very striking Common and quite literally close to the earth encouraged the growth of ecofeminist ideas, as Roseneil has pointed out. This was reinforced by visits from women from the United States who had been involved in the Women's Pentagon Actions and the works of Mary Daly and Susan Griffin which circulated widely in the camp (Roseneil 1995: 67). Like the American actions, the imagery of spinsters and web-weaving were central to many of the Greenham protests, and a countrywide web-like organization was developed that was very effective. As a very temporary resident I can vouch for the visual impact of the Common, which moved me strongly in the direction of ecofeminism. I also saw evidence of the influence of spiritual feminism in a 'Goddess' statue surrounded by offerings. Greenham did, however, share with other feminist, ecofeminist and peace movements an over-representation of white, middle-class activists and an under-representation of Black and working-class adherents (Brown 1984).

One of the most concrete and seemingly successful examples of the link between feminist and green thinking was in Germany, where *die Grünen*, the West German Green Party, sought explicitly to adopt a feminist perspective. Women who had been involved in grassroots action through the Citizens Initiatives, the women's movement and the peace movement were key founding members of the party. The late Petra Kelly is perhaps the best known. When the Green Movement gained significant political representation by taking twenty-eight seats in the German Federal Parliament in 1983, it looked as if feminism was at the heart of green politics in Germany. *Die Grünen* had made a commitment to feminism and the role of women. A central feature of its political programme was the aim of having 50 per cent representation for women throughout the party. Reflecting the origin of many of its members in the women's movement, *die Grünen* called for a society 'built on complete equality of the sexes in the context of an overall ecological policy', thus ending the 'oppression, exploitation, injustice and discrimination that women have suffered for many thousands of years' (Programme of the German Green Party 1983: 40).

In 1984 the national parliamentary group of *die Grünen* was headed by a 'Feminat' of six women. In 1987 women headed all but one of the electoral lists for the *Bundestag*, and twenty-five women and nineteen men were elected. However, in practice this policy was not ultimately successful. Faced with the expectations of politics as defined by men, women – particularly those with domestic responsibilities – found it difficult to take part on equal terms. As early as 1985 Charlene Spretnak and Fritjof Capra reported that the pro-woman policy was not substantiated by any real understanding on the part of the men in the movement of the difficulties women found in taking office (1985: 47). By 1986 Petra Kelly was reporting on the detrimental effect on her health of a high public profile (*Green Line*, no. 48 1986–7). A 1989 profile of the German Greens describes women as a 'special interest group' rather than a core element in the party's membership and programme (Parkin 1989). The experience of the German Greens is unfortunately reflected in many other green parties and in the green movement generally (Mellor 1992c; Seager 1993). Feminism cannot be assumed to be at the centre of green politics; if anything, the German Greens were an exception in this regard. Nor, of course, can the presence of women in a green movement imply that it will adopt an ecofeminist perspective. The relationship between ecofeminism and the green movement will be discussed more fully in Chapter 6.

Despite the involvement of women in grassroots environmental struggles in various parts of the world, including several high-profile conferences and the formation of various networks, there is no formal ecofeminist movement. To the extent that even an informal movement exists, it is represented mainly in a rapidly growing range of publications (Caldecott and Leland 1983; Shiva 1989; Plant 1989; Diamond and Orenstein 1990; Mellor 1992a; Plumwood 1993; Mies and Shiva 1993; Warren 1994). It is a movement of ideas, theories and practices, which builds upon women's actual struggles. While these writings can be criticized for being over-representative of white, middle class women from the North, in mitigation it can be argued that the body of ecofeminist literature forms a critical and radical alternative to traditional, malestream perspectives. As Peggy Antrobus, another of the DAWN founding members, argued at the first Miami meeting in 1991:

The primary task for us as women is to formulate analyses which will help us identify the root causes of our environmental problems. We must clarify the links between environmental degradation and the structures of social, economic and political power. (quoted in Seager 1993: 280–1)

This is what the body of literature that identifies itself as ecofeminist sets out to do.

3

Ecofeminist Thought

Credit for coining the word '*écofeminisme*' in 1974 is generally given to the French feminist Françoise d'Eaubonne, although Janet Biehl makes a claim on behalf of the United States social ecofeminist Chiah Heller (1988). In 'Le Feminisme ou la mort', first published in 1974, d'Eaubonne argued that male control of production and of women's sexuality brings the twin crises of environmental destruction through surplus production, and overpopulation through surplus births (her particular target here was Catholicism). D'Eaubonne called upon women to wrest power from 'patriarchal man', not to replace it with 'power-to-the-women' but 'egalitarian management of a world to be reborn'. Against the 'timid ecologists' who only looked for environmental protection, she argued that what was needed was a 'planet in the female gender' (1980: 64–7).

D'Eaubonne here touches upon a number of issues that would become central to the ecofeminist movement: the crisis of modernity, as the ecological cost of 'progress' became apparent; a critique of (western) 'patriarchal man' as the cause of that crisis; a call to women/female/the feminine/feminism to be the agent(s) of change; a seeming prioritization of the 'female gender', but a commitment to a non-gendered egalitarianism rather than 'power-to-women'. It is *patriarchy* rather than men *per se* that is seen to be the problem. Women are to be the bridge to a reformed and reformulated social order. D'Eaubonne asserted an affinity between woman/femaleness and a benign attitude to the natural world that patriarchal man appeared to lack, while looking to social changes to resolve the problem. This mixture of a near-essentialist conception of a woman–nature affinity and a non-gendered outcome is one of the most complex 'weavings' of the ecofeminist web.

Although ecofeminism emerged in several countries at around the same time, the United States dominated the early development of ecofeminist thinking. The ex-Catholic theologian Mary Daly introduced Boston students to d'Eaubonne's text in 1974. In the same year a conference on 'Women and Environment' was called at the University of California, Berkeley, the theologian Rosemary Radford Ruether was presenting lectures on Women and Ecology at Kalamazoo College, while the poet Susan Griffin was addressing the Department of Agriculture at the University of California, Berkeley on similar issues. Ecofeminism in the United States drew on two main streams. One was radical/cultural/spiritual feminism, which tended to stress the 'natural' affinity of women to the natural world. The second drew on more social constructionist and radical political perspectives, mainly eco-anarchism, but also socialism/Marxism. Socialism/Marxism is, however, much more strongly represented in ecofeminist thought in Europe and Australia and cultural/spiritual feminism less so. Once again, however, categories cannot be watertight. The German Green, Petra Kelly, expressed cultural and spiritual ecofeminist sentiments (1984), while, as we shall see below, United States ecofeminists, even from a theological background, have adopted a socialist politics.

Regardless of their theoretical and political backgrounds, ecofeminists see women as playing a key role in the transition from an unsustainable to a sustainable world, although their perceptions of the mechanisms of change may differ. While spiritual ecofeminists may urge women to call upon the power of the Goddess, social (that is, anarchist) and socialist ecofeminists will be encouraging women to challenge the gender-blindness of male-dominated political organizations. For both groups, however, the ending of women's subordination is a prerequisite of a sustainable society – it cannot be the byproduct of some other struggle. Ecofeminism will not, and cannot, wait until 'after the revolution'.

As I have pointed out, the political impact of ecofeminism has been somewhat hindered by the fact that it has tended to be identified solely with its cultural/spiritual feminist roots and hence subject to critiques of essentialism, romanticism and political naïvety (Biehl 1991; Faber and O'Connor 1989). This is largely due to the domination of ecofeminist debate by literature emanating from North America. In particular, two anthologies – *Healing the Wounds* (Plant 1989) and *Reweaving the World* (Diamond and Orenstein 1990) – concentrated heavily on cultural and spiritual ecofeminism. This was in contrast to an earlier anthology,

Reclaim the Earth (Caldecott and Leland 1983), which concentrated much more on grassroots movements and political struggles.

Some aspects of ecofeminism can certainly be criticized for over-romanticizing women and women's history, for asserting a 'totalizing' image of a universalized 'woman' and ignoring women's differences. Affinity ecofeminists can come very close to biological determinism (although rarely embrace it completely), while being unable to explain why many women are attracted to the western 'patriarchal male' lifestyle. However, it is important not to let these very real criticisms obscure the complexity of the arguments that ecofeminists are making and deflect from the radical perspective that ecofeminism can offer. Although I have made a distinction between affinity ecofeminism based on radical/cultural/spiritual feminism and a social constructionist approach based broadly on socialist/materialist ecofeminism both here and elsewhere (Mellor 1992a: 50 f.), I do not think it is helpful to try to pigeon-hole ecofeminists or ecofeminism. For example, Hilary Rose, a British socialist feminist, and Ariel Salleh, an Australian socialist ecofeminist, have recently been accused of sailing very close to the wind of essentialism (Jackson 1995: 125–6; Davion 1994: 18–20). Maria Mies's and Vandana Shiva's recent ideas are an interesting combination of materialist and affinity ecofeminism (1993), while Rosemary Radford Ruether, one of the earliest ecofeminists, combined feminist theology with a commitment to 'communitarian socialism' (1975). For this reason, in setting out the theoretical debates in this chapter I will treat contributions to the development of ecofeminism broadly chronologically rather than thematically.

Origins and beginnings: connecting women and nature

The emergence of ecofeminism in the early 1970s brought together two crises of modernity. One was the loss of faith in science, technology and development, as reflected in the green critique of western industrialism, the South's critique of economic imperialism and the growing anti-nuclear campaigns. The second was the realization that liberal feminist optimism about women's political and social progress had been misplaced. Education and economic progress had not enabled women to escape from 'femininity', the family or the suburbs (Friedan 1963). For women on the left, 'first wave' feminism was finally defeated by the sexism of the 'new left' of the 1960s, when 'men led the marches and made the speeches and expected their female comrades to lick envelopes and listen' (Coote and Campbell 1982: 13). Equally, the socialist states of Eastern Europe had only produced token representation for women. Facing the powerlessness even of educated and radical women, feminists began to look for a new basis for their struggle. Did there need to be a class struggle between men and women of the same order as that between capital and labour (Firestone 1970)? The problem for the idea of class struggle was that women did not seem to have the same political leverage as the working class. Where, for instance, was the political equivalent of the General Strike or mass class action? De Beauvoir had already pointed out that women had no basis for collective action, scattered as they were among the men (1968). It was not unexpected, therefore, that women turned to reproduction, mothering and nurturing as a basis for their power. Production, apart from being male-dominated, was associated with destructive technologies and lifestyles. Women also began to look for the source and/or origins of male power after it had been named as 'patriarchy' (Millet 1970). Alongside this came a search for female power. If men had patriarchy – the primacy of the father – did women have matriarchy – the primacy of the mother?

One of the earliest celebrations of male/female differences that brought together a critique of male power and a dualist view of men and women in relation to nature was Elizabeth Gould Davis's book *The First Sex*:

> Man is the enemy of nature: to kill, to root up, to level off, to pollute, to destroy are his instinctive reactions.
>   . . . Woman . . . is the ally of nature, and her instinct is to tend, to nurture, to encourage healthy growth, and to preserve ecological balance. She is the natural leader of society and of civilization, and the usurpation of her primeval authority by man has resulted in uncoordinated chaos. (1971: 335, 336)

While Mary Daly recalls the 'incredible impact' that Davis's book had on US feminism in the early 1970s (Collard 1988: xi), Davis's work was subject to heavy criticism, particularly from Black feminists for ignoring Black women's history (Rich 1976/1991: 91). Rich describes Davis as 'the first contemporary feminist myth-maker' whose work is in a direct line from the nineteenth-century German 'patriarchal mythographer' J. J. Bachofen. Rich accepts that Davis's book has 'undoubtedly been an embarrassment to academic feminists intent on working within strictly traditional and orthodox definitions of what constitutes serious knowledge. Yet its impact has been great, beginning with the arresting implications of its title' (ibid.: 91).

Davis's historical claims have been described as 'flights of fancy' (Eisler 1987: 149) but the book did represent a cultural celebration of women which opened up a debate about the relationship between women and nature that has profound implications for feminist theory and practice.

The criticism of modernity implicit in both deep green and radical feminist writing has led to a search for a period in history that was more benign, both socially and ecologically. Sometimes this has been identified with particular historical periods, such as Minoan Crete, sometimes with particular types of human society that may still exist, such as tribal communities. The culture and beliefs of Native American peoples have been particularly influential for spiritual ecofeminism in North America.

Some feminists have claimed evidence of women's power in ancient times (Stone 1976; Daly 1978; Gimbutas 1982). This evidence is drawn from old myths and legends and in archaeological discoveries of a period in early human history when female images abounded (Daly 1973; Reed 1975; Stone 1976). They see women's power as represented in the symbols of women's fertility and sexuality, such as the so-called Venus figurines of 25,000–15,000 BCE, the shrines of the Mother Goddess in Jericho in 7,000 BCE and in evidence from the ceremonial burials of women from 12,000–9,000 BCE (Miles 1988: 19–20). Other feminists have been highly suspicious of this exercise and have seen in the 'myth of matriarchy' a justification for male power (Bamberger 1974). I do not intend to investigate the arguments for and against these claims here, as I have done so elsewhere (Mellor 1992a: 117 f.).

The importance of Davis's ideas and those of other matriarchal theorists to theologians like Mary Daly was that she, like spiritual feminists of the same period, was seeking to reclaim women's spiritual history from patriarchal theology. In Daly's case her aim was to 'spin' an alternative feminist mythology and theology (1973, 1978). Although the woman–nature connection was implicit in Daly's work, it was taken up more fully by other early ecofeminists such as Rosemary Radford Ruether and Susan Griffin.

It is perhaps Griffin's *Woman and Nature* (1978), a poetic exploration of the relationship between scientific/technological man and nature/woman speaking alternately in the male and female voice, that has given ecofeminism its 'essentialist' tag. In her preface Griffin claims that 'this book could not exist had I not read Mary Daly's *Beyond God the Father*, which opened ways of thinking for me' (1978: xii). However, Griffin also cites the socialist ecofeminist Carolyn Iltis

(Merchant) as another influence and her later work makes it clear that she adopts a social constructionist position: 'what I mean . . . is not the biological male and female, but the socially created categories, masculine and feminine, (1990: 87). *Woman and Nature* explores many of the later concerns of ecofeminists such as the relationship between humans and animals, wilderness and wild-ness, sexism and science, the technological destruction of the natural world and woman, bodies, sexuality and knowing. Griffin's work is also a celebration of her own close identification with nature. A prose poem towards the end of the book, entitled 'This Earth What She is to Me' ends with the following:

> This earth is my sister: I love her daily grace, her silent daring, and how loved I am *how we admire this strength in each other, all that we have lost, all that we have suffered, all that we know: we are stunned by this beauty,* and I do not forget: what she is to me, what I am to her. (1978: 219; italics in the original)

Another work which echoes many of Griffin's concerns is Andrée Collard's *Rape of the Wild*. This, too, has often been cited as evidence of the essentialist nature of ecofeminism. Collard, a professor of romance languages, farmer, beekeeper and close friend of Mary Daly, linked the oppression of women with nature in general and animals in particular. The origins of her book lay in a lecture on 'Nature, Animals and Women' given in 1979 in support of Mary Daly, whose employers were causing difficulties following the publication of *Gyn/Ecology* (Collard 1988: xv). *Rape of the Wild* was finally published in 1988, two years after Collard's death. In her view, the domination of woman and nature are directly connected:

> In patriarchy, nature, animals and women are objectified, hunted, invaded, colonised, owned, consumed and forced to yield and produce (or not). This violation of the integrity of wild, spontaneous Being is rape. It is motivated by a fear and rejection of Life and it allows the oppressor the illusion of control, of power, of being alive. As with women as a class, nature and animals have been kept in a state of inferiority and powerlessness in order to enable men as a class to believe and act upon their 'natural' superiority/dominance. (1988: 1)

For this reason 'no woman will be free until all animals are free and nature is released from man's ruthless exploitation' (ibid.: 1). Collard calls on women in the same terms as Mary Daly to re-member and reclaim their biophilic (life-loving) power as 'our destiny as women and the destiny of nature are inseparable' (ibid.: 168). Women's identity with nature is through their bodies as mothers and nurturers. As

Collard's is one of the most explicit statements of affinity ecofeminism, I will discuss her ideas more fully in Chapter 4.

The criticism of both essentialism and mysticism that has been levelled at ecofeminism reflects the fact that several of the early writers were either poets like Susan Griffin, or theologians like Mary Daly. However, one of the earliest attempts to set out a coherent ecofeminist analysis – Rosemary Radford Ruether's *New Woman, New Earth* – shows the importance of not categorizing ecofeminism too readily, even in its earliest days. At the time her book was written in 1974, Ruether was a theology professor and activist in various feminist, peace and global justice organizations. Like Mary Daly, Ruether's starting point was not ecology as such, but sexism, particularly in relation to theology.

For Ruether the subjugation of women is the first subjugation: 'Liberation movements begin at the point of the subjugation of their people. Black Americans begin their story with the slave ships . . . Latin Americans begin their story in the same period. But the subjugation of women begins in prehistoric culture. The woman's story must encompass the entire scope of the human dilemma' (1975: xii). Unlike Simone de Beauvoir, Ruether does not see women's lack of history as a weakness, but as a strength. Arguing that 'women are the first and oldest oppressed subjugated people', she goes on to claim that 'women must be the spokesmen [*sic*] for a new humanity arising out of the reconciliation of spirit and body' (1992: 51). While laying the blame for the human condition on patriarchy, Ruether does not argue for a return to matriarchal pre-history in order to recover an alternative. In fact, she criticizes pre-historical studies for confusing the anthropological literature on matrilineal cultures (family identity and/or location with the mother's family) among tribal peoples and the goddess figurines of classical antiquity among cultures that were hierarchical and civilized (i.e. with power centres in cities). Women's history, she tells us, is broken, but we can pick up the fragments that may 'swell into a real alternative, not just for women, but for humanity and the earth' (1975: xi).

Like Marx, Ruether argues that the task is not to change consciousness (rewrite theologies, reclaim history), as: 'culture and consciousness themselves are merely the ratifiers of a social system . . . the transformation of consciousness is the servant of a struggle to transform this entire social system in its human and ecological relationships' (ibid.: xiv). Ruether calls for the 'fundamental reconstruction of the way resources are allocated within the world community' (ibid.: 31). Women's liberation and the problems of ecological destruction would only be realized in a social revolution. What is needed is a communitarian socialism (by which Ruether means a community-based socialism) that harnesses rather than rejects technology (ibid.: 204–11). She sees the male ideology of western patriarchy as rooted in a 'self-alienated experience of the body and the world' (ibid.: 4). In this, she is setting out a basic tenet of ecofeminist thought, that women have been subordinated with the body and nature as 'man' reaches out for culture and autonomy. Ruether sees the subordination of women as involving three stages: the conquest of the mother, which involved taking away from women over history their economic independence; the negation of the mother through the development of patriarchal religions and philosophies that associated women with carnality and flesh (as in the fall of Eve); and, finally, sublimation of the mother into an idealized image of 'pure womanhood' – the Virgin Mary (ibid.: 6–23).

In describing this 'descent of woman' Ruether argues against seeing women as a class in the Marxist sense. Instead she claims that women are a 'caste within every class and race' (ibid.: 30). Although they have common oppressions such as 'dependency, secondary existence, domestic labour, sexual exploitation', they are also 'divided against each other by their integration into oppressor and oppressed classes and races' (ibid.: 30). Ruether's ecofeminism is therefore a delicate balance, advocating the centrality of women's experience, while taking account of inequalities and differences between women. Nor does Ruether celebrate women, as women. While she sees embodiment and its lack of recognition as crucial, this is not represented as a transhistorical gendered essence, but contextualized within western cultures. And she does not see 'nature' as elemental or essential. In a later work she argues that 'Nature is a product not only of natural evolution, but of human historical development' (1989: 149). She advocates a change in *human* consciousness, 'a historical project and struggle of re-creation' that will remake humanity's relation with nature. Again, Ruether emphasizes the importance of taking account of 'the structures of social domination and exploitation that mediate domination of nature' (ibid.: 149).

Ruether's political solution is a 'communitarian socialism' loosely modelled on the Israeli kibbutz. Women's dependency is to be overcome by 'transforming the relationship among power, work and home' (1975: 207). Women's work would be communalized and collectivized but always under local communal control, as state socialism, like all state power, was potentially fascist. Children would thereby gain 'a tribe while remaining rooted in the family' (ibid.: 207).

All forms of production would return to the local level. Work would be craft-based and non-alienating, organic and non-waste-generating. 'Human society, patterned for a balance through diversity, would be consciously integrated into its environment' (ibid.: 209).

While Ruether has set out a basically socialist and social perspective, other feminists were concerned, like Mary Daly, with the creation of a new spirituality from the perspective of women. Radical political change must first be preceded by profound spiritual change. In 1975, the same year that Ruether's book was published, a women's spirituality conference was held in Boston, which attracted 1,800 women (Christ 1992a: 277).

Feminist spirituality

> Feel your natural tendencies toward multi-layered perceptions, empathy, compassion, unity and harmony. Feel your wholeness. Feel our oneness. Feel the elemental source of our power. Discard the patriarchal patterns of alienation, fear, enmity, aggression, and destruction. It is not necessary to force them away; by merely focusing awareness on the negative, masculinist thoughts as they begin to arise and then opting not to feed them any more psychic energy, their power becomes diminished and they fade . . . The authentic female mind is our salvation. (Spretnak 1982: 573)

> It is the strength of the feminine which can guide us towards a consciousness which, though aware of polarities, is concerned with their interplay and connectedness rather than their conflict and separation. (Leland 1983: 71)

Feminists arguing for a distinctive women's spirituality claim that it will provide a basis for women's empowerment outside patriarchal control. Spiritual ecofeminists maintain we can find this by reclaiming older forms of wisdom that patriarchy has sought to obliterate.

As with ecofeminism generally, the main focus for the critique is Judaeo-Christianity – that is, western religion as symbolic of western patriarchal culture. In the introduction to their anthology *Womanspirit Rising*, which was first published in 1979, Carol Christ and Judith Plaskow see feminist spirituality as addressing four main issues. The first is the problem of an image and language of God that is exclusively male. The second is the division between body and soul (representing also mind and intellect). This is central to Christianity, where the flesh is sin and dwelling upon the Earth is merely a 'travail' in preparation for the Kingdom of Heaven. The third aim is to reclaim women's spiritual experience and history, and the fourth is to create new theology and rituals (1979: vii). Feminist spirituality is earth-based not heaven-directed. It provides a female image of spirituality, often in the form of a goddess, and celebrates the spiritual nature of the physical world and women's bodies.

> What was cosmologically wholesome and healing was the discovery of the Divine as immanent and around us. What was intriguing was the sacred link between the Goddess in her many guises and totemic animals and plants, sacred groves, and womblike caves, in the moon-rhythm blood of the menses, the ecstatic dance – the experience of knowing Gaia, her voluptuous contours and fertile plains, her flowing waters that give life, her animal teachers. (Spretnak 1990: 5)

Many ecofeminists seek to recover the lost mystical world of older earth-based religions of paganism, witchcraft and goddess-worship:

> In ancient times the world itself was one. The beating of the drums was the heartbeat of the Earth – in all its mystery, enchantment, wonder, and terror. Our feet danced in sacred groves, honoring the spirits of nature. What was later broken asunder into prayer and music, ritual and dance, play and work, was originally one. (Eisler 1990: 33)

Spiritual feminists vary as to whether they advocate that there is/was a goddess, or stress the importance of the goddess as a symbol. Carol Christ claims that religion feeds a deep human need which provides 'symbols and rituals that enable people to cope with limit situations in human life (death, evil, suffering) and to pass through life's important transitions (birth, sexuality, death)' (1992b: 274). She sees spirituality as a very important source of empowerment for women, as they realize the 'fierce new love of the divine in themselves' (ibid.: 274).

Christ's case, like many other advocates of feminist spirituality, is that men have their sky/sun gods, therefore why should women not have their moon/earth goddess? She argues that religious symbols have psychological and political effects even for people who don't believe them. Humanity seeks belief systems that make them feel comfortable with current social and political arrangements. If these do not exist as 'the mind abhors a vacuum', other beliefs will take their place. If we are to have symbols, then the goddess, it is argued, is the best one to have. What the goddess represents is the 'acknowledgement of the legitimacy of female power as a beneficent and independent power' (ibid.: 277). She represents 'the affirmation of the female body and the life cycle expressed in it' (ibid.: 279). Male-centred religions are 'anti-*body*' in that they reject the flesh, particularly as represented by women. Like many feminist theologians Christ points to the attack on women launched by the publication in 1486 of the *Malleus Maleficarum* (Hammer of the Witches), prepared by two Dominican monks (Merchant 1983: 134). This tract argued that all witchcraft stemmed from women's 'carnal lust'.

Reclaiming women's bodies and sexuality is very important to spirituality feminists. Rituals involving menstrual blood and other aspects of women's bodies that are declared taboo or unclean in male religions are celebrated. Starhawk, a.k.a. Miriam Somos, is a follower of the pagan religion of Wicca (1982, 1987). She sees rituals as a way of generating the energy for political action and the image of the goddess as a way of understanding the immanence – that is, the 'aliveness' that permeates the natural world:

> [S]pirit, sacred, Goddess, God – whatever you want to call it – is not found outside the world somewhere – it's in the world: it is the world, and it is us. Our goal is not to get off the wheel of birth nor to be saved from something. Our deepest experiences are experiences of connection with the Earth and with the world. (1990: 73)

The phases of women's lives are held sacred: menses, birth and menopause, as represented by the maiden (youth), mother (creativity) and crone (wisdom). It is through the reclaiming of embodiment that women can make the connection between body and nature and realize their own hitherto denied human potential: 'The Goddess as symbol of the revaluation of the body and nature thus also undergirds the human potential and ecology movements' (Christ 1992b: 282).

Does the goddess then exist, or is she a figment of feminist imaginings? Starhawk, first national president of the church of the 'Covenant of the Goddess', responded to this question as follows: 'It depends on how I feel. When I feel weak, she is someone who can help and protect me. When I feel strong, she is the symbol of my power. At other times I feel her as the natural energy in my body and the world' (quoted in ibid.: 278–9). Christ comments that these words may represent 'sloppy thinking' to a traditional theologian, but that they correspond to 'my deepest intuition that tells me they contain a wisdom that Western theological thought has lost' (ibid.: 279). Can a feminist spirituality be consciously created? Doesn't religion have to be something that is handed down as 'god-given'? Should women not seek a rationalist basis for political action rather than a mystical one? While feminist theologians like Mary Daly have argued that women need to create a female mystic power equivalent to the sky-gods

(1973), this search has been condemned as diversionary by social/ist ecofeminists. As Janet Biehl has argued, merely changing our myths from 'bad' ones to 'good' ones will not change our social realities (Biehl 1991: 18). Charlene Spretnak and Starhawk, on the other hand, see spirituality as a source of inspiration for women in their struggle to change social realities. Spiritual energy empowers women. Such energy can, and should, be channelled into political struggle (Spretnak 1990; Starhawk 1990).

Spiritual ecofeminists draw their inspiration from pre-history and from surviving tribal religions, particularly those of Native Americans and original peoples of Australia and New Zealand. This is often expressed as returning to a nature-based spirituality that the modern world has destroyed. Spretnak sees Native American peoples as having 'maintained unbroken practices of earth-based spirituality for more than twenty thousand years' (1991: 89). Unbroken practices perhaps, but they are not unbroken societies, with the beneficiaries being European colonizers. As a European, I feel uncomfortable about drawing spiritual strength from the rituals and beliefs of people whose lives have been so cruelly destroyed. Taking beliefs out of context is also problematic if they are associated with hierarchical or patriarchal views. Vandana Shiva has been criticized for finding inspiration in some aspects of the Hindu religion, such as the ideas of Prakriti (activity and diversity in nature) and Shakti (the feminine and creative principle of the cosmos), while other aspects of the religion support women's subordination and the caste system (Agarwal 1992; Jackson 1995). Green thought has also drawn heavily on Buddhism (Schumacher 1973) and Taoism (Capra 1976), which are also male-dominated.

New Ageism, and the crass commercialism that has accompanied it also poses a problem for spiritual ecofeminism (Seager 1993; Mellor 1992a). And nor is the attack on Christianity unproblematic. White middle-class feminists may find the Christian faith wanting, but other less privileged groups are continuing to find strength and support in Christianity – for instance those in Eastern Europe or the Black churches. Christ and Plaskow, reflecting in 1992 on their *Womanspirit* anthology of 1979, note the absence of the voice of women of colour in their critique of male-dominated Judaeo-Christianity. Barbara Epstein, on the other hand, argues that the development of spirituality within ecofeminism is positive: 'the orientation towards spirituality gives ecofeminism much of its vitality – and also has been the basis for creating bonds between white women and women of colour' (1993: 148). She cites a conference at the

US Woman Earth Institute in 1988 which brought together equal numbers of white women and women of colour.

Affinity and difference

Spiritual ecofeminism is the exemplar of affinity ecofeminism, which tends to combine a celebration of women-centred values (mothering, nurturing, caring) with a celebration of women's bodies. Women's embodiment is then caught up in a cosmology that tends to identify male and female forces (transcendent god versus immanent goddess). Whether these sex/gender differences are insurmountable is more problematic and depends on the perceived origin of patriarchy.

Hazel Henderson, who developed one of the earliest criticisms of western socio-economic systems from a radical 'futurist' perspective (1978, 1980), sees a constant interrelation between human biology and social relations. 'Since, biologically, humans do come in two assymetrical forms, it is obviously different to experience life in a male and female body.' Women's biology means that they 'vividly experience their embeddedness in Nature, and can harbour few illusions concerning their freedom and separatedness from the cycles of birth and death' (1983: 207). Men, on the other hand, 'for the past 6000 years' have had a sense of freedom and relative disembeddedness. Human civilizations in this time have been vastly creative. However, this diversity and creativity has now become destructive and the human species will need to become more androgynous: 'Today we see these alternatives emerging from the world's ethnic and indigenous peoples, from subsistence cultures and traditional wisdom; from the world's women and from the rising female principle, whose nurturant energies can be seen in the new breed of gentle-men' (ibid.: 206). The feminine spirit for Henderson is not only available to women, but to men too if they choose to embrace it. Women have a biological affinity with nature, but the differences between men and women are not ultimately fundamental. Their different historical experiences mean that women have retained a distinctive form of reasoning that is holistic and intuitive, while men have developed a logical, linear and cerebral mode of thought. Sometimes this is expressed as a division of function in the brain itself (Capra 1983).

Henderson's version of affinity ecofeminism sees biological and social differences between men and women, but no ultimate conflict of interests. Women are closer to nature because they never left it. (Western) men have wandered away for a few millennia, but are now returning. For many radical and social/ist ecofeminists, such a view is deeply problematic. Divisions between men and women are not seen either as biologically based or accidents of historical development, but as representing distinct material interests. Social change will not come from a spiritual rebirth, the weaving of dreams or spells or the re-emergence of the 'female' as body or spirit, but from active political struggle against the structures and institutions of current society.

While affinity ecofeminists start from the association between women and nature, social/ist ecofeminists begin from inequalities and dominations within human society. However, once again these categories are not entirely distinct. While social/ist ecofeminists may start their analysis with social forces, their view of the relationship between men and women may lie close to the views of radical difference feminists. For example, while Rosemary Radford Ruether advocates a political solution to gender inequalities and ecological degradation based on a community-based socialism, she does not see the subjugation of women as dependent on any other social forces. It is not a by-product of capitalism, or even western culture, although it has been enhanced by the separation of mind and body in Greek culture. While Ruether sees the origins of women's subordination as lost in pre-history, she does not claim that there is a biologically based division between men and women. Like many ecofeminists, she sees the origins of sex/gender divisions as being historically remote, but socially pervasive.

Affinity ecofeminism offers a strong and a weak version of the relationship between women and nature, affinity and difference. The first is to assert a strong version of both affinity and difference. This would claim a fundamental difference between men and women based on biology and/or cosmological forces that are irreconcilable (immanent goddess versus patriarchal god) and a direct biological or cosmological link between women and nature. A weaker emphasis on both affinity and difference would see differences between men and women as based on biological and/or cosmological differences that are complementary, and therefore reconcilable, as in the Taoist concept of yin and yang. Even where ecofeminists rhetorically claim a strong affinity between women and nature, and deep divisions between men and women often the actual analysis leans towards social constructionism, as differences and divisions in human history are given causal significance such as the patriarchal invasions of ancient matriarchal societies. The clash in this case becomes one of culture and values rather than one of biology or cosmic division. For those ecofeminists who take a social (i.e. anarchist)/socialist/materialist approach, the emphasis is much more on contemporary social inequalities, and the relationship between women and nature is seen as a purely historical phenomenon. It is as if, as Plumwood argues, 'women and nature have been thrown into an alliance' (1993: 21). However, the degree to which that alliance is socially contingent or materially structured becomes crucial. For most ecofeminists, whether they take a strong or weak affinity or social constructionist approach, the relationship between women and the natural world is seen as a material one. For affinity ecofeminists it is a materiality of female embodiment, of blood, birth and sexuality. For those ecofeminists who take a more socially constructed (but not radically constructivist) view of sex/gender, the material relations represent power relations around human embodiment and the allocation of the burdens and responsibilities it represents.

Social/ist ecofeminism

Women have been culture's sacrifice to nature. (King 1990: 115)

Ynestra King represents the link between the ecofeminist movement and radical political activism. She has 'prominently figured in the promulgation of ecofeminism as a position on the American left which is deeply rooted in the politics and practice of the direct action movement' (Noël Sturgeon, quoted in Lahar 1991: 32). King was a founder and organizer of both the Women and Life on Earth Conference in 1980 and the Women's Pentagon Action in 1980–1, which launched ecofeminism as a movement. Before this she had a long history of activism in the feminist and peace movements, and she had worked as a professional community organizer and an academic. Like Griffin, Daly and Ruether, King gave lectures on ecofeminism in the mid-1970s, in King's case at the Institute of Social Ecology in Vermont founded by Murray Bookchin (Merchant 1992: 184). Bookchin has been a formative figure on the green left in the United States, and has theorized a broadly anarchist perspective, although his own background was originally Marxist.

King's ideas were set out in a number of articles (1981, 1983a, 1983b) and have been reproduced or developed in later anthologies (Plant 1989; Jaggar and Bordo 1989; Diamond and Orenstein 1990). Although she takes a broadly social constructionist position on gender relations (that I have described as social/ist), in many of her statements King expresses ideas that are close to affinity ecofeminism. In her earliest writings she records her debt to the writings of Mary Daly and Susan Griffin, praising the former as an inspirational thinker, but dissociating herself from what she sees as Daly's dualistic thinking . She sees Daly as wanting to reverse the truths of patriarchal theology by asserting the truths of feminist theology. King herself holds that 'any truly ecological politics including ecological feminism must be ultimately anti-dualistic' (1983b: 128).

Susan Griffin, on the other hand, King argues, is not a dualistic thinker and has been misrepresented through her poetical expression of the relationship between men/science and woman/nature in *Women and Nature*, into which an unnecessarily essentialist politics has been read. I would agree with King on this matter. In her introduction to the anthology *Reclaim the Earth*, Susan Griffin makes the assertion that human beings (not solely women) are 'flesh and blood of this earth' and goes on to argue the social constructionist case that:

> [W]omen have long been associated with nature. And if this association has been the rationalisation of our oppression by a society which fears both women and nature, it has also meant that those of us born female are often less severely alienated from nature than are most men. (Caldecott and Leland 1983: 1)

This is echoed by King, who sees the building of 'western industrial civilization in opposition to nature' as interacting dialectically with, and reinforcing, the subjugation of women 'because women are believed to be closer to nature in this culture against nature' (1983b: 119). This, King argues, gives women a 'particular stake in ending the domination of nature' (ibid.: 118). She sees the domination of men over women as the 'prototype' of all other forms of domination, so that potentially feminism creates a concrete global community of interests through interconnection with other dominations, 'its challenge . . . extends beyond sex to social domination of all kinds because the domination of sex, race and class, and nature are mutually reinforcing' (ibid.: 120). Ecofeminism can form the basis of 'a decentralized global movement founded on common interests but celebrating diversity and opposing all forms of domination and violence' (ibid.: 119/20).

King's work presents the main elements of ecofeminism: a critique of the dualism of (western) patriarchal society that makes a distinction between humanity (man) and the natural world; the subordinate position of women in that dualism, so that women are associated with, and materially experience, a relationship with the natural world; the necessity of creating a non-destructive connectedness between humanity (man) and the natural world; the centrality of women to creating that connectedness. King rejects the idea of women abandoning their association with nature and joining men on an equal basis in the 'public world', as that would mean embracing women-hating and nature-hating cultural forms. Also, given that women's 'ecological sensitivity and life orientation' is socially constructed, it 'could be socialized right out of us depending on our daily lives. There is no reason to believe that women placed in positions of patriarchal power will act any differently from men' (1983b: 122–3).

The core of social/ist ecofeminism that brings it close to affinity ecofeminism is that all human beings are rooted in nature, they are embodied beings. However, for social/ist ecofeminists women are not more rooted *essentially* than men, it is just that men are less rooted in practice. To put it another way, (some) men have used their power to escape the consequences of their rootedness or embodiment. Like Ruether, King argues that women are particularly connected to nature through the process of the patriarchal rejection of embodiment: 'it is as if women were entrusted with and have kept the dirty little secret that humanity emerges from nonhuman nature' (1990: 116).

Patriarchal society's rejection and objectification of women and the natural world means that women have a 'deep and particular understanding' of nature-hating patriarchy, 'through our natures and through our life experience as women' (1983a: 11). It is clear from such a statement that King is bringing together elements of affinity (our natures) and social construction (our experience). Women as 'keepers of the home, the children and the community' develop 'nurturant powers', which they use daily whether or not they are biological mothers – a similar point is made by the affinity ecofeminist Andrée Collard. Through their particular experience and understanding, King argues, women can develop an attitude to the natural world that is 'about connectedness and wholeness of theory and practice. It asserts the special strength and integrity of every living thing' (ibid.: 10). In the process of nurturing the 'socialisation of the organic' women form the 'bridge between nature and culture' (1990: 116).

King praises the contribution to ecofeminism from radical cultural feminism. She sees it as a 'deeply woman-identified movement' which, by celebrating what is different about women, has challenged male culture rather than, as liberal feminism, 'strategising to become part of it' (ibid.: 111). Acknowledging that radical cultural feminism

tended to overlook the differences between women, King argues that
the feminist spirituality movement that grew out of radical cultural
feminism has been better able to bridge the gap between western and
non-western women. However, feminist spirituality is weakened by
its emphasis on personal transformation as a route to emancipation.
This cannot provide a solution to current forms of domination without a confrontation with political realities, as 'human beings can't
simply jump off, or out of history': 'These indigenous, embodied,
Earth-centred spiritual traditions can plant seeds in the imaginations
of people who are the products of dualistic cultures, but White
Westerners cannot use them to avoid the responsibility of their own
history' (ibid.: 113). To confront history King turns to a socialist
analysis: 'Ecofeminism takes from socialist feminism the idea that
women have been *historically* positioned at the biological dividing
line where the organic emerges into the social. The domination of
nature originates in society and therefore must be resolved in society'
(ibid.: 116–17; italics in the original). However, King feels that the
analysis of women's domination has been better expressed in Murray
Bookchin's anarchist analysis of the origins of hierarchy in society
than in traditional socialist analysis. Bookchin sees the origins of
hierarchy in the subordination of women by men and the young by
the old (1982, 1989). The socialist emphasis on class domination, on
the other hand, has focused on the sphere of production, with
women's role in the sphere of reproduction seen as secondary if not
diversionary.

Despite the long history of women's subordination, like Hazel
Henderson, King does not in the end see any fundamental conflict
between men and women. A cultural form has emerged which is
ecologically destructive and socially unjust. In response, 'thoughtful
human beings must use the fullness of our sensibility and intelligence
to push ourselves intentionally to another stage of evolution' (1990:
121). In this process women are to play a special role:

> It is the moment where women recognise ourselves as agents of history –
> yes even unique agents – and knowingly bridge the classic dualism
> between spirit and matter, art and politics, reason and intuition. This is the
> potentiality of a *rational re-enchantment*. This is the project of ecofeminism.
> (1990: 120–1 italics in the original)

From her earliest writings King rejects the assertion that women
'naturally' align themselves with nature, but argues that they can
make the conscious political choice not to reject that alignment.
Women can:

recognize that although the nature/culture opposition is a product of culture we can, nonetheless *consciously choose* not to sever the woman nature connections by joining male culture. Rather we can use it as a vantage point for creating a different kind of culture and politics that would integrate intuitive/spiritual and rational forms of knowledge, embracing both science and magic insofar as they enable us to transform the nature/culture distinction itself and to envision and create a free, ecological society. (1983b: 123; italics in the original)

From a socialist feminist perspective Carolyn Merchant agrees with Ynestra King that: 'Although cultural feminism has delved more deeply into the woman–nature connection, social and socialist ecofeminism have the potential for a more thorough critique of domination and for a liberating social justice' (1992: 184). Carolyn Merchant was an early advocate of the compatibility of socialism and ecofeminism. However, her best-known work was a feminist critique of the idea of nature in the scientific revolution, in which she only discussed socialism briefly in reference to the socialist-feminist aim of 'revolutionizing economic structures in a direction that would equalize female and male work options and reform a capitalist system that creates profits at the expense of nature and working people' (1983: 294). In a later essay Merchant expands on the relationship between ecofeminism and other feminist perspectives (1990), and in her book *Radical Ecology* argues for socialist ecofeminism as part of a radical ecology movement (1992).

For Merchant, socialist ecofeminism sees environmental problems as 'rooted in the rise of capitalist patriarchy and the ideology that the Earth and nature can be exploited for human progress through technology' (1990: 103). The basic source of the problem is the sexual division of labour, as humanity tries to divorce itself from nature through the productive system. Men predominate in the sphere of commodified production, while the domestic sphere is serviced by women's unpaid labour. As a result, women and men become alienated from each other and from their labour. The productive process itself is alienated from the natural world. The natural world is, in turn, transformed, eroded and polluted in the course of production for profit. Even so, although nature remains the basis of human life, it is at the same time the result of historical and social forces. It is both a 'natural' and a social construct. The same is true for gender. It is created by biology *and* social practices. As a result, socialist ecofeminism sees the natural world and the human world as active agents, as material forces. Ecological and biological conditions, social production and reproduction are all forces creating and shaping human society. What is required, therefore, is a multilevelled structural analysis that sees a dialectical relationship between production and reproduction as well as between society and nature.

Socialist ecofeminism, Merchant argues, steers a course between a natural conception of 'nature' and the idea of social construction as well as between patriarchy and capitalism as systems of exploitation. While claiming that a materialist analysis of women's social position provides the best basis for an ecofeminist politics, and that a spiritual assertion of women's difference as 'a politics grounded in women's culture, experience and values could be seen as reactionary' (1990: 102), Merchant, like King, does not seek to divide the ecofeminist movement: 'Weaving together the many strands of the ecofeminist movement is the concept of reproduction construed in its broadest sense to include the continued biological and social reproduction of human life and the continuance of life on earth' (1992: 209). Merchant sees ecofeminism as part of a broader movement of 'radical ecology' that embraces theoretical and practical struggles across the globe. This movement has not yet produced 'a worldwide socialist order', but it does offer 'an alternative vision of the world in which race, class, sex and age barriers have been eliminated and basic human needs have been fulfilled' (ibid.: 235–6). The task of the movement is to raise public consciousness of the dangers to human health and non-human nature of maintaining the status quo and to 'push mainstream society toward greater equality and social justice' (ibid.: 235).

Social/ist ecofeminism has developed in a number of directions. Much of its work has taken the form of a critique of Marxism and/or male-oriented versions of ecoMarxism and ecosocialism (Merchant 1992; Thrupp 1989; Mellor 1992b) or of deep ecology (Salleh 1984). More recently, socialist ecofeminist analysis has been developed using a neo-Marxian framework (Salleh 1994; Mellor 1992a/b), or drawing on critical theory (Plumwood 1986, 1993). These ideas will be discussed more fully in later chapters.

Although affinity and social/ist ecofeminists have differed in their emphasis, they have mainly addressed the position of women in western societies. As Seager has argued, ecofeminism is in danger of being a 'particular first world philosophy' (1993: 316). However, it is perhaps right that (mainly) white middle-class feminists should challenge patriarchy and privilege (including their own) in their own societies. In 1975 Ruether called upon feminists in the United States to challenge patriarchal power within their own society. Maria Mies, a German with a long history of involvement with, and support for, women in India asks that western women challenge power 'in the heart of the beast' (Mies and Shiva 1993: 1). However, given the importance of women from the South in grassroots struggles over the environment and the global nature of patterns of socio-economic exploitation, racist oppression and ecological degradation, an ecofeminist analysis from a South perspective is vitally necessary.

Ecofeminism: a South perspective

> Third World women are bringing the concern with living and survival back to centre-stage in human history. In recovering the chances for the survival of all life, they are laying the foundations for the recovery of the feminine principle in nature and society, and through it the recovery of the earth as sustainer and provider. (Shiva 1989: 224)

While ecofeminism has largely been identified with white women in the North, the Indian ecofeminist Vandana Shiva has been one of its most influential voices worldwide. She is, perhaps, best known for her book *Staying Alive* (1989). Inspired by 'the many women, peasants and tribals of India who have been my teachers in thinking ecologically', Shiva abandoned her career as a nuclear physicist and devoted herself to campaigning against ecologically destructive 'maldevelopment'. Examples of maldevelopment are agricultural technologies that are unsustainable and reproductive technologies that interfere with the integrity of women's bodies.

Maldevelopment, for Shiva, has been created by the North's imperialist imposition of its model of modernity on the whole globe. The 'twin pillars' of this model are economic development and modern scientific knowledge. As a result, the world is becoming effectively a 'monoculture' with a consequent loss of diversity of plant and animal life and of peoples and cultures (1993). At the heart of this development is violence, a violation of nature and women: 'this violence against nature and women is built into the very mode of perceiving both, and forms the basis of the current development paradigm' (1989: xvi). The diversity of the natural world is sacrificed for industrialized agriculture and genetically engineered crops. The subsistence, use-value-based way of life of women and peasant peoples is sacrificed for profit-driven commercial production and trade. The West, she argues, has justified its intervention by the assumption that traditional economies are poor economies: 'The paradox and crisis of development arises from the mistaken identification of culturally perceived poverty with real material poverty, and the mistaken identification of the growth of commodity production as better satisfaction of needs' (ibid.: 13). Western 'developers' have also made false assumptions about the economic position of women in the South. Drawing on Ester Boserup's analysis of women's role in subsistence production (1970), Shiva shows how western patriarchal assumptions about male domination of production processes destroyed the resource base for women's subsistence. This denial of the 'feminine principle' in development leads to a one-sided view of resources and resource use. Maldevelopment only sees a river as a resource to be dammed and put to technological use, and not as a 'commons' – that is, a communal resource that meets the water needs of local communities. As women are the main users and carriers of water, they suffer most if supplies are interrupted. Maldevelopment, is 'a development bereft of the feminine, the conservation, the ecological principle' (ibid.: 4). The aim of the development process is to pull all resources and labour into the commodity form, to be circulated via the market. This leaves no resources for women's subsistence or for 'nature to maintain her production of renewable resources' (ibid.: 9). While economic development undermines the subsistence base through pulling all resources into the capitalist market, scientific development applies technologies conceived in laboratories without any real understanding of the 'web of life' on the ground.

Shiva particularly criticizes the green revolution for developing species of crops that demanded high chemical inputs of fertilizers and pesticides, and huge amounts of water. The hybrid seeds that had been developed were also sterile so that farmers had to buy new seeds each year rather than retain seeds from their crops. The loss of diversity and species and the commercial control of seeds has been a particular concern of Shiva's (1994). The commercial production of seeds affects both diversity and the autonomy of farmers, particularly women, who do not have the resources to buy seed. Worse, Shiva argues, vital knowledge is also being lost as the livelihood of subsistence farmers is destroyed. The domination of the North then becomes not just commercial domination, but a domination of knowledge itself. The monocultures of the green revolution and commercialized agriculture are being joined by a 'monoculture of the mind' (1993).

For Shiva, the whole process of maldevelopment rests on the patriarchal assumptions of western culture. This is in contrast to the world-view of women and non-westernized peoples, as represented by the Chipko movement:

> In the world-view personified by the Chipko women, nature is Prakriti, the creator and source of wealth, and rural women, peasants, tribals who live

in, and derive sustenance from nature, have a systematic and deep knowledge of nature's processes of reproducing wealth. (1989: 219)

There is a confusion in Shiva's ideas between the relationship between women *per se* and nature, and between women as representative of non-westernized peoples (peasants, tribals) and nature. Women are, of course, part of the North as well as the South. Following Mies (1986), Shiva argues that western patriarchy has effectively conquered women, through the dualistic nature of its philosophy and science, and the sexual/gender division of labour under industrialism. Western patriarchal culture broke the connection between society and nature and between women and nature. Again following Mies, Shiva argues that women have a particular connection to nature through their experience of the 'production of life' because:

(a) Their interaction with nature, with their own nature as well as the external environment, was a reciprocal process. They conceived of their own bodies as being productive in the same way as they conceived of external nature being so.

(b) Although they appropriate nature, their appropriation does not constitute a relationship of dominance or a property relation. Women are not owners of their own bodies or of the earth, but they co-operate with their bodies and with the earth in order to 'let grow and to make grow'.

(c) As producers of new life they also became the first subsistence producers and the inventors of the first productive economy, implying from the beginning social production and the creation of social relations, i.e. of society and history. (Mies 1986: 56; quoted in Shiva 1989: 43)

Shiva's ideas are therefore a mixture of affinity ecofeminism and an assertion of the social construction of inequality through western models of science and economic imperialism.

Mies and Shiva have elaborated their ideas in a book of essays on ecofeminism (1993). For them 'an ecofeminist perspective propounds the need for a new cosmology and a new anthropology which recognizes that life in nature (which includes human beings) is maintained by means of co-operative, mutual love and care' (1993: 6). They reject any division within the ecofeminist movement based on 'spiritual' versus 'political' ecofeminism. While criticizing the commercial appropriation of 'oriental spiritualism', they claim that an assertion that the earth should be treated as sacred is not in conflict with a materialist and active politics. Against feminists such as Seager, who have argued that spiritual ecofeminists are in danger of stressing the importance of personal transformation to the exclusion of collective political action (1993: 249), Mies and Shiva claim that:

'The ecological relevance of this emphasis on "spirituality" lies in the rediscovery of the sacredness of life, according to which life on earth can be preserved only if people again begin to perceive all life forms as sacred and respect them as such' (1993: 17/18). Political change will come from a spiritual approach combined with political struggles over the fight for immediate survival. In the end everyone can unite on the 'material base' that 'all women and all men have a body which is directly affected by the destructions of the industrial system' (ibid.: 20).

Mies and Shiva also combine an affinity perspective on women's relationship with nature, with an emphasis on women's social experience. Both are triggered in political action:

> Wherever women acted against ecological destruction or/and the threat of atomic annihilation, they *immediately* became aware of the connection between patriarchal violence against women, other people and nature . . . We have a deep and particular understanding of this both through our *natures* and our *experience* as women. (ibid.: 14 italics added)

The enemy of nature and women is the 'white man' of patriarchal capitalism. The main focus of Mies and Shiva's political strategy is to oppose the hegemony of capitalist patriarchy through the defence of women-based subsistence communities in the South and the development of economic alternatives to the capitalist system in the North. The new politics would unite around fundamental needs such as food, shelter, clothing, affection, care, love, dignity, identity, knowledge, freedom, leisure and joy, which are common to 'all people, irrespective of culture, ideology, race, political and economic system and class' (ibid.: 13).

In maintaining that there is the basis for a common global politics, Mies and Shiva reject the postmodern claim that such ideas are 'totalizing' and denying of difference. Drawing upon the experience of the women of the Chipko movement, they argue strongly against the postmodern turn to cultural relativism:

> These women spell out clearly what unites women worldwide, and what unites men and women with the multiplicity of life forms in nature. The universalism that stems from their efforts to preserve their subsistence – their life base – is different from the eurocentric universalism developed via the Enlightenment and capitalist patriarchy. (ibid.: 13)

It is not universalism *per se* that is at fault, but the false universalism of western hegemony.

Common themes in ecofeminist thought

Women's values, centred around life-giving, must be revalued, elevated from their once-subordinate role. What women know from experience needs recognition and respect. We have generations of experience in conciliation, dealing with interpersonal conflicts daily in domestic life. We know how to feel for others because we have been socialised that way. (Plant *Green Line*, No. 48 1986–7: 15)

The everyday struggles of women for the protection of nature take place in the cognitive and ethical context of the categories of the ancient Indian world-view in which nature is Prakriti, a living and creative process, the feminine principle from which all life arises. (Shiva 1989: xviii)

Women are devalued first, because their work cooperates with nature's processes, and second because work which satisfies needs and ensures sustenance is devalued in general. (ibid.: 7)

The divisions within ecofeminism between a biological and a social construction of the relationship between women and nature (affinity versus social/ist ecofeminism) are not easy to separate, as the above statements show. Plant begins by asserting an affinity and woman-centred perspective, referring to women's nature and their life-giving role, but goes on to talk of women's social experience and ends up by arguing the social constructionist case that women have been socialized into their role and values. Shiva's first statement sees women as embodying an ancient cosmic expression of the feminine, but within a few pages we are presented with a socially constructed view of the devaluation of women's work, not just because it is associated with nature, but because it is concerned with basic needs and sustenance.

Whichever perspective is taken – strong or weak affinity, or purely social constructionist – ecofeminism necessarily engages with women's embodiment as sexed beings. Ecofeminists start from the importance of human embodiment (as reflecting biological existence) and embeddedness (within the surrounding ecosystem) and direct their attention to the impact of both on women. The case ecofeminism is making is that women represent the dilemma of human embodiment in a sexed and gendered society. Human embodiment, in turn, represents the fact that human beings live not only in an historical and social context, but also an ecological and biological one. The needs of human embodiment have to be met within an encompassing ecosystem. Differences in the historical and social position of human beings mean that their relationship to their ecosystem may be very different. The rich middle-class drinker of sparkling mineral water is in a very different relationship to her/his water ecosystem from the wo/man who relies upon local intermittent rains. However, they are both embodied and need water, however it is obtained.

Where there are inequalities and/or differences based on sex/gender, the consequences of human embodiment and embeddedness mean different relationships between women and 'nature' in terms of their sex/gender-related work in different contexts. In industrial societies women's distinctive role lies mainly in the area of childbirth, childcare and unpaid domestic work generally. This work is also represented in low-paid and sexually segregated occupations in the formal economy. In the South many women combine their 'biological' roles of motherhood and nurturing with a wide range of activities that directly relate to their environment, such as water-fetching, farming, wood-gathering, rearing small animals, etc. It is important, therefore, not to let the issue of women's oppression on the basis of her reproductive role in the North obscure the wide range of ecological issues that impinge on many women in the South in addressing the 'women and nature' debate.

The common core that unites ecofeminist thought worldwide is its critique of the patriarchal nature of western society. The current threat to the natural world is seen as resulting from the existence of hierarchical dualisms in western society (man/woman, public/private, society/nature, mind/body) and western patterns of knowledge (reason/emotion, abstract/concrete, expert/vernacular). Although ecofeminists may differ in their focus, sex/gender differences are at the centre of their analysis. In confronting western dualism, affinity and social/ist ecofeminists want to revalue the experience of women in patriarchal society. For some affinity ecofeminists this becomes an end in itself, the realization of the 'feminine' in women's bodies or natures or as a spiritual force. For other affinity ecofeminists and social/ist ecofeminists the revaluing of women's experience is a political challenge to dualism.

While differing in their focus and approach to western dualism, ecofeminists are in agreement about the kind of society they want, although most ecofeminist writings are much more concerned with eliminating the negatives of present society than envisaging the specific positives of a new one. An ecofeminist society would be egalitarian and ecologically sustainable. There would be no sexual/gender division of labour, and any necessary work would be integrated with all aspects of communal life. Relationships between humans and between humans and nature would be harmonious and co-operative. These ideals would be shared with most feminists, who 'would advocate a view of nature that emphasized harmony and cooperation with other living things' (Birke 1986: 149; Soper 1995). In ecofeminist writings there tends to be an implicit optimism that once dualist structures are removed there will be no inherent imbalance between the human and the natural worlds, an assumption that I would not make.

However, overemphasis on the particular role of women in challenging the dualist divisions in western society could marginalize the importance of other inequalities and oppressions. Most ecofeminists are at pains to point out that they see sex/gender as being part of a matrix of oppressions. While some affinity ecofeminists may seem to adopt a reductionist position, seeing sex/gender as the original or most universal oppression, I would want to argue that attention to sex/gender can reveal structural dynamics that are helpful in confronting other oppressions. This is not, however, to claim a priority for sex/gender, it is simply *one* starting point.

Addressing the relationship of woman and nature as ecofeminism has done is problematic for feminists who have sought to minimize or destroy this connection. From the perspective of feminists who deny the social relevance of sex difference and claim equality with men in the 'public' world, ecofeminism is in danger of returning to the old essentialist arguments that denied women's equality in the first place. In the next chapter I will look at the feminist debate around 'nature' and biology and its implications for ecofeminist thought. Another debate that is very important in contemporary feminism is the question of sex/gender identity as the basis of political action or as the foundation for particular kinds of knowledge. I will look at ecofeminism in the context of this debate in Chapter 5.

4

Women, Biology and Nature in Feminist Thought

I know I have the body of a weak and feeble woman, but I have the heart and stomach of a king. (Elizabeth I, 1588. Speech to the troops at Tilbury on the approach of the Armada)

One essential feature of all ecological feminist positions is that they give positive value to a connection of women with nature which was previously, in the west, given negative cultural value and which was the main ground of women's devaluation and oppression. (Plumwood 1993: 8)

The fundamental difference between the attitude of Elizabeth I to her body, which has had many echoes through the ages, and Plumwood's summary of the ecofeminist position is their acceptance or rejection of female embodiment. While strong affinity ecofeminists would see female embodiment as positive in itself, most ecofeminists (including Plumwood) would see it as standing for the dilemmas of human embodiment generally.

The debates around the nature of sex/gender differences and the impact of women's biology on their social position has been very much a feature of western feminism. As I have pointed out, for women in other parts of the world and for poor women in western societies, embodiment is much more about obtaining basic sustenance and avoiding disease, disability through overwork and death. To discuss the woman–biology–nature debate within feminist thought is very much to embrace the concerns of relatively privileged western feminists with the danger of ignoring more fundamental problems which the majority of women face. To look at the debate between feminism and ecofeminism in this context must necessarily marginalize or exclude the interests and experiences of many groups of women (hooks 1984). My motivation for returning to these issues is to open up the agenda and break through the preoccupations of western 'equality' feminism. To do this it is necessary to go back to some classic texts and re-examine the woman–biology debate. This is particularly important given the almost total domination of current western feminist thought by postmodern cultural questions (Barrett and Phillips 1992). Embodiment in the sense used by ecofeminists, as a material problem for human beings, is not a focus in many contemporary feminisms. Explicit discussion of human embodiment and the relationship between woman, biology, nature and culture is more common in older feminist texts.

To the extent that western society has created the dualisms of nature/female/feminine and culture/male/masculine, women have found themselves subordinated through their alliance with nature/biology. Upper-, middle-, and upper-working-class white women have historically been prevented from playing a full part in public life on grounds of their biology. This has ranged from allegations of their innate wickedness, innate purity or physical frailty, to the requirements of motherhood (Ehrenreich and English 1979). Poor working-class women, on the other hand, were associated with nature as a justification for their hardship and hard labour. Similar arguments have been used by racists and colonizers to justify their exploitative and oppressive behaviour in terms of their 'superior' culture. In this sense the biology/nature association and its consequences are of more critical political importance than just representing the frustrations of middle-class women whose problem had 'no name' (Friedan 1963).

Transcending nature

The case for ignoring the alleged relationship between women and nature has been made by liberal feminists such as Mary Wollstonecraft. She argued that men and women share a common humanity, capabilities and capacities, and therefore deserve equal rights. In common with Enlightenment thinking of the time, she framed her claim for a common humanity in terms of the distinctiveness of human beings from 'brute nature'. This was not just a feature of liberal thinking; Marx also advocated a common human nature, which was set against 'mere' animal life (Marx 1844; Benton 1993). Although later feminists have not felt the need explicitly to separate themselves from the natural world, the case for equality between men and women, whether on a liberal or a radical/socialist model, has tended to involve a rejection of the association of women with nature. From Mary Wollstonecraft to de Beauvoir and beyond, feminists have been at pains to help women escape from the constraint of their biology (de Beauvoir 1968; Firestone 1970). What was most firmly rejected was biological determinism, in Freud's terms that anatomy was destiny. Feminists particularly rejected the assumption that motherhood should be the determining factor in women's lives and that women's ability to bear children should determine their social role. It was argued that 'women are no more innately gifted for intensive childcare than men' (Barrett and McIntosh, 1982: 145) and that 'the biological experience of childbirth does not necessarily generate maternal emotions and behaviour in the form idealised in the west' (Jackson 1995: 138).

To enable women to escape their domestic role women's liberation movements have argued for equal opportunities in access to economic and social life, together with collective provision of childcare and other domestic support (Coote and Campbell 1982). This strategy is directly threatened by the ecofeminist positive re-evaluation of the association of women with nature. Critics have argued that an ecofeminist reassertion of women's association with the natural world, whether through their bodies, their caring role as mothers or nurturers, or their traditional subsistence work, far from being an agent for change in society, could become a reaffirmation of women's present position:

> Ecofeminist prescriptions are for women to reject transcendence, embrace the body, bond to our mothers, remain embedded in our local ecosystems, abandon the goals of freedom and autonomy, rely on and care for our kin and community and remain in subsistence production. Such conservatism can hardly claim empowerment for women. (Jackson 1995: 129)

I hope to show that such a programme can be empowering and that assumptions that a transcendent 'freedom and autonomy' can exist outside of human embeddedness and embodiedness is ecologically, socially and theoretically unsound (Mellor 1996a).

As a starting point I want to return to the debates within feminism around women, biology and nature, and the relationship of all three to men and culture. Central to this debate are issues of commonality/common interest/sameness and difference/inequality/power, as between men and women and between women. The general short-hand of 'difference/equality' belies the complexity of these issues (Gatens 1991a; Bock and James 1992). Difference/equality is not even a coherent dualism: difference is the opposite of sameness, and inequality of equality. I would agree with Joan Scott that equality does not imply the elimination of difference, and difference does not preclude equality (1991: 138). In this chapter I will be dealing mainly with the divisions between culture/man and woman/nature/biology; in the next chapter the divisions between women and the difference/equality debate within feminism will become more important.

Iris Marion Young has described androgynous 'humanist' feminism with its stress on the equality of men and women, as being in 'revolt against femininity'. By arguing for the 'superiority of the values embodied in traditionally female experience', she sees difference, 'gynocentric' feminism on the other hand, as a potentially more radical position (1985: 173). When first putting forward this argument in 1985, Young still felt that the danger of a woman-centred feminism in an anti-feminist reactionary context outweighed its advantages. However, writing in 1990 she finally 'climbed off the fence to the gynocentric side', arguing that humanist, androgyny feminism did not challenge the assumptions of patriarchal culture (1990: 7). I would want to make a distinction between humanist and androgyny feminism in this context, seeing humanist feminism as claiming the existence of a common hu(man)ity that ignores dualism. Androgyny (derived from the Greek for man–woman) on the other hand, does try to resolve the problem by combining male and female values, experience or labour in some way as the word implies.

While both humanist and androgynous feminism may represent a 'revolt against femininity', ecofeminism is more concerned about the revolt against biology/nature in dualist society. All ecofeminism is gynocentric to the extent that it opens up the question of human embodiment and its particular relevance to the sexed body and women's position in society. Opening up this debate, as Young pointed out, holds the danger of being taken as a reactionary perspective. I would argue that it is a risk worth taking if a deeper radicalism is to be achieved.

Uniting women and nature: Andrée Collard

The identity and destiny of woman and nature are merged. (Collard 1988: 137)

Andrée Collard presents a strong affinity ecofeminism that seeks to revalue and reclaim women's biology and reproductive role. Her book, *Rape of the Wild* was written as a 'burning protest' against animal cruelty, ecological damage and the oppression of women (1988: 1). It provides an example of the kind of arguments that many feminists would see as undermining all their generations of struggles to escape from their association with biology. Far from wanting to put some distance between women and nature, Collard celebrates women's bodies and their biologically linked roles such as motherhood. Patriarchy is the enemy of nature while woman is to be its rescuer through her biological links to the natural world: 'Nothing links the human animal and nature so profoundly as woman's reproductive system which enables her to share the experience of bringing forth and nourishing life with the rest of the living world' (ibid.: 102). Collard recognizes that not all women are mothers, or want to be, but argues that each woman is united in a common mother-identity, 'whether or not she personally experiences biological mothering', as 'it is in this that woman is most truly a child of nature and in this natural integrity lies the wellspring of her strength' (ibid.). Patriarchy, on the other hand, is also biological; it is a disease that reveals itself in the treatment of women and animals (ibid.: 1).

As with much ecofeminist analysis, Collard sees the fundamental problem as lying in the separatist mentality and dominating dualism of patriarchy. It sets itself apart from nature (and women) in a way that allows for the development of cruel and oppressive behaviour towards both. Nature, on the other hand, 'has worked out a self-regulated flow of birth and decay, striking a balance between death and rejuvenation' (ibid.: 2). Whereas patriarchy is immoral, nature is innocent because it acts out of 'inherent need' not conscious behaviour – it is a 'wild and free spirit'. Collard sees the breakdown in the relationship between humanity (as patriarchy) and nature as the cause of all 'divisive "isms" – sexism, racism, classism, ageism, militarism, etc.' (ibid.: 3). If the 'isms' are to be overcome, nature must be reclaimed as sacred and valued for its own intrinsic worth. It must no longer be regarded as something that is dead, to be used and exploited. Humanity must re-establish a 'universal kinship' with nature that would see nature as similar and equal, and not different and inferior: 'It is ultimately the affirmation of our kinship with nature, of our common life with her, which will prove the source of our mutual well-being' (ibid.: 137)

Like many cultural and spiritual feminists, Collard finds evidence for the possibility of 'universal kinship' between humanity and the natural world in the example of ancient and tribal societies. She also accepts the case for the existence of an 'ancient gynocentric way of life' (ibid.: 14) which exhibited 'nurturance-based values which women experienced and projected not only on their goddesses but on to every creature among them' (ibid.: 8). For Collard, 'the history of women's oppression must continually be juxtaposed with what came before. Only then can we have a vision of what we were and therefore what we can be' (ibid.). As with other accounts of a gynocentric pre-history, patriarchy emerges as a cultural clash between the male culture of a transcendent god that separates 'man' and nature and the more egalitarian, earth-loving culture of the goddess. Patriarchy replaced the gathering society associated with women's values and launched the cultural forms associated with hunting, war and violence. This, Collard argues, is what created the division of labour between men and women.

Collard offers us no material explanation of why men launched upon this cultural change. A psychological explanation is hinted at. Men are jealous of the creative potential of women and nature as represented in the goddess. This leads to a fear of female autonomy, 'the enemy within that must be held in check by compulsory hetero-sexuality and compulsory fertility' (ibid.: 106). 'Womb envy' lies behind 'man's scientific divine intervention' ranging from microbiology to animal experimentation (ibid.: 126). Collard also quotes Virginia Woolf's observation that 'male vanity needs female mirrors to reflect men at twice their size' (ibid.: 21). Patriarchy's denial of its material dependence on women and nature has further psychological consequences: 'A tradition that encourages us to free our bodies from the limitations of nature is one that plucks us from the web of life, leaving us stranded and longing for the very biophilic connections we are taught to repudiate' (ibid.: 47). Her answer to the ecological destruction that patriarchy has created is a reassertion of motherhood: 'Ecology is very much a motherhood issue since women and nature have been linked in our consciousness since pre-history . . . Good women have kept good houses on the model of Mother Nature for as long as there have been mothers' (ibid.: 147, 37). Such ideas can be criticized as embracing a biologically determinist and universalist essentialism. Collard sees all women as 'biologically' mothers and her universalism is evident in such statements as: 'all women are victims of degradation. All women are experts in the art of survival' (ibid.: 148). She advocates the values and principles that 'are distilled from women's experiences everywhere and of all times' (ibid.: 137). However, on other occasions she is less absolute and suggests that women's experience of oppression and abuse, as well as mothering, makes them more 'sensitive' to the oppression and abuse of nature (ibid.: 138).

Although she praises the women's peace camps, Collard does not advocate women-only activity or a separatist solution. Instead, she advocates direct action campaigns that reflect deep ecological politics, particularly wilderness preservation. 'Women and men' are also urged to refuse to endorse the values that drive 'sexism, racism, classism and speciesism' (ibid.: 137). Implicitly, she also absolves those scientists and ecologists who have broken free of destructive science, particularly those who endorse a nature-centred perspective. She also has praise for the peasant farmers of Europe (ibid.: 143). The main enemy is modern scientific/technological systems, which separate people from a direct experience of nature: 'The way out of this morass is to strive with all our might to become as independent as possible of all those technologies that threaten life on earth' (ibid.: 146). There are no details of what alternative society could develop, except that it should celebrate wildness (freedom, self-regulation) and not be civilized; people must resist becoming 'tamed city-dwellers' (ibid.: 156).

Collard's assertion of the universal and essential relationship between women and nature is certainly problematic for most feminist perspectives. She believes, however, that feminism is weakened by not seeing these connections. I would agree with her that ecofeminism has the grounds for a more fundamental critique of patriarchy than feminisms which do not have an ecological perspective. Although most feminist texts do not dwell on ecological arguments, at some point the ecologically destructive nature of patriarchal society is often touched upon together with the assumption that women would be more ecologically sensitive. As Kate Soper has pointed out: 'Despite the pervasive resistance of feminism to any naturalization of gender relations, there has been an equally widespread sense that there is an overall affinity and convergence of feminist and ecological aims' (1995: 121). The time has come to make these hidden assumptions explicit, which means examining the 'pervasive resistance' within feminism to any association of woman with biology/nature.

Transcending Biology: Simone de Beauvoir

Men have presumed to create a feminine domain – the kingdom of life, of immanence – only in order to lock up women therein. But it is regardless of sex that the existent seeks self-justification through transcendence . . . what [women] demand today is to be recognised as existents by the same right as men and not to subordinate existence to life, the human being to its animality. (de Beauvoir 1968: 90)

Simone de Beauvoir, writing in the late 1940s, bridged the gap between first- and second-wave feminism. While echoing liberal feminism's rejection of the social and political limitations placed upon women through their association with their bodies, her analysis of the power relations between men and women did not allow for a simple equality model. Although her analysis accepted the dualism between nature and culture and the biologically based difference between men and women, she does not anticipate radical cultural feminism in arguing for the superiority of women's nature or culture. In fact, she does quite the opposite: 'in truth women have never set up female values in opposition to male values; it is man who, desirous of maintaining masculine prerogatives, has invented that divergence' (ibid.)

At the heart of 'male values' is the distinction between transcend-ence and immanence. The cultural world is created through tran-scendence of the immanence of humanity's embeddedness in nature and biology. Rejection of immanence means that human society is always constructed over and against the natural world. Far from celebrating women's connection with the immanence of the natural world, as in Starhawk's spiritual ecofeminism, de Beauvoir saw women's biology as the source of their inequality. If women are to be free, they must escape their embodiment: '[T]he female, to a greater extent than the male, is the prey of the species: and the human race has always sought to escape its specific destiny' (ibid.).

The rejection of women's embodiment was central to de Beauvoir's feminism in her life and her writing. This rejection extended to domestic work (de Beauvoir prided herself on never having learned to cook), marriage and child-bearing, although not to her (hetero)sexuality. As Mary Evans has pointed out, this means that, effectively, de Beauvoir's sentiments and aspirations 'are derived from male expectations and assumptions about the organi-zation of the material and emotional world' (1985: 56). For de Beauvoir, women achieved liberation by 'living like a childless, rather singular, employed man' (ibid.: 57). Taken at face value, she could be seen as a very uncritical liberal feminist who has a very poor view of women who succumb to their marital and maternal roles. However, within the complexity of *The Second Sex* is a view of biology and male–female relations that comes much nearer to the perspective of radical feminism, and certainly gives a hint towards an ecofeminist analysis.

In de Beauvoir's view, the basic difference between men and women lies in procreation and reproduction. Sharing the western liberal view of individual autonomy as central to human freedom, she sees pregnancy and motherhood as necessarily alienating experiences. The child growing within the mother is a colonizing force. The essential difference between men and women is that men, once coitus has been achieved and the sperm deposited, withdraw back into their own autonomy. The male stays free and independent, while the female has the responsibility of species reproduction thrust upon her. Woman is 'first violated . . . then alienated – she becomes, in part, another than herself . . . tenanted by another, who battens upon her substance throughout her pregnancy, the female is at once herself and other than herself' (1968: 50).

This is certainly not the nurturing mother of Collard's ecofeminism. The implication for de Beauvoir is that if a woman does not experience pregnancy as alienation, then she is colluding with the biological imperative that is the cause of her subordination. The only answer, therefore, is to escape, to abandon biology, to become a man. For 'it is male activity that in creating values has made . . . existence itself a value: this activity has prevailed over the confused forces of life; it has subdued Nature and Woman' (ibid.: 91). From an ecofeminist perspective, the withdrawal from biology and the subjugation of nature and woman is not an option. All humanity is embodied and the cycles of birth, nurturing and death have to be continued if the species is to survive. De Beauvoir herself has written most movingly about senescence and death.

Despite the criticisms that can be made of her rather limited solution to women's subordination, her uncritical valuing of male-dominated culture and her dismissal of the problems of embodiment, de Beauvoir does come very close to an ecofeminist position in seeing that there are similarities in the way man both needs and rejects woman and nature:

Man seeks in woman the Other as Nature and as his fellow being. But we know what ambivalent feelings Nature inspires in man. He exploits her but she crushes him, he is born of her and he dies in her; she is the source of his being and the realm that he subjugates to his will. (1968: 144)

Drawing on the existential philosophy that underlies her analysis de Beauvoir sees masculinity and femininity as irreducibly linked to each other. Male domination must be accompanied by female subordination, the one cannot exist without the other. Woman is the Other which creates identity for Man. This relationship is a unique one in human history. Whereas other oppressed groups can unite around a common history, language or culture, or can organize politically, women have no history and no independent base of organization. They are separated and isolated in their family units. Their histories are always and, essentially, intertwined with those of men; there is no woman's history without man, and no revolution can 'overthrow' the sex structure in the way that class revolution can overthrow economic structure.

Although at the time of writing *The Second Sex* de Beauvoir described herself as a socialist arguing that the term feminist was not relevant, her existential analysis takes her towards a radical feminism which hovers somewhere between a cultural and a materialist analysis. This is a move that she confirmed towards the end of her life (Simons and Benjamin 1979). The complexity of her analysis has made her an inspiration to many other feminists.

Escaping biology: Shulamith Firestone

One of the earliest second-wave radical feminists, Shulamith Firestone, saw de Beauvoir as 'the most comprehensive and far-reaching' of all feminists (1970: 16). However, she rejected the idealism of de Beauvoir's existential use of the Hegelian concept of Otherness in favour of the more material implications of human biology, as reflected in the sexual division of labour.

Firestone's *Dialectic of Sex*, first published in 1970, argued that 'biology itself – procreation – is at the origin of the dualism'. 'Sex class', unlike economic class, 'sprang directly from a biological reality: men and women were created different and not equal' (ibid.: 16). Pregnancy, she believed, was 'barbaric', and the only way to escape 'fundamental biological conditions' and the 'tyranny of the biological family' was to use reproductive technology to eliminate sex/gender differences. She also saw productive technology as a liberating force that would free men and women from useless toil. She looked forward to a 'cybernetic communism' that would 'abolish economic classes, and all forms of labour exploitation, by granting all people a livelihood based only on material needs' (ibid.: 224).

Some twenty-five years later Firestone's optimism about reproductive technology looks rather naïve, and productive technology is seen as the cause of, rather than the solution to, human need and the relationship between humanity and the natural world. However, it is wrong to condemn Firestone for not foreseeing the future and in many ways she did show an early awareness of critical issues. One of the sections of her book is entitled 'Feminism and Ecology' and although she reflects the preoccupations and prejudices of her time on the ecology issue, she can be seen as one of the earliest advocates of a feminist position on the ecological crisis. She argues that the tyranny of biology that affects women is also reflected in humanity itself. Humanity is facing an ecological crisis which nature has imposed, compounded by cultural factors. Reflecting the optimism of the age (late 1960s), Firestone sees the solution as 'human mastery of matter', so that an artificial ecological balance can be created where the natural one failed. However, this technological solution is only possible if it is part of a feminist revolution:

> The double curse that man should till the soil by the sweat of his brow and that woman should bear in pain and travail would be lifted through technology to make humane living for the first time a possibility. The feminist movement has the essential mission of creating cultural acceptance of the new ecological balance necessary for the survival of the human race in the twentieth century. (ibid.: 192)

Firestone was writing at a time when there was considerable (and highly alarmist) concern about the 'population explosion'. She argued for women's control of contraception as a solution to the 'crisis', while recognizing the political implications of birth control programmes. She does, however, call on her erstwhile Marxist colleagues to recognize behind the 'population explosion' rhetoric the issue of ecological imbalance.

The elements of Firestone's analysis are also very similar to that of affinity ecofeminists. She starts from the observation that nature produced the fundamental inequality between men and women: women give birth, men do not. This 'natural division of labour' has continued throughout human history, causing great damage to the psyches of both men and women: 'The division of the psyche into male and female to better reinforce the reproductive division was tragic: the hypertrophy in men of rationalism, aggressive drive, the atrophy of their emotional sensitivity, was a physical (war) as well as a cultural disaster' (ibid.: 193). This is very different from de Beauvoir's rather benign view of hu(man) culture. For Firestone a feminist revolution would redress this balance, not through the superiority of women's culture, but through a material challenge to the sex–class division: 'Women were the slave class that maintained the species in order to free the other half for the business of the world' (ibid.: 192). This statement reflects Firestone's Marxist framework, and like Marxist feminists she sees a communist revolution as the political solution, although in reproduction as well as production. If, however, as ecofeminists would now argue, such solutions are not available, then Firestone's analysis leaves a material conflict of interest between men and women in the relation of society/culture to nature/biology. If reproductive technologies have proved to be as much a mechanism of patriarchal control as 'natural' reproduction, and the technologies of production are ecologically damaging, how are women to escape their 'slave–class' role as maintainers of the species? While contemporary feminists would want to quarrel with the assumption that all women are in a sex–class relationship to all men, the dilemma of transcendence as identified by de Beauvoir remains. In creating 'humanity', where do women stand in relationship to nature and culture?

Women, nature and culture

Within the dualisms of male/culture and female/nature, culture is used rather loosely to mean all aspects of the public world, religion, science, technology, militarism, production, knowledge, etc. This leaves unclear whether the critical factor in differences of power between men and women lies in social structures or in value systems. Equally, do those social structures or value systems rest on an assumed biological relation between women and nature (women as mothers) – a material/structural relation (women as a gendered slave class) – or is it purely a cultural association (women as motherly), in the narrower sense of culture?

As we have seen, de Beauvoir hovers between a biological and a cultural explanation. She seems to be arguing both that biology is the cause of the male–female dualism (the autonomy–procreation dilemma), and that it is a cultural phenomenon (the creation of identity through Otherness). Firestone on the other hand, has emphasized the biological and material base of male–female differences. Biology divides the sexes and male-dominated society builds on this, exploiting women's slavery to free itself for 'the business of the world'. Sherry Ortner, writing shortly after Firestone, takes up the cultural side of de Beauvoir's analysis in an influential paper first written in 1972 'Is Female to Male as Nature is to Culture?' (1974, reproduced in Evans 1982).

The basic tenet of Ortner's analysis is that women are subordinate to men in all societies and that this subordination is directly linked to women's association with 'nature'. However, this does not imply biological determinism read as genetic determinism. Men are not genetically determined to be dominant or women to be inferior. Biological difference only becomes problematic when it is overlaid by 'culturally defined value systems' (ibid.: 489). Having maintained that women's subordination is universal, but having rejected biological sex differences as an explanation, Ortner tries to show how cultural forms can achieve universality. For this she goes back to biology in the sense of embodiedness and embeddedness (although she does not name these as such):

> If we are unwilling to rest the case on genetic determinism, it seems to be that we have only one way to proceed. We must attempt to interpret female subordination in the light of other universals, factors built into the structure of the most generalized situation in which all human beings, in whatever culture, find themselves. For example, every human being has a physical body and ... must engage in some relationship, however mediated, with 'nature', or the non-human realm, in order to survive. (ibid.)

For Ortner this biological imperative means that human societies must dominate nature, and she goes on to make 'an assertion in all human cultures of the specifically human ability to act upon and regulate, rather than passively move with and be moved by, conditions of natural existence' (ibid.: 490). As humanity 'transcends the givens of natural existence, bends them to its purposes, controls them in its interest', so every human culture devalues nature in the process of that domination. Although Ortner uses the word 'human' in this context, it is clear that she means 'man', as women are devalued along with nature as a symbolic reflection of human dependence on, and dominance of, nature: 'My thesis is that woman is being identified with – or, if you will, seems to be a symbol of – something every culture devalues, something that every culture defines as being of a lower order than itself ... "nature" in the most generalized sense' (ibid.). The idea of women being a symbol of association with nature, rather than being identified as nature, is very important to Ortner.

They are 'merely' seen as closer to nature, not as embodying nature. Culture (still equated relatively unambiguously with men) 'recognizes that women are active participants in its special processes, but at the same time sees them as being more rooted in, or having more direct affinity with nature' (ibid.: 491). Despite wanting to keep women's relationship to nature as 'merely' a cultural artefact, Ortner's explanation of the subordination of women comes close to biological determinism. She shares with de Beauvoir a distaste for women's physicality and a support for 'culture' as a symbol of humanity. She agrees with de Beauvoir that women are trapped in their role as mundane producers of repetitive life. In this sense women are 'more enslaved to the species than the male' (quoting de Beauvoir in ibid.: 493), suffering considerable discomfort in the process. Men, on the other hand, escape the biological role of the repetition of life and can concentrate on what for both Ortner and de Beauvoir is the real focus of human existence – life as culture:

> [M]an assures the repetition of Life while transcending Life through Existence (i.e. goal-oriented meaningful action); by this transcendence he creates values that deprive pure repetition of all value . . . in serving the species the human male also remodels the face of the earth, he creates new instruments, he invents, he shapes the future. (ibid.)

Still quoting de Beauvoir, Ortner argues that women want to share the cultural world of men:

> For she, too, is an existent, she feels the urge to surpass, and her project is not mere repetition but transcendence towards a different future – in her heart of hearts she finds confirmation of the masculine pretensions . . . Her misfortune is to have been biologically destined for the repetition of Life, when even in her own view Life does not carry within itself its reasons for being, reasons that are more important than life itself. (ibid.: 494–5)

Like de Beauvoir, Ortner celebrates the transcendence of culture as 'Life', accepting the hierarchical dualism of nature and culture. Rejecting nature/biology as inferior, their solutions are to urge women to move towards the world of culture of 'creativity and transcendence' (ibid.: 506), which means accepting 'masculine pretensions'. Ecofeminism is in a much stronger position because it can use the celebration of nature and 'Life' as a critique of the human-centred and nature-hating world of 'masculine pretensions'.

Ortner argues that the masculine association of females with nature is unconscious – that is, men are not to be blamed. There is no sense of male interest here even though it is a universal cultural occurrence.

Women are intermediate between male/culture and woman/nature in that they share the cultural world of men (albeit through confirming their own subordination), while at the same time being unable to shake off the encumbrances of their biology, 'because of woman's greater bodily involvement with the natural functions surrounding reproduction, she is seen as more a part of nature than man' (ibid.: 495). There is a near-affinity perspective here; should 'seen as' be replaced by 'is'? Ortner goes on to argue that women's 'physiological functions' (particularly birth and lactation) lead to a 'logic of cultural reasoning' which limits her mobility and confines her to domestic space. Men, 'since they lack a "natural" basis for a familial orientation' (ibid.: 498) and cannot create 'naturally' from within their own being, are forced into cultural reproduction, to 'create artificially' (ibid.: 495). Ortner attempts to escape the biologically determinist implications of this argument by drawing on Nancy Chodorow's analysis of the psychological impact of early childhood development (1974, 1978). Chodorow based her analysis on a version of psychoanalytic thought: object relations theory. She argued that the exclusive involvement of women in early childcare meant that boys and girls were socialized in different ways. While both sexes had to break from the mother to establish their own identities, this was easier for boys than girls. Girls, sharing the same sex as their mother, did not manage to establish their separateness and were always drawn empathetically to nurturing relationships with others. Males, on the other hand, develop stronger ego boundaries and a more abstract, universalistic orientation to the distant world of masculinity. By emphasizing childhood socialization rather than Freudian drives or instincts in the development of the male and female psyche, Chodorow's approach was more sociological. The importance of her analysis for Ortner is that it gives a social explanation for women's cultural differences rather than seeing it as representing a biologically determined response.

Ortner, following Chodorow, argues that the socialization patterns in child-rearing produce a response in women's psyche that perpetuates their subordination and traps her into the repetitive cycle of reproduction. The obvious solution is to 'spring' women out of the intermediate role they have been 'forced' into. Ortner argues that as women's reproductive role is culturally imposed, it could be shared between the sexes. The problem is, what would motivate men or women to transcend the dualism? Can 'nature' be dissolved away? Like de Beauvoir, Ortner defines culture as transcendence of nature, 'culture being minimally defined as the transcendence, by means of systems of thought and technology, of the natural given means of existence' (1974: 503). Yet it is this transcendence that Ortner sees as producing *culturally* the nature/culture distinction. How does a culture that is created by a separation from nature become the forum which creates that dualism or can resolve it? If culture is created against nature, and women are always more embodied in natural cycles than men, then such a culture can never liberate women.

Ortner, de Beauvoir and Chodorow can all be criticized for asserting a false universalism. They are projecting the concerns of white middle-class women on to 'women' generally. Ortner has been particularly criticized for her assertion of the universality of cultural forms (MacCormack 1980). MacCormack criticizes Ortner and de Beauvoir for tending towards an essentialist view of woman/nature, male/culture and of having a very westernized view of culture as individual achievement. For many cultures, historical continuity is a collective social achievement through extensive family and group structures (1980). Pointing out that there are vast cultural differences in the way gender, sex, culture and nature are perceived, MacCormack argues against universalizing statements about women's subordination and the woman/nature relation. Equally, Chodorow has been criticized for focusing on the specifically western child-rearing model of the isolated nuclear family (Spelman 1988: 85; Young 1990: 40).

While MacCormack criticizes the universalist assumptions in Ortner's work, she does praise Ortner's identification of women's role in mediating between culture and nature. She sees this as a retreat from essentialism, but argues that it is not something done exclusively by women. Given that both men and women are a combination of nature and culture, they are both involved in mediation. While this may be true, what is more important is whether men and women are *equally* involved in mediation. The idea of women as mediating between culture and nature is a very important one in ecofeminist thought. Ynestra King referred to women as a 'bridge'. For Ortner, women's mediating role is a purely cultural one, socializing children to bring them from nature into culture. Later theorists (including myself) would want to argue that women's mediating role is a much more material one. Their work in production and reproduction is much more wide-ranging than childcare, and it is through this work that women (among others) have been the 'bridge' upon which 'transcendent' culture has been built.

While early feminists such as de Beauvoir, Firestone and Ortner saw women's liberation as the rejection of women's biology, a new wave of radical feminism began to argue that women should reclaim their bodies and their 'biological' role, particularly mothering. Speaking of the American context, Ann Snitow has argued that the 'demon texts' attacking motherhood were very shortlived within the women's movement and were replaced from the mid-1970s by an overt or covert pro-natalist stance (1992).

Reclaiming the body: Adrienne Rich

[F]emale biology – the diffuse, intense sensuality radiating out from the clitoris, breasts, uterus, vagina; the lunar cycles of menstruation; the gestation and fruition of life which can take place in the female body – has far more radical implications than we have come to appreciate. (Rich 1976: 39)

Adrienne Rich's *Of Woman Born* sought to reclaim women's bodies from patriarchal domination. Rich claimed that the institutionalization of motherhood and compulsory heterosexuality had alienated women from their bodies. The alienation that de Beauvoir identified in pregnancy is not the existential destruction of women's autonomy, but the loss of control by women over their own bodies. When feminists have 'recoiled' from their bodies, they are reflecting the rejection of female biology in patriarchal thought. Rich argued that women have to reclaim and gain control over their bodies. Like many affinity ecofeminists she wants to revalue the repressed half of the dualism. Women are called upon to explore and understand 'our biological grounding, the miracle and paradox of the female body and its spiritual and political meanings' (ibid.: 284). Rich wants them to be able to 'think through the body', so that 'every woman is the presiding genius of her own body' (ibid.: 285).

Rich can be read as seeking to 'upend' the man–woman dualism by giving priority and creativity to women, and as seeking to transcend that dualism. There are two endings to her book. In the final chapter she appears to be seeking to bring men's and women's lives into complementarity, to 'release the creation and sustenance of life into the same realm of decision, struggle, surprise, imagination, and conscious intelligence, as any other difficult, but freely chosen work' (ibid.: p. 280). This is followed by an Afterword, which ends with a more women-centred sentiment: 'we need to imagine a world in which . . . women will truly create a new life . . . the visions, and the thinking necessary to sustain, console and alter human existence' (ibid.: 285–6).

Rich, therefore, gives us two versions of how women's embodiment is to be an agent of change. One is to dissolve the dualisms of patriarchal society by according women's work of motherhood the same status as other valued aspects of human life. The second is to upend the dualism by giving women responsibility for 'visioning' the future. However, in yet another part of the book she offers a different alternative, where humanity embraces its embodiment: 'In order to live a fully human life ... we must touch the unity and resonance of our physicality, our bond with the natural order, the corporeal ground of our intelligence' (ibid.: 39). In so far as (some) men have transcended their physicality, they have lost contact with the natural order. As Rich points out women too, have lost touch with their physicality in patriarchal societies, experiencing motherhood as 'alienated labour'. If women can 'think through their bodies' and 'the corporeal ground of our intelligence', can men not also do so?

For Rich, motherhood in a patriarchal society is damaging to men and women. Mothering by subordinated women interferes with the process of maturation for men. Women infantilize men, who have become dependent on the unconditional love of women. Rich recalls a story told by Olive Schreiner in 1890. A woman is trying to cross a deep river while suckling a child. She is told 'no, you will lose your life trying to save him; he must grow into a man and save himself, and then you will meet him on the other side.' Rich urges men to break out of these dependent patterns 'not for me, or for other women, but for themselves, and for the sake of life on the planet Earth' (ibid.: 215).

The fear of embodiment: Dorothy Dinnerstein

As we have seen, the destructive impact of mothering on men and women has been a recurring theme in feminist thought. Dorothy Dinnerstein sees the whole process of human maturation as a 'human malaise'. When human beings are torn from the womb they experience a crisis of separation from which they never recover. Dinnerstein links this to humanity's ambivalent relationship to the natural world. Starting with the image of the mermaid and the minotaur, Dinnerstein sees humans as hybrids both continuous with, and different from, other animals. It is necessary to explore this human dilemma, because 'in these continuities, and these differences, lie both our sense of strangeness on earth and the possible key to a way of feeling at home here' (1987: 2). Humanity, and particularly 'man', has made the mistake of trying to run away from this malaise, this loss of continuity with 'life'.

Failure to confront human frailty is leading humanity into destructive patterns. This is particularly true for men. Women retain their connectedness through mothering and childcare. Men are cast adrift to rule the world in their terror. Men, and to a lesser extent women, are trying to console themselves for 'a peculiarly human loss – the loss of infant oneness with the world' – and to assert themselves 'against a peculiarly human discovery – that the most important features of existence elude control' (ibid.: 8). Humans are by nature unnatural. As tool-users they walk upright, although they were designed to walk on all fours. Forced by biology into division by sex in order to reproduce, humanity is a species against itself. It has immense creativity, but causes destruction. Humanity is the only animal species that knows it will die and is unable to bear the emotional weight of this enigma. Like Rich, Dinnerstein sees the failure to confront the dilemmas of human existence as infantilizing humanity: '[W]hat we have worked out is a masquerade, in which generation after generation of childishly self-important men on the one hand, and childishly play-acting women on the other, solemnly recreate a childs-eye view of what adult life must be like' (ibid.: 87).

For Dinnerstein, the almost exclusive role of women in early childcare means that 'for virtually every living person it is a woman . . . who has provided the main initial contact with humanity and with nature' (ibid.: 26). This means that the mother is an ambivalent figure: she gives love and security, but she also takes it away: '[T]he early mother, monolithic representative of nature, is a source, like nature, of ultimate distress as well as ultimate joy. Like nature, she is both nourishing and disappointing, both alluring and threatening, both comforting and unreliable' (ibid.: 95). Woman is the 'dirty goddess', the 'carnal scapegoat-idol' for human mortality. She is despised by men and women. Dinnerstein draws on de Beauvoir in claiming that 'from the day of his birth man begins to die: this is the truth incarnated in the Mother' (ibid.: 127). While Dinnerstein finds a great deal of commonality with de Beauvoir, she does not see the answer in transcendence of the biological world. Instead, she comes nearer to the ecofeminist notion of immanence, connectedness. Embracing embodiment is the way to 'contain the two sides of our central ambivalence toward what we are . . . inside each individual human skin where they belong'. If humanity is able to come to terms with its 'flawed life', it may be able to save itself and the web of life in which it is embedded, from extinction (ibid.: 228).

Although an ecofeminist perspective was implicit in Dinnerstein's book, which was first written in 1976, in a chapter written for an ecofeminist anthology in 1989 she addresses these ideas more directly: 'Central to a humanly whole feminist vision is awareness that our traditional uses of gender form part of an endemic mental and societal disorder . . . that is killing our world . . . the rageful, greedy murder of the planet that spawned us' (1989: 193).

The political control of reproduction: Mary O'Brien

Another writer who challenges the masculine and individualist bias of de Beauvoir's thinking about nature/culture dualism is Mary O'Brien. She is particularly critical of the notion of transcendence where 'the significant movement in masculine history is *anti-physis*, that male values have been created in the course of a historical struggle to overcome nature' (1981: 68). O'Brien argues that biological history – species history – is as important as cultural history and goes further to argue that masculine domination of cultural history reflects male frustration at not being able to control species history. Men's insecurity at their rather limited involvement in procreation leads to male domination as a 'doctrine of potency': 'at the heart of the doctrine of potency lies the intransigent impotency of uncertainty' (ibid.: 191).

Taking her cue from the Marxian dialectics of production, O'Brien argues that what is needed is a dialectics of reproduction. While Marx argues that 'man' is alienated from production, O'Brien argues that man is alienated from reproduction and thus from nature in general. Although she does not explicitly embrace an ecofeminist perspective, her concerns are the ecologically destructive effect of the nature/culture divide: 'the problem is to move from the war against nature and against life to policies of integration with nature and with life' (ibid.: 201). She also shares with ecofeminists a belief that 'female consciousness' is the key to the alienation of 'man' from 'nature': '[I]n a world in which the need for reintegration with nature is becoming more and more apparent, it may well be an urgent task, and one for which integrated female consciousness is pre-eminently suited' (ibid.: 64). Women's role is to transcend the dialectical oppositions that reflect 'the history of male attempts to impose order on contingency' (ibid.: 192). O'Brien argues that Marx was wrong to claim that the sphere of production was the origin of human sociability, rather it is grounded in reproduction: 'A feminist philosophy of birth must ground sociability and the ethics of integration where they belong: in the essentially social process of reproduction' (ibid.: 40) Reproduction is the key for O'Brien because, as a 'material process, biological reproduction necessarily also sets up an opposition between those who labour reproductively (women) and those who do not (men)' (ibid.: 36). She sees this division of labour as the key to understanding western dualism and the domination of women. She argues that the dialectic of reproduction can be materially analysed from the 'standpoint of women . . . women working from within women's reality' (ibid.: 188) through the creation of 'a transformed universal, feminine consciousness' (ibid.: 190). I will return to the debate about women's standpoint in the next chapter.

Following Marx, O'Brien argues that women in the sphere of reproduction hold the key to political agency in the same way that the proletariat relates to production, through their labour. Women's long history of oppression can now be ended because they can control their reproductive power by means of contraception. She describes this as a *'world historical* event', echoing Engels's claim that male control over women's fertility resulted in the world-historic defeat of women (ibid.: 189 italics in the original; Engels 1884).

In advocating a technological solution to the dialectic of reproduction, O'Brien is coming close to the 'cybernetic' world of Shulamith Firestone. However, the main difference between O'Brien's ideas and Firestone's (which both take a Marxian framework) is that women's biology is no longer to be escaped, instead it has become a site of struggle. A similar conceptual division between nature and culture is, however, evident in O'Brien's work. Echoing de Beauvoir and Firestone, she asserts that now women are 'freed from the brute contingency of biological compulsion', they are 'free' to join men in the making of history by embarking upon 'the elaboration of their second nature' (1981: 194). However, they are not to join the masculine world of culture, rather women's historical task is a very ecofeminist one: 'It is becoming increasingly clear that the struggle of feminism is not the struggle for liberation, or for some abstract humanism, but a historical force whose task is the regeneration and reintegration of historical and natural worlds' (ibid.: 195). These words are echoed in the work of Maria Mies, writing more than ten years later.

The political control of reproduction: Maria Mies

[W]omen strove originally for liberation from exploitative and oppressive male–female relations, we now deal with the question of 'emancipation' from the uncontrolled reproductive potential of the female body, of 'emancipation' from our female nature. (Mies and Shiva 1993: 221)

Maria Mies is concerned at the way the feminist argument for a woman's right to choose – reproductive autonomy – is linked to a notion of self-determination that represents a bourgeois conception of rights and privileges. As the structures that support communal and social relations break down, women are forced to gain their reproductive autonomy by placing their bodies in the hands of 'technodocs', who can manipulate fertility through the new reproductive technologies. Mies is concerned that the long-term effect of this process is that women stand to lose control of their bodies to commercial interests, technological manipulation and state regulation. Bodies are beginning to be seen as composed of commodifiable bits from eggs, sperm and womb, through blood plasma and body tissue to kidneys, which can be bought and sold on a 'free' market. They can be manipulated by governments and international agencies, as in sterilization programmes, or by patriarchal interests, as in the abortion of female foetuses.

While acknowledging that reproductive technologies have been seen as being of great benefit to women, particularly in relation to fertility treatment and safe abortion, Mies argues that the dangers outweigh the benefits: '[W]e can no longer argue about whether reproductive technology or genetic technology as such are good or bad; the very basic principles of this technology have to be criticized no less than its methods' (ibid.: 175). She argues that the reproduction of 'living relations' with the natural world and in human communities will enable women to regain control over their bodies without recourse to the technodocs. Men and women are urged to come to the realization that 'nature is not our enemy, our bodies are not our enemy, that our mothers are not our enemies' (ibid.: 229).

Mies contrasts de Beauvoir's Enlightenment view of transcendence (self-determination, freedom, the universal) with the idea of immanence (life, nature, the organic, the animal, the particular) that de Beauvoir sought to escape. De Beauvoir's solution to the Otherness of women in relation to men must necessarily entail the maintenance of, or the creation of, new Others to sustain the self of the transcendent (middle-class) woman:

> [S]elf-determination of the social individual, the subject, was – and is – based on the definition of the 'Other', the definition as object, of certain human beings . . . autonomy of the subject is based on heteronomy (being determined by others) of some Other (nature, other human beings, 'lower' parts of the self). (ibid.: 223)

The concept of freedom in Enlightenment thought sets mind against body, culture against nature. Far from the Boston Women's Health Collective's notion of 'Our Bodies' as 'Our Selves', a woman's body has become her enemy; 'Its "wild" generative capacities' threaten her independence and self-determination (ibid.: 226). The rejection of the female body is part of the whole rejection of embodiment in Enlightenment thought: that 'humans are born from women and must die, that they have a body, senses, emotions'. What the Enlightenment is rejecting is the 'living relationship' that humanity has with the environment: 'the earth, the water, the air, plants, animals, and other human beings' (ibid.: 224). This rejection meant that the Enlightenment was built upon a structure of exploitation, oppression and repression: '[T]he rise of man was based on the descent of woman. Europe's progress was based on the regression of colonies. The development of productive forces (science, technology) was based on robbery, warfare and violence, at home as well as in the colonies' (ibid.: 223). Mies argues for a revaluing of the woman–nature–culture connection, as well as offering a materialist analysis of the structures of exploitation that have created the freedom, self-determination and autonomy that many feminists have sought. Individualized self-determination rests on the paraphernalia of western culture from science and technology, capitalist economic relations, to militarism and the state. For Mies, all are male-dominated structures of violence and control. Western notions of freedom are based on a structure of exploitation, including the oppression and exploitation of women, based on class, 'race' and colonization.

From an ecofeminist perspective it is not possible to avoid confronting the woman–nature–biology connection if the material contradictions of human embodiment and embeddedness are to be addressed, which brings into question the relationship between ecofeminism and other feminist perspectives.

Ecofeminism and essentialism

[B]iological arguments are all too frequently adduced to provide justification for women's continued oppression and in that sense feminism has had to confront biology. (Birke 1986: vii)

[T]he problem for feminist materialists is to admit nature, particularly the body – that is, a constrained essentialism – while giving priority to the social, without concluding at the same time that human beings are infinitely malleable. (Rose 1994: 22)

It may be that the danger of essentialism will always be present in ecofeminism simply because we are engaged with such fundamental grand questions – questions like the relationship between humanity and non-human nature (interview with Barbara Holland-Cunz in Kuletz 1992: 10)

As Barbara Holland-Cunz points out, in bringing ecology and feminism together, ecofeminism engages in a contradictory approach to the political freedoms associated with the Enlightenment. While much of feminism has sought to gain 'freedom and autonomy' for women through social and technical 'progress', ecology, and particularly deep ecology, has launched a profound critique of modernity (ibid.: 3). Ecofeminism must necessarily be seen as acting against the interests of one or other of its constituent parts; it has to convince (most) feminists to let go of their Enlightenment-based commitment to 'freedom and autonomy' (Mellor 1996a) and convince (most, particularly male) green thinkers that male dominance is a central problem (Mellor 1992c).

Confronting biology, for women, means confronting the structures of power that have rested upon women's association with nature, animality and human embodiment. Bringing the mind and body, nature and culture back into a direct relationship must open up charges of essentialism. From an ecofeminist perspective, feminism (and all other political and social theories) have to address the mermaid/minotaur issue. How do human beings cope with their physicality and the consequences of it, their embodiment and their embeddedness? It is no use feminists trying to avoid these issues in case it reaffirms women's oppression. In ecological terms, ignorance (ignoring) is destructive.

In its emphasis on 'body politics' ecofeminism is very close to radical feminism, even when its analysis takes a predominantly social/ist rather than an affinity perspective. Given that human beings are sexed animals, any discussion of biology must open up the question of whether women are in a different relation to their physicality than men. This seems to be the point at issue for all the writers discussed above. Collard sees women's bodies as connecting them directly with the natural world, whereas men are in a destructive relation to it. For de Beauvoir, women are more ensnared by their biology than men and have to transcend their physicality by denying it. Firestone argues that biology always potentially condemns women to the barbarity of pregnancy and must be escaped. Ortner believes that male culture's fear of nature pushes women into an identification with it, a point that Dinnerstein also makes, but in a different way: men and women's fear of embodiment creates a rejection of woman as mother. Rich begins the re-evaluation of mothering and the assertion of a potential maternal culture freed from male control. O'Brien observes a difference in male and female psyches based on procreation, and Mies sees women's bodies as a site of struggle and one that cannot be avoided if ecological sustainability is to be achieved.

Feminism has moved, as we have seen, from a rejection of women's biology/sex to a reassessment of their relationship to biology/ nature, at least by radical feminists and ecofeminists. Is such an approach necessarily essentialist? This charge contains at least three different elements: biological determinism, universalism and reductionism (Eisenstein 1984; Ferguson 1993).

Biological determinism is the concern of most critics of cultural/ radical feminism and affinity ecofeminism (Davion 1994). Biology is seen as producing particular patterns of behaviour and ways of thinking: women as nurturing and loving, men as aggressive and competitive. This is easily dismissed by the observation that not all mothers are loving and caring and not all men are aggressive and destructive. Writing like that of Collard does appear to imply innate male–female differences, but as with most writers who assert the existence of a pre-historic matriarchy, the differences are seen as basically cultural. Men and women are not locked into some biologi- cally determined eternal dance of death.

Feminists are rightly concerned that discussion of biology may feed the prejudices of patriarchal biological determinism. As Sayers argues, feminists cannot ignore biology, but they do not need to embrace explanations based in biology. What is needed is a concrete understanding of how women are oppressed in sexual and family relations (1982: 201). Ecofeminism widens this critique to understand the position of women in human–nature relations. The danger of reactionary conservatives taking advantage of this debate is less likely where the discussion of human, and particularly women's embodiment, takes place in the context of a fundamental critique of the male-dominated, unequal and ecologically destructive world that excludes women in the name of biological determinism.

The criticism of essentialism on the basis of universalism in femin- ist thought is a potentially more damaging critique. The critique of universalism has been levelled at radical feminism and ecofeminism, led by Black feminists and postmodern theorists (hooks 1981; Riley 1988). Universalism involves the claim that all women share a com- mon experience of subordination. Often this reflects what Eisenstein has called a false universalism, where the preoccupations of some (white, middle-class) women are projected on to all women (1984: 132). The Bangladeshi campaigner against population control, Farida Akhter, for example, points out that the western feminist campaign for reproductive rights has no meaning for women who have to accept sterilization as a way of getting food (quoted in Mies and Shiva 1993: 219).

The third way in which some feminisms have been seen as essentialist is in making reductionist claims that the male–female dualism is the ultimate and determining one. This is certainly true of many ecofeminists, including Collard, who see sexism as the basis of all other 'isms'. There are two ways that this could be read. One is that women's subordination was the *first* subordination, the other that it is *at all times* the primary subordination. I would not wish to defend ecofeminists on either of these points. I would argue that slavery is as old as women's subordination, as far as we know, and that class, 'race' and colonialism are arguably more oppressive and exploitative than sexism in many contexts.

Rethinking essentialism

Elizabeth Spelman has pointed to the irony that while masculine cultures have seen women as inessential in relation to what it means to be hu(man), feminism has claimed an essentialized 'generic' woman as its political 'subject'. As has been pointed out many times in critiques of white middle-class feminism, a generic concept of 'woman' denies differences between women, or as Spelman prefers 'heterogeneity' (1988: 174). As with Eisenstein's false universalism, it presents the particular experience of white middle-class women as standing for all women. As most ecofeminists are white and middle class and expound a theory of 'women' as pivotal in addressing the ecological crisis, it is obviously a target of this type of criticism.

For Spelman, far from the body representing an essentialized woman, it is rejection of the body that is central to an essentialized view of women. The heterogeneity of women in their particular lives and locations are real people in real bodies: 'Once the concept of woman is divorced from the concept of woman's body, conceptual room is made for the idea of a woman who is no particular historical woman – she has no color, no accent, no particular characteristics that require having a body' (ibid.: 128). Spelman sees 'somatophobia' disdain for, and rejection of, the body as being symptomatic of sexist, racist and classist attitudes. Inferiority is assigned to those associated with the functions of the body, sex, reproduction, appetite, secretions, excretions and those who serve the bodily functions of others: '[W]hen a group views its liberation in terms of being free of association with, or responsibility for, bodily tasks, its own liberation is likely to be predicated on the oppression of other groups – those assigned to do the body's work' (ibid.: 127–8). Feminists who reject human, and particularly female embodiment, are following the division between culture and embodiment as set out by Plato and Aristotle. For Aristotle (male and female) slaves were responsible for the needs of embodiment, while 'free' women were excluded from participation in the *polis* on the grounds of their embodiment. Women could become philosopher-kings in Plato's republic, but only by rejecting and transcending their embodiment.

'Somatophobia' is not overcome by identifying an essential woman-ness, 'a "woman" substance that is the same in each of us and interchangeable between us' (ibid.: 158). For Spelman it is impossible to speak 'as a woman', only as a particular woman whose heterogeneity is based on 'identity in terms of race, class, ethnicity, sexual orientation, language, religion, nationality' (ibid.: 187). It is interesting that this list leaves out the sexed and gendered body. Do statements about women's embodiment necessarily fall into the trap of essentialism? Are embodiments always particular embodiments – is there no context in which we can speak of the embodiment of women as *women*? Is there a middle way between asserting a generalized biological determinism (women's innate natures, a generic 'woman', etc.) and a totally contextualized auto/biographical view of individual women?

Diana Fuss has argued that the distinction between essentialism and social constructionism is not a watertight one. She shows convincingly that those who make an essentialist case rest on an implicit constructionism, and vice versa. She argues that social constructionists should not assume that their concepts escape essentialism. To the extent that constructionist ideas are determinist, they are equally as essentialist as 'natural' theories. At the same time it would be wrong to assume that 'nature' is fixed, immutable and determining: '[T]here is no compelling reason to assume that the natural is, in essence essentialist and that the social is, in essence, constructionist' (1989: 6). The problem rests on the difficulty of theorizing the social in relation to the natural (ibid.: 1). Fuss shares with ecofeminists a concern that the question of women's biology must be addressed. Nor is such a debate necessarily essentialist:

[O]ne can talk about the body as matter, it seems to me, without presuming that matter has an essence.

. . . substituting social determinism for biological determinism, and replacing sex with gender, may not be the most productive ways to deal with the question of biology. Biology will not simply go away, much as we may wish it to; it has to be theorized. (ibid.: 51)

While not offering us her own theorization of biology, Fuss has attempted to open up a dialogue between social constructionism and essentialism which allows for the strategic use of essentialist arguments. I would agree with Elizabeth Carlassare that Susan Griffin also uses essentialist arguments in this way, as a poetic illustration of the scientific/abstract–rational/male voice as against the poetic/embodied–embedded/female voice (Carlassare 1994).

Postmodern feminists have been most marked in their criticism of essentialist universalism in feminist thought, as represented in the category woman/the feminine or even feminist (Riley 1988). Despite her claim that sexual division is a 'bifurcation of the discursive world', Riley is still left with the 'obstinate core of identification . . . the concept of the female body. Even if it is allowed that the collective "women" may be an effect of history, what about biology, materiality?' (ibid.: 101) Her answer is that bodily materiality is not a constant for women, that 'women only sometimes live in the flesh distinctively of women' (ibid.: 105). She also points to the fact that the experience of embodiment generally is not sexed. Malnutrition, for example, is only sexed when it affects women as women, as in the case of amenorrhoea. The ecofeminist concern with embodiment is also not limited to questions of sexual difference. Embodiment involves everything that we have to do as humans to express our biological being-ness: sex, procreation, feeding, excreting, dying. These can be incorporated into socio-economic systems, or be carried out with personal love and caring or even cruelty, but they need to be done.

To focus exclusively on sex/sexuality or procreation/mothering ignores the areas of human life that involve other kinds of oppression and exploitation, particularly production and consumption. An emphasis on sexuality and early child-rearing represent the preoccupations of a bourgeois sexualized culture in a society which separates the public from the private and limits (some) women to a domestic/mothering role. From the perspective of a concern with the ecological consequences of human activity and the socio-economic inequalities that people face in meeting their physical needs, it is an ethnocentric diversion. A wider conception of embodiment interconnects with many forms of oppression and avoids the reductionist view that sex oppression is the most fundamental. Certainly sex/gender is important in relation to the particular embodiment that relates to sexed bodies, but that is by no means the whole story of humanity's relationship to biology/nature.

It is ironic that postmodern feminists, who have been central to the critique of essentialism and universalism in feminism, have themselves been accused of essentialism (Hekman 1990). This is particularly true of the work of Luce Irigaray and Hélène Cixous, who take the Lacanian position that all culture represents a patriarchal world. Language itself represents the symbol of the phallus: all knowledge, culture and language is phallocentric. When the child leaves the world of the imaginary and enters the world of the symbol, woman is lost. Feminist postmodernism has taken the division between culture and woman to its logical extreme. All culture as represented in the 'word' or the 'text' is male. The dualism between man–woman, culture–nature is complete: all culture is man; any representation of woman in culture must be a construct of patriarchal thought. So where is embodied woman to go? For Irigaray and Cixous, the embodied woman and particularly her sexuality, is the only aspect of woman which escapes male control. All that she is left with is her pre-social self. This rests in her sexed and sensual difference, her *jouissance*. For Irigaray (1985) this means celebrating women's 'otherness' as an ontological condition, and expressing women's desire as the 'sex that is not one' – that is, the multi-sited sexuality of the female, as against the phallus-centred one sex of the male. However, this is limited as a mechanism of political action because it is, by definition, outside the phallocentric world. To engage with the Logos/Symbolic is to succumb to patriarchy. As Lynne Segal has argued, the influence of psychoanalytic thinking in feminism has had the effect of a move away from engaged politics and has also encouraged an idealist and essentialist view of sexual difference (1987: 133).

Julia Kristeva takes a less sexually essentialist view by turning not to sexuality, but to the biological role of the mother. Denying that she is a feminist, she argues that both men and women can reclaim the pre-Oedipal experience of the maternal body. The symbolic world of the male can be escaped by turning to the repressed feminine in all of us (Butler 1990: 82). Despite these engagements with the body, French postmodern feminism does not engage with biology/nature in a way that will answer the ecological problems raised by ecofeminism. By ontologically prioritizing cultural struggle within the human community, or more precisely within language and culture, postmodern feminism cannot begin to address the relationship between humanity and nature. It is a human-centred and radically social constructivist perspective, which denies the natural world or human biology any independent agency. This does not mean to say that the postmodern critique of modernity is not important, particularly its attack on the unitary Enlightenment 'subject' and the dualist logic that underpins it. However, this critique can be made without a psychoanalytic and/or a linguistic 'turn'.

Conclusion

Ecofeminism starts from a recognition of the centrality of 'nature' to human existence. Nature is untranscendable in de Beauvoir's sense. It will always be part of the human condition and must be addressed directly. The question then becomes how the nature–culture dualism that has marginalized women and nature can be confronted. An analysis of the relationship between male domination, women and nature is at the heart of ecofeminism. Women's relation to human embodiedness and embeddedness provides the key to understanding and confronting the hierarchical power relations that characterize western society and make it so oppressive to women and destructive to the environment.

If women's (and men's) position in the nature–culture dualism is seen as biologically determined or essentially different, it is clear that the dualism will never be bridged. The only solution is a separatist one. Men and women will have to follow their own paths. If the nature–culture dualism is seen as being socially constructed either on the basis of different (but not essentially different) value systems as between men and women (mothers and warriors), or on the basis of social inequalities (capitalism, hierarchy), then at some point the value systems could be changed or the inequalities ended. Values could be substituted (mother's values for warrior values), or could be seen as complementing each other (yin and yang, androgyny). The idea of balance and complementarity are very common in green thinking and I will discuss them in Chapter 6. A social/ist solution would eliminate the oppression of women and nature through the elimination of social inequalities (I will discuss these ideas in Chapter 7).

A third possibility is that the culture–nature dualism is directly related to women's subordination, that dominant men materially need women (and other groups) to be in a subordinate position. Ecofeminists argue that women form the link with nature, in that women's work keeps hu(man)ity's 'dirty little secret' of its embodiment, (women as Dinnerstein's 'dirty Goddesses'). Non-human nature contains the dirty secrets of hu(man)ity's consumption and excretion. The focus in this context turns from a biologically based view of woman to a biologically based view of humanity. Transcendence cannot be achieved without an 'Other' as Mies pointed out. The 'Other' is not a psychic or cultural mirror in the creation of identity (de Beauvoir), but carries out the basic work of embodiment that makes transcendence possible for *some* people. The outcome of this view of culture–nature relations would be a political struggle over the sexual/gender division of labour. Whereas an emphasis on sex, sexuality and mothering must necessarily return to sex-based biological differences, a focus on women's work as representing hu(man) embodiment can be linked to the way in which many peoples and groups unequally bear the burden of the embodiment of so-called 'free', 'autonomous', transcendent 'Subjects' (Mellor 1997). I would argue that to see women and nature as being in a material relation brings together the biological and social aspects of embodiment (Mellor 1996b). I will discuss this further in Chapters 7 and 8.

Central to ecofeminist thought is the argument that to the extent that women stand in a sex/gendered relationship to human embodiment, they have a special awareness of the nature and consequences of human embodiment either as differently bodied beings (as birth-givers, incarnation of the female), or as people differently concerned with human embodiment (as mothers, care-workers, etc.). To claim that women have a privileged perspective on the ecological dilemmas facing humanity is a contentious one for feminism, a debate that I will explore further in the next chapter.

5

Women and Nature: A Privileged Standpoint?

We know that women suffer disproportionately from the many different manifestations of the global ecological crisis . . . The question is no longer what is the 'correct' position on the woman/nature relation, but rather how we situate ourselves as women and agents committed to fundamental change . . . the vantage point of women and environment has been a particularly useful perspective from which to criticize the western development model. (Harcourt 1994: 153)

If women's lived experience were . . . given legitimation in our culture, it could provide an immediate 'living' social basis for (an) alternative consciousness. (Salleh 1984: 340)

Women's experience with oppression and abuse, as well as their experience of mothering, can make them more sensitive to the oppression and abuse of nature, as well as better situated to remedy it. (Collard 1988: 138)

Women know from the inside out what it is like to weave the Earth into a new human being. (Swimme 1990: 21)

All the above statements are arguing for a privileged epistemological perspective for women in relation to the natural world and for women's positioning as effective agents in confronting the ecological crisis. By raising the question of epistemic privilege in the context of gender and knowledge in relation to the natural world, ecofeminism is entering a contentious field for feminist theory (Jaggar and Bordo 1989; Nicholson 1990; Harding 1991; Alcoff and Potter 1993). From a postmodern perspective, feminists are asking whether it is possible to claim a privileged epistemological viewpoint on any basis (Hekman 1990). From a difference perspective, epistemological claims on the part of, or on behalf of, women can be seen as denying differences between women by essentializing their 'natures', universalizing their 'experience' and taking a reductionist position in prioritizing their viewpoint over that of other oppressed groups.

On what basis are ecofeminists claiming an epistemological privilege for women? The statements above offer a number of options: women as disadvantaged and oppressed; women as mothers, birthgivers and nurturers; women's 'lived experience'. To argue that women as *female* are the source of epistemic privilege would certainly be open to the criticism of being universalizing and essentializing. The same criticism is made of those who see women as having a distinctive culture or ethic (Gilligan 1982; Noddings 1984). A great deal of the criticism directed at ecofeminism reflects the way in which much of its rhetoric seems to be making such claims. However, in more considered statements this rhetoric tends to be qualified. For example, Charlene Spretnak, a proponent of ecofeminist spirituality, states that 'what cannot be said, though, is that women are drawn to ecology simply because we are female' (1990: 4).

While Spretnak urges us to 'embrace the body' and talks of the 'elemental power of the female body' as representing the goddess and the 'Earthbody', this is open to men as well as women (1991: 143). Spretnak, who like other cultural feminists asserts the previous existence of a goddess-based matriarchy, sees patriarchal society as emerging through socialization rather than 'inherent masculine behavior'. Men can therefore become re-socialized to embrace the 'Earthbody' (ibid.: 128). For Starhawk, 'earth-based spirituality' is based on immanence, interconnection and community. Immanence is the aliveness of the earth, connectedness is the way that immanence is expressed, community is the goal of a human society in harmony:

> When we understand that everything is interconnected, we are called to a politics and a set of actions that come from compassion, from the ability literally to feel *with* all living beings on the Earth. That feeling is the ground upon which we can build community and come together and take action and find direction. (1990: 74)

Starhawk does adopt a standpoint perspective but not only on the part of women: 'Environmental issues cannot be intelligently approached without the perspectives of women, the poor, and those who come from other parts of the globe, as well as those of all races and cultural backgrounds' (ibid.: 83). For Ariel Salleh, a socialist ecofeminist, the important aspect is 'women's lived experience' linked to women's subordination. Like Harding and Haraway, Salleh calls for 'an episte-mology from below'. She argues that women's experience in capitalist patriarchal societies has given them a materially grounded base which privileges them 'temporarily as historical agents par excellence'. Women are in a contradictory position in that they are both inside and outside patriarchal systems. From this position, whether they are 'dominated' or 'empowered', they are well placed to 'take up the case for "other" living beings' (1994: 120). Salleh denies that this is an essentialist position. It is not women's bodies that locate them politically, but their position within the sex/gender division of labour. Nor do women spontaneously recog-nize this contradiction; they have to develop an 'ecofeminist conscious-ness'. Salleh therefore follows the Marxist model of distinguishing between a sex/gender in itself and a conscious sex/gender 'for itself', or rather 'for nature'. Women hold a privileged standpoint, but they may not necessarily 'see' it.

Similarly, Ynestra King, a social ecofeminist, does not assert a 'natural' affinity between women and the natural world, arguing instead that the socially constructed identity of women and nature could be consciously used as a 'vantage point' for 'creating a different kind of culture and politics that would integrate intuitive, spiritual and rational forms of knowledge, embracing both science and magic insofar as they enable us to transform the nature-culture distinction and to envision and create a free, ecological society' (1983b: 123). Vandana Shiva, writing from the perspective of Asian women, claims that 'the intellectual heritage for ecological survival lies with those who are experts in survival'. It is 'women as knowers' who are the experts in survival: 'women producing survival are showing us that nature is the very basis and matrix of economic life' (1989: 224). In stressing that women are experientially 'knowers', holding the intel-lectual heritage of subsistence societies, Shiva sometimes seems to be leaning towards making a claim for an essentialized embodiment of the feminine principle in women *per se*. However, in Mies's and Shiva's 1993 book *Ecofeminism*, Mies states that such knowledge is gained in struggle, quoting Shiva:

> As Vandana Shiva points out in this book, a new vision – a new life for present and future generations, and for our fellow creatures on earth – in which praxis and theory are respected and preserved can be found *only* in the survival struggles of grassroots movements. (1993: 297; my italics)

This knowledge can be developed wherever people are marginalized and seeking earth-centred alternatives, even in countries in the North.

This would seem to imply that experience of a struggle for survival or subsistence defined as 'life-producing and life-enhancing work' (ibid.: 298) is the most important element in establishing 'praxis and theory'. In the case of people struggling for survival, poor men as well as poor women could as much be repositories of an alternative knowledge. However, elsewhere Mies argues for a more woman-based knowledge:

> in defying this patriarchy we are loyal to future generations and to life and this planet itself. We have a deep and particular understanding of this both through our natures and our experience as women [such that] wherever women acted against ecological destruction or/and the threat of atomic annihilation, they *immediately* became aware of the connection between patriarchal violence against women, other people and nature. (ibid.: 14; my italics)

Mies and Shiva leave us with confusing messages about the relationship between women, nature and knowledge. Nature-oriented knowledge is seen as resting with those (particularly women) who still retain direct links with the natural world. However, political struggle is also an important source of realization of this knowledge, which can be shared by women who are not in immediate contact with nature or the struggle for survival. In which case, it would be perfectly possible for western men to disengage from their dominant forms of knowledge and embrace a 'subsistence perspective'.

Standpoint: the view from below

As we have seen, ecofeminism hovers between an approach that seems to prioritize the idea of *women's* experience reflecting an essential representation of women's embodiment, and an approach that looks at women's *experience* in a more historical and contextual way. However, this raises questions of how women's experience is to be galvanized and on what basis. The implication of most of the ecofeminist theorists surveyed above is that the main criterion is experience of disadvantage. Disadvantage is deemed to produce a perspective on society which is denied or obscured for the advantaged. This line of argument is reflected in feminist standpoint theory, which stands in direct lineage to Marxist theories of the epistemic privilege of the working class and Hegel's analysis of the master–slave relationship (Harding 1991: 120 f.). For ecofeminists, women, because of their structural disadvantage, can see the dynamics of the relationship between humanity and nature more clearly than can (relatively) privileged men.

Hartsock originally framed the idea of a 'feminist standpoint' in *Money, Sex and Power* in 1983, with a revised version published in 1987. Following Iris Young, she developed her standpoint perspective as a feminist extension of Marx's historical materialism. Young's and Hartsock's starting point was the sex/gender division of labour, which is also central to social/ist ecofeminist analysis. For Hartsock, the limitation of Marx's materialism was that it did not focus on the whole of human activity in humanity's interaction with nature and each other. As human interaction with nature is socially mediated and shapes both human beings themselves and their knowledge, the sex/gender division of labour means that 'women's lives differ systematically and structurally from those of men' (1983: 231). Women's dual role in production and reproduction means that they have a wider understanding of the range of activities within human existence, which 'represents an intensification and deepening of the materialist world view' (ibid.: 236). Drawing on Nancy Chodorow's work, Hartsock sees men as withdrawing from the concrete world of women's lives and experience to the socially constructed world of 'abstract masculinity':

> Masculinity must be attained by means of opposition to the concrete world of daily life, by escaping from contact with the female world of the household into the masculine world of politics or public life. This experience of two worlds, one valuable, if abstract and deeply unattainable, the other useless and demeaning, if concrete and necessary, lies at the heart of a series of dualisms–abstract/concrete, mind/body, culture/nature, ideal/real, stasis/change. (ibid.: 241)

Women's role as 'mediators' between men and nature provides the epistemological base for 'a specifically historical materialism, a materialism that can provide a point from which to both critique and work against phallocratic ideology and institutions' (ibid.: 234). The concept of women as mediators of nature has already been raised by Ortner and has been developed by Salleh (1994) and Mellor (1997). It is a concept that is central to a materialist ecofeminism and one to which I will return.

Women's mediating role in the sex/gender division of labour has rendered relations between humanity and the natural world invisible in malestream theory, so that the 'biological, bodily component of human existence' is in danger of 'evaporating' (Hartsock 1983: 233). In order to develop an analysis that does not separate nature from nurture, or biology from culture, Hartsock follows Sara Ruddick in separating those social forms that are virtually universal yet changeable (such as women's role in child-rearing) from those that are universal and less easily changeable (such as men's inability to bear children). Hartsock argues that it is only when the changeable aspects of the sex/gender division of labour have been tackled that the reality of biological limitations can be revealed. She recognizes the problem of universalism in her analysis, but with 'reluctance' proposes to 'lay aside the important differences among women and instead search for central commonalities across race and class boundaries' (ibid.).

A feminist standpoint, Hartsock argues can expand an understanding of human materiality and expose the 'perverse and deadly forms' of patriarchal institutions and ideology (ibid.: 231). However, such a standpoint is not readily available as 'raw data'. Knowledge based upon women's experience is not just 'there', it has to be struggled for intellectually and politically:

> the vision available to the oppressed group must be struggled for and represents an achievement that requires both science to see beneath the surface of the social relations in which all are forced to participate and the education that can only grow from struggle to change those relations . . . an engaged vision, the understanding of the oppressed, the adoption of a standpoint . . . carries a historically liberatory role. (ibid.: 232)

A materialist understanding, Hartsock argues, gets women off the hook of being seen as either natural or social: 'as embodied humans we are of course inextricably both natural and social' (1987: 158). It has, however, been strategically necessary for women to emphasize the social aspect of their lives, rather than the natural. What is needed now is a revaluing of women's experience as the basis of a revolutionary politics that begins with 'the sexual division of labour . . . as the real, material activity of concrete human beings' in order to produce 'a fully human community, a community structured by connection rather than separation and opposition' (ibid.: 175). If 'women's experience' will guide humanity to 'a fully human community', this still leaves open the question of the relationship between experience and knowledge.

For Patricia Hill Collins, the most important distinction is between knowledge and wisdom. In defining an afrocentric feminist epistemology, she sees experience as the 'cutting edge' between them: 'Knowledge without wisdom is adequate for the powerful, but wisdom is essential to the survival of the subordinate' (1990: 208).

Collins sees the basis for Black women's wisdom in the connectedness of Black communities that emphasizes an ethic of caring and the importance of personal accountability, a 'connected knowing' based in holistic ideas: '[R]ooted in a tradition of African humanism, each individual is thought to be a unique expression of a common spirit, power, or energy inherent in all life' (ibid.: 215). Like Hartsock, Collins argues for the importance of the standpoint of subjugated knowledges not as answers in themselves but as a challenge to the 'truth' of dominating knowledges and as the basis of a wider picture. If Black women can claim a privileged perspective, it is as 'outsiders-within'. On the basis of their experience of exploitation and subordination at the hands of racist, patriarchal and capitalist societies, and drawing on their own cultural histories, Black women 'have a distinct view of the contradictions between the dominant group's actions and ideologies' (1990: 11).

Knowledge and action

One of the main criticisms that can be made of standpoint theory is that it sets up *a* privileged view from *a* specific oppression – a woman's voice, a Black voice – that is essentializing, universalizing and totalizing. Collins argues against the idea of *a* specific oppression by seeing afrocentric feminism as part of a matrix of struggles against oppression. This does not, however, overcome the problem of there being *a* specific view from any particular position, or of whether such a view can obscure differences between women. More importantly, perhaps, it leaves unclear the responsibility of the oppressed for producing the solutions to their own, and others', oppression and in the case of ecofeminism, the survival of the planet.

Although not referring specifically to ecofeminism, Uma Narayan has pointed to conflicting dangers in claims for women's epistemic privilege, which argue that 'our location in the world as women makes it possible for us to perceive and understand different aspects of both the world and human activities in ways that challenge the male bias of existing perspectives' (1989: 256). The first danger is that women who are not suffering a particular form of oppression will seek to 'speak for' the oppressed, while not being aware of their own role in subordinating other women. Such a danger seems apparent in both Hartsock's and Harding's work. Harding sees standpoint theory as 'not women's experience, but the view from women's lives' (1991: 269). The critical question is, whose view and from which women's lives? Harding meets this criticism by arguing that knowledge should always be socially and politically self-conscious, thereby exhibiting 'strong objectivity' (1993). Certainly, for ecofeminism there is always a temptation to prioritize the ecological question over issues of differences between women and the power relations they represent.

The second danger that Narayan sees is a false assumption about the political efficacy of oppression. It cannot be assumed that because subordinated people live in two cultures or on both sides of their divided lives (as Collins claims) that this will result in a radicalizing or dialectical experience: 'The thesis that oppression may bestow epistemic advantage should not tempt us in the direction of idealizing or romanticizing oppression and blind us to its real material and psychic deprivations' (1989: 268). Similar concerns are raised by Flax (1990) and Braidotti et al., who argue that 'subjugation does not necessarily result in superior vision' (1994: 120). Also, to claim a superior voice for poor women is merely to reverse the hierarchies of knowledge and not transcend them. Braidotti et al. also see dangers in what they perceive as the way in which organizations such as DAWN claim to speak on behalf of poor women in the South, and they call upon 'all those concerned to facilitate pro-environmental changes' to take up their 'political and historic responsibility' to analyse critically their *own* position in the wider power structure in order to identify 'points of leverage' (ibid.: 171–2). They identify 'a radically differentiated female-embodied materialism', whereby 'the embodiment of the subject is the political standpoint which allows for the critique of dualism' (ibid.: 174). The proposition that ecofeminists should engage in political action within their own societies has already been made by both Mies and Ruether, but the argument of Braidotti et al. is somewhat undermined by a postmodern perspective. In seeing 'the body as a construct, an interface between symbolic and material forces' (ibid.: 174) it is not clear how such a struggle can be broadened without adopting a 'totalising perspective'. How would a struggle over her body by a middle-class white woman connect with the struggle of a young girl sold into sex slavery, or the exploitation of the natural world?

What Hartsock seems to be arguing is that the starting point is not *women's* experience, by virtue purely of their female embodiment, or women's *experience* as a subjective phenomenon, but *women's experience* as a historical and material relation, which may be built upon either by women themselves or by politically conscious activists (including men). Such an analysis will not satisfy radical difference and postmodern feminists who would want to return to the subjective phenomenon of women's experiences and to decentre the concept of 'women'. It would also not satisfy the postmodern critique, in that the feminist standpoint perspective is clearly within the western humanist tradition. Standpoint theory locates 'subjugated knowledges', which by definition have to be 'realized'. This can be done either by subjugated groups themselves or by others, often from more privileged groups, who 'reason dialectically' or search for the voices of others. Standpoint theory therefore offers two seemingly contradictory positions: knowledge is located or 'situated' with those who are oppressed or subordinated, yet that knowledge remains available to all those who would search for it.

The important element here is the subjugation rather than the situation. If knowledges are merely situated, then they are relative to the positions/perspectives of particular social locations. A relativist position would be appropriate as there would be no reason to prioritize any particular location. Starting from a position of subjugation, the material 'fact' of inequality is the starting point. As Haraway has argued: ' "Subjugated" standpoints are preferred because they seem to promise more adequate, sustained, objective, transforming accounts of the world' (1991: 191). Ecofeminist epistemology argues that situatedness, while representing context and diversity, also has concrete things to say about social and ecological location. Situatedness is not just about 'raw' experience, but is always located in social relationships and in relation to the natural world: 'A situated self is a self-reflective self; a self that always attempts to explore her relationship to others and the world' (Gruen 1994: 128). As Harding argues, dominant groups need to 'systematically interrogate their advantaged social situation' which in any event renders them 'epistemologically disadvantaged' (1993: 54). Like Haraway, Harding argues that less privileged positions are epistemologically advantaged: '[T]he activities of those at the bottom of . . . social hierarchies can provide starting points for thought – for *everyone's* research and scholarship – from which humans' relations with each other and the natural world can become visible' (ibid.; italics in the original). Like Hartsock and Gruen, Harding and Haraway do not claim that the subjugated have 'raw vision'. Vision reflects the *power* to see, not just sight itself, 'there is no immediate vision from the standpoint of the subjugated' (Haraway 1991: 193). The perspective of the subjugated is not 'innocent' it is not a mirror, a truth, but neither is it a relativism where every position/perspective tells a different story. Haraway argues that every located position gives only a partial view. The case for solidarity rests in putting together all the partial views to get a picture of the whole. Haraway describes this as 'embodied objectivity' (ibid.: 188). Because the concept of 'objectivity' implies a positivist framework, I would prefer to see this as a realist rather than an objectivist perspective. Also, as the ecofeminist perspective refers not only to embodiment, but embeddedness within an interconnected ecological framework, I would prefer Starhawk's (and, ironically, de Beauvoir's) concept of immanence. An immanent realism would be revealed through patterns of subjugation and the perspectives they generate within the human community, and through an awareness of the interrelatedness of humanity and nature in ecological processes.

In asserting with Ynestra King that women are a 'bridge' between culture and nature, ecofeminists are arguing that women provide a 'critical position' in terms of the natural world. This is not to deny individual and collective differences, but, as Hartsock argues, to look for commonalities because the overall problem is so great. Haraway writes: 'We need the power of modern critical theories of how meanings and bodies get made, not in order to deny meanings and bodies, but in order to live in meanings and bodies that have a chance for the future' (1991: 187). The kind of critical perspective taken by standpoint epistemology must necessarily draw on elements of the western intellectual tradition, i.e. realism and materialism/structuralism. Yet ecofeminists also see the western tradition and its epistemological framework as the source of women's subordination and the ecological crisis. This would appear to put ecofeminism politically nearer to a postmodern than a modernist position. One perspective which ecofeminists and postmodernists share is a critique of dualism within western culture (Hekman 1990).

Dualism: the logic of domination

Western culture has treated the human/nature relation as a dualism and . . . this explains many of the problematic features of the west's treatment of nature which underlie the environmental crisis, especially the western construction of human identity as 'outside' nature. (Plumwood 1993: 2)

As we have seen, ecofeminists trace the destruction of the natural world to the hierarchical dualisms of western society, although they may differ in the historical period and origins identified. The debate around western dualism has been the point at which poetic ecofeminism meets academic ecofeminism, the latter being particularly represented in the work of environmental philosophers such as

Val Plumwood (1986, 1990, 1993) and Karen Warren (1987, 1990, 1994).

Both Plumwood and Warren see dualism as representing a cultural institutionalization of power relations. This is described by Warren as a 'logic of domination' and by Plumwood as a 'logic of colonization'. Such a logic not only divides categories of thought and life, but also prioritizes one over the other. Plumwood refers to this as hyperseparation or radical exclusion (1993: 49), calling instead for a 'critical ecological feminism' that will resolve these dualisms by exposing the assumptions that underpin them.

Plumwood, like Ruether, sees the origin of dualism in western thought as lying with the Greeks, particularly Plato. What Plato did was to separate off the sphere of ideas from the rest of human existence, and particularly human embodiment, both as subsistence and (hetero)sexuality. As women were associated in Greek culture with both subsistence as household production and carnal sexuality (as opposed to Plato's idealized sexuality of the young male), women were by definition not part of the world of ideas. According to Plumwood, this has led to a 'hyperseparated conception of the human', which forms the 'master identity' of western culture (ibid.: 72). The master culture emphasizes rationality, freedom and transcendence of nature, and Plumwood argues that the fatal flaw of western dualism was to tie these ideas to domination.

Plumwood shares with many other feminists a critique of masculinity as the hidden dimension of the western definition of the 'human' (Hartsock 1983; Lloyd 1984; Ruether 1975; Irigaray 1985). She is also concerned that male green thinkers are tending to look uncritically and with approval towards Greek society as a model of ecological sustainability, in the same way that male political theorists have praised Greek democracy without appreciating its gendered (and slave-based) nature. For Plato, the world of ideas and of order through reason (*logos*) is separate and superior to the inferior sphere of matter. It is the *logos* that gives order to the world. The body and materiality, on the other hand, are essentially chaotic. *Logos* (world-soul) must be superior because it (he) must maintain order. The elements of Plato's dualism of soul and nature can clearly be seen in Christianity, and his separation of ideas and nature in western rationalism. However the world of materiality (like sin) is always with us and must be continually repressed by the *logos* both within society and within the individual.

Plumwood explains the origins of Plato's dualism in the war-based character of Greek society. The dominant classes of Greek culture could only maintain their society through war and domination. If an elite male were to live 'the life of the master, his ability to lead a life above slavish necessity depended on war' (1993: 97). He must always be ready to fight and die (gloriously) in battle. Life, therefore, could not be valued for itself. Instead the 'order' of society that transcended individual human existence was accorded the highest value. Plumwood, like Hartsock, argues that Platonic theory is a justification for the valorization of death over life. But she believes that this type of thinking has led to an 'existential homelessness' (ibid.: 71) in western thought, 'an alienated account of human identity in which humans are essentially apart from or "outside of" nature, having no true home in it or allegiance to it' (ibid.). This alienation is made all the worse by the fact that 'modernity has dispensed with the other world' (ibid.: 101). There is no longer a transcendent world of *logos* or soul, there is no form or father in heaven. Instead, modern society has to face the meaninglessness of death: 'Modernity, despite its pride in throwing off the illusions of the past, has not provided an earthian identity which gives a life-affirming account of death, or comes to terms with death as part of the human condition' (ibid.: 102). What is needed, Plumwood argues, is an 'ecological identity' which is based not on alienation from the natural world, but connection with it. However, masculinist culture is not moving in this direction. Instead, it is struggling to take control of the world of nature and the body through 'progressive' science and technology, while still denying the materiality of human existence. This 'backgrounding' of nature has had destructive consequences. Economic systems have developed in ways that have 'externalized' nature from economic calculations and concern. Depletion of resources or pollution of the environment is not treated as a responsibility of companies, or, until recently, of governments.

Another key figure identified by Plumwood in the incorporation of dualism into western philosophy was the French mathematician/ philosopher René Descartes (1596–1650). While Plato's dualism had focused upon the 'other world' of soul/*logos*, Descartes directed his attention towards developing human knowledge and control of the natural world. What was distinctive about humanity, he argued, was the existence of mind, read as consciousness with the ability to think and reason. As nothing else in existence possesses mind, the natural world, including the human body and all other animate life, is seen as an inert object to be controlled and manipulated. Mind becomes disembodied and body/nature becomes mindless, a machine. Plumwood sees Descartes as undertaking a 'stripping out' process, whereby all similarities between human mind and body/nature are defined out to leave only pure disembodied consciousness 'I'. This is the autonomous human-centred form of consciousness that both deep ecologists and ecofeminists see as lying at the heart of the destructiveness of western thinking. All agency is denied to the natural world, so that nature has no 'originative power' within itself (ibid.: 115):

> *Consciousness* now divides the universe completely in a total cleavage between the thinking being and mindless nature, and between the thinking substance and 'its' body, which becomes the division between consciousness and clockwork. Gone is the teleological and organic in biological explanation. Mind is defining of and confined to human knowers, and nature is merely alien. (ibid.: 116; italics in the original)

Susan Bordo has decribed Cartesian dualism as a 'flight to objectivity', where (as in the case of Plato) all possible distractions from pure consciousness are removed (1987). Like Bordo, Plumwood sees the 'objective' self as implicitly masculine, with the separation of the masculine mind not only from 'female' body but from all other forms of animate life, including the 'mind's' own body. As a socialist ecofeminist, Plumwood also broadens the idea of the 'mind' as masculine by seeing it as representing a 'master' identity that encompasses a much wider framework of domination: 'The body is "feminine-associated" but it is even more clearly associated with other oppressed groups, such as "primitives", animals, slaves and those who labour with their bodies' (ibid.: 116). The hyperseparated, disembedded master identity presents us with a 'self' in western philosophy which not only represents the 'ideals' of masculinity, but of 'class, race and species colonisation' (ibid.: 152).

Despite this very material basis to her analysis of the master identity and her call for a critical ecological feminism, towards the end of her book, Plumwood moves to a more poststructuralist language and orientation. She seeks to challenge the 'master's story' that has been built out of the dualisms of western thought. However, she rejects the spiritual ecofeminist's 'story'. Nature is not to be seen as representing 'spirit' or a 'Goddess' (ibid.: 126). Plumwood also rejects 'extreme holism', where humanity is to be sunk into nature to such an extent that it is indistinguishable. Instead, she wants to extend the 'concepts of autonomy, agency and creativity to those who have been denied them under the Cartesian division of the world', so that 'we reconceive ourselves as more animal and embodied, more "natural", and that we reconceive nature as more mindlike than in the Cartesian conception' (ibid.: 124).

The Greek/Enlightenment concept of 'humanity' needs to be challenged from a feminist perspective, since it has been constructed in a 'framework of exclusion, denial and denigration of the feminine sphere, the natural sphere and the sphere associated with subsistence' (ibid.: 22). How is the concept of the 'human' to be challenged? Not, argues Plumwood, by the assertion of an alternative 'woman's culture', which she calls 'uncritical reversal' (ibid.: 31). She makes the criticism that many other feminists have made of ecofeminism, that to celebrate the feminine is to celebrate what is only a distortion of the masculine/feminine dualism (Davion 1994). To celebrate womanhood is to celebrate something that has been created by inequality. Making the same point as Ynestra King, Plumwood argues that the challenge must be to the dualism itself, i.e. to the master's story. It will be no easy task to challenge the 'cultural bondage to the logic of the master' that reflects the 'deep structures of mastery':

> Although the super-rich increasingly own both the world and the word, the master identity is more than a conspiracy: it is a legacy, a form of culture, a form of rationality, a framework for selfhood and relationship which, through the appropriation of culture, has come to shape us all. (ibid.: 190)

The implication in Plumwood's analysis is that the deep culture of master identity appeared with the Greeks, but built on a pre-existing pattern of elite domination, which was male-dominated and slave-owning. It would appear, then, that being preceded consciousness, i.e. that the cultural form came to represent a pre-existing pattern of domination and not the other way round. By the end of her book Plumwood, despite the poststructuralist language, combines a material and a cultural analysis. One solution she gives is that the master story will falter through inherent *material* contradictions: 'After much destruction, mastery will fail, because the master denies dependency on the sustaining other; he misunderstands the conditions of his own existence and lacks sensitivity to limits and to the ultimate points of earthian existence' (ibid.: 195). However, such a materialist analysis is undermined by the use of much weaker concepts. Mastery has moved from being a colonization and domination to a 'story' or an 'identity', in which women are complicit. The focus of political action is also directed away from material struggle to personal and political transformation. Plumwood asks 'active and intentional subjects . . . to recognise and eject the master identity in culture, in ourselves, and in political and economic structures', and instead to develop 'forms of rationality which encourage mutually sustaining relationships between humans and the earth'. Such alternative frameworks would be based on examples of 'care, friendship and love . . . radical democracy, co-operation, mutuality' (ibid.: 195–6). These are not specifically limited to women, although Plumwood does refer to 'women's stories of care' (ibid.: 196). She is calling on all those men and women who share ecofeminist and related perspectives to join forces. However, the specific focus of that struggle is not made clear and the elements of a specifically materialist analysis are lost. A politically undifferentiated 'we' are to engage in struggle over identities and stories, not material relations.

For Plumwood, the ecological impact of the 'logic of colonization' lay in western patriarchy's 'mastery of nature' through its male-dominated knowledge systems. This 'mastery' has been exemplified by western science and technology, of which one of the earliest critiques was made by the socialist ecofeminist Carolyn Merchant, a view that has been echoed in the work of other feminist critics such as Evelyn Fox Keller (1983, 1985, 1992) and Hilary Rose (1986, 1994).

Masculinist science and the death of nature

> The removal of animistic, organic assumptions about the cosmos constituted the death of nature – the most far-reaching effect of the Scientific Revolution. (Merchant 1983: 193)

Carolyn Merchant's book *The Death of Nature* was first published in 1980. While acknowledging the destructive framework of Judaeo-Christian religion and culture as well as western rationalism, Merchant's particular target was the scientific revolution of the sixteenth and seventeenth centuries. She argues that the emergence of scientific rationality was the final twist that released the full destructive potential of western patriarchal culture. Until the scientific revolution, exploitation of the natural world had been restrained by an organic view of nature as both female and alive. Nature was revered as a nurturing 'Mother Earth', and feared as a wild and tempestuous spirit. But the scientific revolution brought about a disenchantment of 'Nature'. Wild and alive Nature was replaced by a mechanistic world view that saw the natural world as dead and passive. Whereas the organic view had restrained exploitation, or at least made it self-conscious, the mechanistic view, associated with Descartes and Newtonian mechanics, led to the 'death of nature', as an idea and in practice.

The aliveness of Nature before the scientific revolution had been represented through the 'female principle', which 'emphasized the interdependence among the parts of the human body, subordination of the individual to communal purposes in the family, community, and state, and vital life permeating the cosmos to the lowliest stone' (ibid.: 1). The alternative perspective of vitalism, represented by philosophers such as Gottfried Wilhelm von Leibniz and Lady Anne Conway, were eclipsed (ibid.: 253 f.). The wisdom of those, particularly women, associated with the old organic relationship was also lost or destroyed. Merchant argues that the scientific revolution was legitimated by Judaeo-Christianity, which had bequeathed to 'Man' the God-given right of the domination of nature. This could finally be achieved through the development of modern science. The Christian faith and other patriarchal faiths had already destroyed women-based myths and religious images, and had even gone as far as persecuting and massacring women in large numbers as witches (ibid.: 127 f.). For Merchant, the women persecuted as witches represented the chaotic and wild aspect of nature, particularly as represented in women's sexuality. This was a period of transition:

> [T]he old organic order of nature in the cosmos, society and self was symbolically giving way to disorder through the discoveries of the 'new science', the social upheavals of the Reformation, and the release of people's animal and sexual passions. In each of these realms, female symbolism and activities were significant. (ibid.: 127–8)

One of the main exponents of the new methods was Francis Bacon, who, as Merchant notes, was Attorney-General to James I during a wave of witchcraft trials. Bacon's language is rife with the imagery of torture and even makes reference to the persecutions:

> For you have but to follow and, as it were, hound nature in her wanderings, and you will be able when you like to lead and drive her afterward to the same place again . . . Neither ought a man to make scruple of entering and penetrating into these holes and corners, when the inquisition of truth is his whole object – as your majesty has shown in your own example. (quoted in ibid.: 168)

Merchant's critique of Newtonian mechanics and the early exclusion of women from modern science has been followed by a number of feminist critiques of science (Alic 1986; Harding 1991; Keller 1985; Rose 1994).

The feminist critique of science

In the overall critique of dualism within western culture, science represents the 'hard edge'. As with most feminist critiques of male-dominated society, the first level of criticism was at the exclusion and marginalization of women in science. Feminist historians found evidence of women's hidden contribution (Alic 1986), the history of women's experiences and role in the area (Rose 1994) and their distinctive perspectives (Keller 1983). As Keller and Rose point out, it was only later that the critique moved to a more fundamental concern with the nature of science itself. The major jump was from the exposure of the exclusion, exploitation and marginalization of women in a male-dominated scientific world to a critique of science itself as a masculinist project. Keller describes how in 1975, almost overnight, she moved from being a mathematical biophysicist, committed to physical laws as the 'apex of knowledge', to a questioning of whether the masculine basis of science destroyed its integrity as a subject. This change occurred through life changes such as taking leave to accompany her husband on a sabbatical and teaching interdisciplinary studies. In confronting her experience as a woman in science, Keller began to question the legitimacy of the scientific model in which she had been trained, in particular, its claim to produce disembodied knowledge that was self-detached, impersonal and transcendent (1992: 19). The detachment of the scientific model, Keller argues, has led to the technologies of life or death such as nuclear physics and molecular biology (1985), a concern shared by many feminists, eco-logists and anti-militarists (Easlea 1983).

Following Chodorow, Keller sees the masculinization of science as resulting from childhood socialization. Women, given their gendered socialization, are likely to approach their study of the natural world with less detachment. Scientific knowledge does not have to be impersonal and transcendent; it can reflect both love and feeling. Keller draws on her study of the work of the geneti-cist Barbara McClintock to illustrate her case (1983). McClintock saw the natural world as infinitely complex, with organisms having a life and order of their own. Scientists who wish to understand them should 'listen to the material' and have a 'feeling for the organism' (Keller 1983). By contrast, masculinist science rests on a detached claim to be able to produce a 'copy theory' of reality that is both objective and objectifying. Unsurprisingly, McClintock's failure to follow the accepted scientific model led to accusations of 'personality difficulties' and marginalization in her profession (Keller 1985: 159).

Keller argues that the idea of science as a 'mirror of nature', or as reflecting the 'laws of nature', is purely a metaphor for the prevailing hierarchical assumptions of western culture, with humans as the discoverers and interpreters of a subordinate natural world. Words, argues Keller, are far too limited a resource to permit a faithful representation of the cultural world of our own experience, let alone the hugely complex structure of the natural world (1992: 29). In fact, the assumption that science can reflect and explain the world must mean that the development of knowledge is being artificially restricted: 'To assume . . . that all perceptible regularities can be represented by current (or even future) theory is to impose a premature limit on what is "naturally" possible' (ibid.: 30). Science is on stronger ground if it relates itself to practice: 'good science is science that effectively facilitates the material realisation of particular goals' (ibid.: 5). However, she goes on to point out that these goals can be good or bad.

One example of the destructive impact of the use of science to achieve certain goals is the 'green revolution', of which as I have pointed out Vandana Shiva has been a particularly influential critic (1989). Like many feminist critics of science, Shiva was herself a scientist, a nuclear physicist. The green revolution is an example of what Shiva has called 'maldevelopment'. Central to the problems of the green revolution were crops designed in western laboratories without an understanding of local environmental and economic conditions in the South. At first, the green revolution appeared to be a huge success, as heavily cropping varieties of rice and wheat seemed to be the answer to the widespread Malthusian fear of human population growth outstripping the resources of the planet. However, the limitations of the policy soon became clear. The new varieties needed vast amounts of water, which quickly depleted the 'once and for all' resource of ground water. Rapid and constant evaporation in hot climates left residues of salt on the ground which poisoned the soil. Heavy cropping caused soil erosion, and the crops were susceptible to pests. Only wealthy landowners could afford the necessary fertilizers and pesticides.

Alongside the scientific agriculture went large-scale water-management schemes, such as dams and hydroelectric plants that displaced large numbers of people. The Narmada dam scheme in India, for example, threatened 250,000 people with relocation and was the subject of fierce opposition. Women farmers were particularly vulnerable, as their needs were not recognized. In the case of the Mahaweli Irrigation and Development Project in Sri Lanka, for example, men were given resettlement land as 'heads of households', while women received nothing. As a result, women have to work even harder on the newly irrigated land without gaining any of the benefits (Jayaweera et al. 1994).

Shiva's criticism of 'scientific' agriculture and western development programmes generally is that by projecting themselves on the basis of a universal, rational, value-free, objective knowledge, they displace other belief and knowledge systems that are more ecologically sustainable:

> Modern reductionist science, like development, turns out to be a patriarchal project, which has excluded women as experts, and has simultaneously excluded ecological and holistic ways of knowing which understand and respect nature's processes and interconnectedness *as science*. (1989: 14–15; italics in the original)

Like Merchant, Shiva traces this violence back to the destruction of women 'knowers' in the witchcraft purges, and sees it as represented in the elimination of tribal and peasant cultures today. For Shiva, the violence of science is achieved through both epistemological and ontological reductionism. Epistemologically, science fragments knowledge, subjects it to particular rules of evidence and holds only western scientists to be 'knowers'. Ontologically, it sees the natural world as itself fragmented and inert, disconnected from humanity and subject to universalistic mechanical laws: 'Reductionist science is a source of violence against nature and women because it subjugates them and dispossesses them of their full productivity, power and potential' (ibid.: 22). Reductionist science, Shiva argues, violates women, tribal peoples and peasants by designating them non-experts and non-knowers, even within their own lives and experience. It impoverishes the poor and women, even when claiming that they will be the ultimate beneficiaries. Reductionist science commits a violence against nature by destroying its integrity. Ultimately, reductionist science is self-defeating because it does violence to knowledge itself. By claiming universal control of knowledge in the name of western superiority, it achieves a 'monoculture of the mind' (Shiva 1993) which denies alternative ways of knowing.

Shiva sees the process of colonization and the 'White Man's burden' of responsibility for 'development' in the South as a trap for the North as much as for the South. The trap comes from the fact that 'processes of wealth-creation simultaneously create poverty, processes of knowledge creation simultaneously generate ignorance, and processes for the creation of freedom simultaneously generate unfreedom' (in Mies and Shiva 1993: 264). Decolonization of the South must be accompanied by 'decolonizing' of the North if new forms of knowledge and social structure are to be created.

Maria Mies, like Shiva, also sees a direct relationship between reductionist science, colonization, patriarchy and capitalism. Mies echoes Plumwood's critique of the idea of mastery as central to western thought. She sees the violence of western science towards nature as representing western man's need to establish himself as separate and 'above' his embodiment:

> [I]n order to be able to do violence to Mother Nature and other sister beings on earth, *homo scientificus* had to set himself apart from, or rather above, nature . . . The modern scientist is the man who presumably creates nature as well as himself out of his brainpower. He is the new god, the culture hero of European civilization. (ibid.: 47)

Echoing Dinnerstein, Mies sees the key to European scientific man as his negation of his 'symbiosis' with nature and with his human mother. It is in this denial of symbiosis that European models of emancipation and liberation have been created. It is not just science that Mies critiques, it is the whole development of western liberalism as well as the basis of capitalism in colonial exploitation. For Mies, all are linked:

> Without turning a reciprocal, symbiotic relationship between humans and nature into a one-sided master-and-servant relationship, the bourgeois revolutions would not have been possible. Without turning foreign peoples and their lands into colonies for the White Man, the capitalist economy could not have evolved. Without violently destroying the symbiosis between man and woman, without calling woman mere animal nature, the new man could not have risen as master and lord over nature and women. (ibid.: 47)

Like Plumwood, Mies sees western knowledge as being 'purified of all traces of the fact that we are born of women and that we shall die, that we are carnal, mortal beings'. All embodied ways of knowing are therefore rejected: 'sensuous knowledge, our experience, all feelings and empathy, all power of imagination and intuition' (ibid.).

Sandra Harding has identified three approaches within the feminist critique of science and its masculinist epistemology. The first is feminist empiricism, which tries to correct the failings of masculinist science as 'bad science'. There is no basic problem with the idea of science, it has just been distorted by the male interests and prejudices that have dominated it. The second is standpoint theory, which aims to produce a successor science based on 'strong objectivity' that is from a contextualizing and positioning of knowledge. The third is a postmodern rejection of the Enlightenment epistemological framework on which the scientific model rests, that there is *a* truth which can be objectively identified (1991). As McLennan has argued, feminist standpoint epistemology stands rather uneasily between feminist empiricism and postmodernism (1995) and Harding herself has hovered uneasily between leaning towards feminist empiricism and postmodernism (Maynard 1994). For Harding:

> Knowledge claims are always socially situated, and the failure by dominant groups critically and systematically to interrogate their advantaged social situation and the effect of such advantages on their beliefs leaves their social situation a scientifically and epistemologically damaged one for generating knowledge. (1993: 54)

Clearly, from this statement Harding is expecting 'knowledge', although it is not clear if it is *a* knowledge. The debate on objectivity and science is very much focused around the problems of subjectivity as against objectivity. For ecofeminists, the more critical question is human subjectivity/objectivity in relation to the subjectivity of nature as an object. If humanity is part of an immanent reality, an interconnected whole, then, while epistemological questions are vital for humanity, they do not affect the dynamics of the whole. There is a 'truth' about those relations that is at present beyond hu(man) grasp.

Gender, nature and knowledge

> He says that woman speaks with nature. That she hears voices from under the earth. That wind blows in her ears and trees whisper to her. But for him this dialogue is over. He says he is not part of this world, that he was set on this world as a stranger. He sets himself apart from woman and nature. (Griffin 1978: 1)

> I am a woman born and shaped by this civilization, with the mind of this civilization, but with the mind and body of a woman, with human experience. (Griffin 1989: 17)

Griffin here points to three levels of experience, embodiment, humanity and civilization. Her argument is that male domination has withdrawn not only from embodiment, but from human experience in its widest sense. Civilization has been created over and against nature. Women hang half in and half out of that process as 'insider–outsiders' in Collins's sense, as the 'bridge' between 'man as stranger' and embodied nature. In *Woman and Nature* Griffin is poetically exploring the two voices of 'man as science' and 'woman as nature'. These stand figuratively, although Griffin has been taken as essentializing male/female in this context. The point that she is making is not that women are closer to nature, but that (some aspects) of male-dominated culture and society is further away.

The (eco)feminist critique of science leaves the problem of whether science *per se* is the problem, or the fact that it is a (white, western, bourgeois) male-dominated scientific project. Within feminism, this dilemma is represented by a division between those such as Rose (1994), Keller (1985) and Harding (1993), who are arguing for a successor science, and those who dismiss science as part of the failed foundationalist project of the western Enlightenment (Hekman 1990). The feminist critique of science is left between the Scylla of postmodern 'social relativism' and the Charybdis of Enlightenment 'scientific objectivism'.

Keller's answer is to judge science according to its efficacy against a framework of cognitive, psychosocial, economic, political and technical interests (1992: 90). Her aim is to re-embody and locate science as a socially constrained phenomenon. However, Keller also wants to avoid going the whole way towards social relativism. While science is most certainly not a 'mirror of nature' according to the copy theory, it is also not a cultural artefact. To see science as a purely cultural artefact is to see nature in the same light. This would not be acceptable from an ecofeminist perspective, which sees in the natural world not only a distinct identity, but an identity which embraces humanity. Humanity is inside, not outside nature, immanent not transcendent. This issue has been addressed by Donna Haraway, who describes herself as trying to hang on to both ends of the dichotomy of a 'usable doctrine of objectivity . . . a successor science', and postmodernist accounts of difference. She wants simultaneously to have 'an account of radical historical contingency for all knowledge claims . . . *and* a no-nonsense commitment to faithful accounts of a "real" world' (1991: 187).

Haraway points out that social constructivism can only go so far. While social relationships may be culturally constructed, to see knowledge in this way destroys the ability to talk about knowledge at all, except as stories: '[T]hose of us who still like to talk about reality

. . . would like to think our appeals to real worlds are more than . . . .an act of faith like any other cult's' (ibid.: 185). This is even more of a problem when the 'real world' is non-human nature. While postmodern arguments may be persuasive for social reality, physical reality has a concrete existence. Postmodernists like Hekman may argue that all experience of the natural world is interpreted socially and culturally (1990: 142), but this assumes a dead and malleable 'nature' – 'dumb reality', in Foucault's terms. For ecofeminists the natural world is not dumb; it not only has existence, but agency. Humanity may variously interpret and respond to natural phenomena, but cannot ultimately construct them or itself. As Keller argues, the natural world is too complex. From this perspective, postmodernism is as human-centred and arrogant as the Enlightenment science that Merchant condemned.

While ecofeminists would want to challenge the false application of 'natural laws' such as in the attitude of biological science to women (Birke 1986; Sayers 1982), it would not want to deny that the natural world has its own independent processes. For ecofeminists, the natural world is a material force in itself. It is actual and real in its consequences. There is therefore a 'truth' about human–nature relations – the problem is, what epistemological framework would best reveal (or glimpse) it? From an ecofeminist perspective, Haraway points to the mortality and ultimate lack of control that human embodiment represents. The natural world is not just a resource to be exploited or even something that can be interpreted in a positivist or objectivist sense. Humanity cannot 'know' nature. Its active dynamic agency is always beyond our grasp. Haraway sees the natural world as a 'Coyote or Trickster' with an independent sense of humour with whom humanity must learn to converse. Knowledge of the natural world is a 'conversation', not a discovery.

Conclusion

What ecofeminism would criticize is the transcendent objectivity of male-dominated science that Haraway has called the 'god-trick of seeing everything from nowhere' (1991: 189). She argues for an 'embodied objectivity', which I have called immanent realism. Embedded and embodied human beings, as part of the natural world, will never be able to grasp the whole, but can struggle to gain knowledge about the limits, potentialities and responsibilities that immanence entails. Haraway argues that transcendent objectivity represents 'a story that loses track of its mediations', it is disembodied, abstract and unlocatable and therefore irresponsible. 'Embodied objectivity', in contrast, represents knowledge that can provide an 'earth-wide network of connections' (ibid.: 187). It is objective because it is knowledge that is locatable and responsible. The possibility of sustained, rational, objective knowledge rests in such an interconnected web of knowledge.

I would agree with Haraway that knowledge as 'vision' was always an element of science and that such a vision needs to be reclaimed. Green versions of science are emerging that take a much more holistic view (Lovelock 1979; Capra 1976). However, for knowledge to be locatable and responsible it also needs to be situated. The case for taking the standpoint of the subjugated is that it is less likely to be irresponsible and unlocatable. If superordination, as I have suggested, is based on transcendence, it is, by definition, a process of detachment. However, taking a standpoint in this way only makes sense if the subordinate and superordinate are structurally and materially related. Standpoints are not just stories or perspectives, they are different aspects of a material relation. It is the material relation that is the object of knowledge, not the particular perspective of particular people. Haraway's conception of bringing together partial perspectives makes no sense unless there is a whole to be grasped. The whole for ecofeminism is the structure of relationships that surround human immanence and 'create' transcendence.

The problem with the radical social constructivist critique of knowledge is that the epistemological problems raised have come to stand for ontological questions about human existence. Consciousness (in the form of symbolic structures) is seen as determining 'being' from bodies to social institutions and practices, such as science. From an ecofeminist perspective, just because hu(man)s have a problem about understanding their environment, it does not mean that it doesn't exist. Postmodernists warn against committing the conceptual fallacy of confusing the representation with the real. However, in avoiding the error of naturalizing the cultural, it is important not to end up committing the reverse error of socializing the natural. I will make the same point in the context of Marxist social constructionism.

'Nature' within western philosophy and science may be a social construction but the natural world has its own agency and dynamic (Soper 1995: 149 f.). As Keller argues, 'the locus of real force in the world [is] physical not mental' (1992: 25). It may be that formal scientific knowledge-gathering systems are not the best way to understand the human interrelationship with nature. A spiritual or some other body-based intuitive approach may be more appropriate in raising awareness, although more detailed information-gathering would require experiential or (appropriate) scientific knowledge. The critique of masculinist science is not just that it has not disentangled the 'real force' of the physical world from the conceptual and social biases of the dominant groups that scientists represent, but that it has not seen that detachment from nature is central to the Enlightenment view of the world. To the extent that the material position of most women enables this detachment to be made on the part of (some) men and even fewer women, then the power relations surrounding the sex/gender division of labour and women's 'difference' cannot be just another 'story'. I will elaborate upon this in Chapters 7 and 8. In the next chapter I will look at ecofeminism in relation to those who put humanity's relationship with nature at the forefront of their analysis and take the 'real force' of the physical world as a starting point: green theorists and particularly deep ecologists.

6

Feminism and the Green Movement

The relationship between feminism and the green movement needs to be discussed in terms of women's involvement in green politics and the place of feminism in green thought. As Seager has shown, women provide much of the grassroots support for environmental campaigning, but fall away when organizations become more formal and bureaucratized (1993: 176 ff.). Women predominate where activism is local and free or low paid. When involvement becomes more demanding in both time and distance and positions are salaried, men begin to take control. Rosemary Teverson has confirmed this process in her British study of the employment structure of groups such as Greenpeace, World Wide Fund for Nature and Friends of the Earth (1991). She found a high level of participation by women in the more junior clerical and administrative posts, but a much reduced proportion in the campaigning, fundraising and senior management posts. The women who did achieve senior posts found themselves under pressure to commit themselves wholeheartedly to the organization and, in particular, not to 'burden' themselves with children. Part of the pressure came from a concern within these organizations not to 'divert' precious funds to pay for maternity leave and other forms of childcare support.

Men also figure strongly in the hagiography of environmental movements – for example, Christopher Manes's his-tory of Earth First! (1990). Although women are well represented in direct action movements, her-story remains to be told. Seager argues that the high profile of men in organizations such as Earth First! both creates and reflects a bias in their campaigning towards issues such as wilderness and wildlife preservation rather than concerns with human health and habitat which are often the focus of women's local campaigning (1993: 180–1).

The German green party, as I have shown, provides depressing evidence of the problems women face when the movement engages directly with existing power structures. Headed by high profile women such as Petra Kelly, *die Grünen* came to power in 1983 committed to a feminist programme. Among its aims were ending 'the oppression, exploitation, injustice and discrimination that women have suffered for many thousands of years', and the formation of a society 'built on complete equality of the sexes in the context of an overall ecological policy' (*Programme of the German Green Party* (PGGP) 1983: 40). The programme had policies on the recognition and sharing of housework, abortion rights, laws on rape and violence in marriage and sexual discrimination. Women should no longer be condemned to 'passive femininity', watching silently as men disregarded their interests. *Die Grünen* argued that women must play an equal role in the economic and political arena if the life of the next generation was to be safeguarded, instead of the present system where 'men are at the centre of a patriarchal world, North, South, East and West' (Kelly 1988: 111).

Despite the centrality of feminism to theory and practice in *die Grünen* the early momentum was not maintained. Although the intention was to have 50 per cent representation for women at all levels of the party, this was difficult to achieve given the domestic pressures on women. Even within the parliamentary party men were marginalizing the feminist agenda, seeing abortion and other social issues as 'less political' (Spretnak and Capra 1985: 48). As with the history of other parts of the green movement, feminism and women's experiences are being marginalized in the histories of *die Grünen* (Hülsberg 1988; Parkin 1989). Women are also disappearing, or never appear, as a political 'fact' in surveys of green politics, for example one British survey of contemporary green politics included only two references to women (Rudig 1990).

Women may be present in large numbers in the green movement, but sex/gender issues are not central to the (malestream) green political agenda (Mellor 1992c). In a patriarchal society, failure to recognize the interests, experience and needs of women must mean that the values and experience of men will determine the direction of green politics by default. Although many men in the green movement may think they have transcended masculinist politics, without an avowedly feminist perspective dominant male attitudes and priorities will prevail. Evidence that women's contribution to green politics is being marginalized can be found in the male domination of green literature. Women's input into green thinking is becoming ghettoized into ecofeminism, rather than being at the core. Compilations of green thinking only include a few women contributors (Button 1990; Dobson 1991; Sachs 1993) and journals like the UK *Ecologist* or even the more radical US-based *Capitalism, Nature, Socialism* are dominated by male writers who rarely include a feminist or ecofeminist perspective. More women green writers are represented in the area of environmental philosophy and ethics (Warren 1994, 1996) and there are some individual exceptions, such as Carolyn Merchant's critique of the scientific revolution, Vandana Shiva's critique of development and Robyn Eckersley's politics of deep ecology, which are frequently cited.

Where women do enter malestream green political thought it is often in connection with their role in the family and on population issues. Women's interests are seen as directly connected with the need to reduce population: 'education and employment opportunities for women lead to smaller families' (Paehlke 1989: 266) there is a 'happy correlation' between women's liberation and 'population control' (Irvine and Ponton 1988: 23). The importance of family structures are stressed in the development of sustainable societies, with 'the extended family as the basic unit of socialization and production' (*The Ecologist* 1993: 189) and as the central unit of the 'vernacular community' (Goldsmith 1992). The latter example represents the most conservative version of malestream green thought which even defends the caste system as an institution of vernacular society (ibid.: 338). Goldsmith makes the teleological assumption that communities that he sees as emerging 'naturally' are ecologically benign, part of an evolutionary process, whereas human attempts to make conscious progress (science, the state) are ecologically destructive. Women's position is ordained within the family. For Goldsmith, hierarchy is part of nature – 'the Way' – and must not be challenged. Fritz Schumacher's highly influential work *Small is Beautiful* used Buddhist ideas to argue that a woman's place is in the home: 'to let mothers of young children work in factories while the children run wild would be uneconomic in the eyes of a Buddhist economist' (1973: 51–2).

There are some exceptions. Feminism has been claimed as a 'guiding star' for ecology (Dobson 1995: 29) and has been described as 'the deepest current expression of a personal tie to the natural world' (Tokar 1987: 85). However, where male green writers do draw upon ecofeminism, it is often more associated with the 'feminine' than 'feminism' (Mellor 1992c). Ideas of masculine–feminine complementarity do not draw on modern feminist thinking, but on much older ideas of the unity/partnership of the masculine and feminine influenced by Eastern philosophy, particularly Taoism. Influential male green writers such as Fritjof Capra (1983) and Jonathon Porritt (1984) draw on the Taoist idea of yin and yang, the feminine and the masculine. Human society has become destructive because of the predominance of the masculine/yang principle. The aim is not the feminist one of overthrowing the masculine principle or male power, but of restoring the balance between them. Drawing on Capra, Porritt sees this balance as being restored by men and women reclaiming the 'feminine principle', the 'soft/yin' qualities of 'co-operation, empathy, holistic thinking, emotion and intuition' (1984: 201). For Porritt, the problem is not male domination of women, but the lack of 'balance' within the human psyche, with men being too tough and hard (competitive, assertive, rational, analytical, materialist and intellectual) and women too gentle and soft. For both men and women the path lies in individual personal transformation, not the politics of personal relations. From this perspective there is no inherent conflict between men and women. Patriarchy is not a system of power, it is a system out of balance. Although some ecofeminists have used a similar language to that of Capra and Porritt, none would be so optimistic about the ease with which patriarchal systems could be opposed. Most affinity ecofeminists draw on the idea of the goddess as representing (defeated) female values rather than Eastern ideas of benign balance.

Ecofeminism and ecological thought

Ecofeminism has generally been identified as part of a 'deeper' or more radical approach to the ecological crisis (Merchant 1992; Eckersley 1992; McLaughlin 1993; Dobson 1995). Although, as I intend to show, there is no necessary conflict between a radical and a 'deeper' approach to human–nature relations, there are tensions between them in practice. The source of these tensions is the priority given to human–nature relations as opposed to human–human relations. A radical approach to ecology would incorporate a fundamental reorganization of human–human relations as an essential aspect of reformulating human–nature relations. Deep ecology, on the other hand, would see human–nature relations as the critical element.

McLaughlin has identified five branches of 'radical environmentalism': human-centred environmentalism, social ecology, ecological feminism, bioregionalism and deep ecology (1993: 198). Human-centred environmentalism is based on radical *social* change, with resolution of the ecological crisis as an outcome of that process. Social ecology also prioritizes social relations, but sees these as based on a dialectical relationship between society and nature. Both these approaches will be discussed more fully in the next chapter. Bioregionalism argues that humanity must organize itself socially and geographically in relation to its ecological context. The primary focus is the identification of distinctive bioregional ecosystems within which to locate sustainable human communities, a process that is not without fundamental conceptual and political difficulties (Mellor 1992a: 109 f.). Deep ecology seeks to reformulate completely humanity's relationship to the natural world, and will be the main focus of this chapter.

Carolyn Merchant sees 'radical ecology' as emerging from a sense of crisis in the industrialized world that 'confronts the illusion that people are free to exploit nature' (1992: 1). However, as a socialist ecofeminist, she also goes on to point to patterns of inequality and exploitation in human society. Social/ist ecofeminists by definition, take a radical social approach, focusing on failures in human–human and particularly sex/gender relations as both cause and consequence of failures in human–nature relations. Affinity and spiritual ecofeminists such as Charlene Spretnak and Starhawk tend to lean more towards deep ecology and a much more elemental cosmology. As I have stressed, these perspectives should not be seen as exclusive, and most ecofeminists offer a combination of deep ecology sentiments and proposals for radical social change. However, this is not true for some male deep ecologists, where there is a tendency to stress the relationship between humanity and nature at the expense of a consideration of social relationships. Ecofeminism's emphasis on the centrality of sex/gender relations is either ignored or at best seen as a weak contributing factor.

Deep ecological thinking has mainly been associated with male writers such as Arne Naess, George Sessions, Bill Devall and Warwick Fox. Deep ecologists have drawn a distinction between their 'deep' approach to the natural world and the 'shallow' human-centred perspective of those who are merely concerned with the effect on human communities of specific environmental problems. This distinction was first drawn by Arne Naess in 1972 (published in 1973) and has been represented by Robyn Eckersley as anthropocentrism versus ecocentrism. For Eckersley, anthropocentrism represents human-centredness in the sense that 'intrinsic value is taken to reside exclusively or at least pre-eminently in humans', such that human interests become favoured over the interests of the non-human world (1992: 2).

The ecocentric perspective, on the other hand, does not single out the human species for special treatment or see it as distinct from the rest of the natural world. Instead, the world is seen as 'an intrinsically, dynamic, interconnected web of relations in which there are no absolutely discrete entities and no absolute dividing lines between the living and the nonliving, the animate and the inanimate, or the human and the nonhuman' (ibid.: 49). This echoes Naess's formulation that: 'In the Deep Ecology Movement we are biocentric or ecocentric. For us it is the ecosphere, the whole planet, Gaia, that is the basic unit, and every living being has intrinsic value' (1990: 135). From the perspective of feminist spirituality Charlene Spretnak also stresses the principle of interconnectedness and intrinsic value:

> Deep ecology encompasses the study of Nature's subtle web of interrelated processes and the application of that study to our interactions with Nature and among ourselves. Principles of deep ecology are that the well-being and flourishing of human and non-human life on earth have inherent value, that richness and diversity of life forms contribute to the realization of these values and are values in themselves, and that humans have no right to reduce this richness and diversity except to satisfy vital needs. (1985: 233)

For deep ecologists bio/ecocentrism is not just a statement of the ontological condition of humanity, it is a source of knowledge: 'Deep ecology goes beyond the so-called factual level to the level of self and earth wisdom . . . to articulate a comprehensive religious and philosophical worldview . . . the basic intuitions and experiencing of ourselves and Nature which comprise ecological consciousness' (Devall and Sessions 1985: 65). Deep ecology has not only produced a number of philosophical treatises, it has also inspired direct action movements such as Earth First! Deep ecological principles have led many activists to put their own lives at risk in defence of the biosphere: forests, animals, oceans, landscapes. However, sometimes concern for the natural world and the critique of anthropocentrism has become associated with anti-humanism (Tokar 1990). Ecocentrism is no longer identified with the whole web of life, as in Eckersley's formulation, but solely with non-human life and/or nature. This is particularly reflected in the prioritization of wilderness which tends to be identified as 'nature' unspoilt by 'man'. Ecocentrism therefore has to hold a difficult balance between enhancing the intrinsic value of the natural world, both as a whole and in its constituent parts, without devaluing humanity to the point where its own intrinsic right to existence is threatened.

The intrinsic right to existence of all life is expressed as 'biospheric egalitarianism', one of the seven principles of deep ecology first set out by Arne Naess. Biospherical egalitarianism reflects 'the equal right to live and blossom' of all living things (Naess 1973: 95). This concept was later rephrased by Warwick Fox (1990) and Robyn Eckersley (1992), among others, as ecocentric egalitarianism to embrace non-living nature. The other six principles include the assertion of the importance of seeing 'man' as being part of the natural world, in Naess's words, rejection of the 'man-in-the-environment image' in favour of 'the relational total-field image'. This shares the ecofeminist rejection of the 'man'/nature dualism of western thought and reflects Starhawk's notion of immanence, humanity as embedded and embodied in the alive-ness of the natural world as a whole. Like Starhawk's notion of connectedness, it reflects an ecological holism. Everything is connected to everything else in the web of life. Naess called for humility in humanity's approach to the complexity of the natural world and stressed the importance of diversity and symbiosis, that is, the mutual coexistence of all living forms. He argued against inequalities between 'man and man' and called for a fight against pollution and resource depletion, which he argued could only be resolved through local autonomy and decentralization. While Naess's ideas have remained at the heart of deep ecological thinking, the importance of the inequalities between 'man and man', and particularly between man and woman, have been marginalized, if not ignored completely.

In 1988 Naess reiterated his ideas in an eight-point 'platform for deep ecology'. His first four points are:

1 The flourishing of human and non-human life on Earth has inherent value. The value of non-human life-forms is independent of the usefulness of the non-human world for human purposes.
2 The richness and diversity of life-forms are also values in themselves and contribute to the flourishing of human and non-human life on Earth.
3 Humans have no right to reduce this richness and diversity except to satisfy vital needs.

4 The flourishing of human life and cultures is compatible with a
substantial *decrease* of the human population. The flourishing of
non-human life requires such a decrease.

He goes on to call for less 'human interference with the non-human
world', a change in 'basic economic, technological and ideological
structures' towards a 'more joyful experience of the connectedness of
all things', and a stress on 'life quality' rather than standard of living
(Naess 1988: 128–32). For deep ecologists the problem in following
Naess's platform lies in making the jump from an ontological assertion of 'man's' interconnectedness with the natural world to a political programme, a politics of ecology. A central theme of much deep
ecology writing has been to establish the philosophical grounds for
political action (Devall and Sessions 1985; Devall 1990; Fox 1990;
Eckersley 1992) that goes beyond the extension of human values such
as rights into the natural world (Singer 1976).

For Naess, deep ecology was more than just the development of an
environmental ethics, a moral code from which to address the natural
world. Instead he argued for the 'supremacy of environmental ontology and realism over environmental ethics' (quoted in Fox 1990:
218). Fox also points to Sessions's concept of 'ecological consciousness' and Devall's notion of 'ecological realism' as examples of
perspectives that transcend the rational/liberal approach of moral
extensionism. Eckersley also points to the weakness of according
intrinsic value to the natural world, including the classic intrinsic-
value approach, Aldo Leopold's 'land ethic', first set out in 1949: 'A
thing is right when it tends to preserve the integrity, stability and
beauty of the biotic community. It is wrong when it does otherwise'
(quoted in Eckersley 1992: 61). Eckersley sees Leopold's land ethic as
too human-centred, particularly in its concept of beauty. Any approach that extends ethical values developed within the human
community, such as rights and obligations, must necessarily be
human-centred. 'Values' have to be accorded by the human viewer.
A problem for any ethical approach to the natural world is that in the
end a reformulation of human–nature relationships must be human-
generated, if not human-centred (Hayward 1994: 68). Eckersley also
argues that the concepts of integrity and stability in Leopold's 'land
ethic' could justify 'ecofascism', in the sense of requiring the sacrifice
of individuals for the good of the whole.

Eckersley sees a more hopeful way forward in Warwick Fox's
transpersonal ecology, which is itself a development of Naess's ideas.
Fox calls for a new cosmology and a change in psychological atti-

tudes: 'The primary concern of transpersonal ecology is the cultivation of a wider sense of self through the common or everyday psychological process of *identification* with others' (quoted in Eckersley 1992: 61; italics in the original) Fox's 'wider sense of self' does not come from the individual but from the cosmos: '[D]eep ecologists emphasize identification within a cosmological context – that is, within the context of an awareness that all entities in the universe are part of a single, unfolding process' (1989: 11). Despite such holistic statements, at the heart of Fox's cosmology, as with Naess's, is an atomistic, ahistoric and teleological notion of each organism/structure unfolding its own preordained destiny with which humans must not interfere. This is in conflict with the notion that all are part of the cosmic whole where 'all entities . . . are relatively autonomous modes of a single unfolding process' (ibid.: 12). Following Naess, Fox sees biological egalitarianism as 'an attitude that, within obvious practical limits, allows all entities (including humans) *the freedom to unfold in their own way unhindered by the various forms of human domination*' (ibid.: 6; italics in the original). Fox's teleological and ahistoric approach to the natural world is clear in his statement that: 'all life forms are the production of *distinct* evolutionary pathways and . . . should be thought of as more or less perfect (complete) examples *of their own kind*' (1990: 200; italics in the original). Such a conception leads to the problem of what happens if evolutionary pathways start to conflict and Fox clearly puts interpretation of nature's 'real' intent in human hands: '[I]f a particular entity or life form imposes itself unduly upon other entities or life forms . . . one has no real choice but to *oppose* even in extreme cases, to terminate the existence of, the destructive or oppressive entity or life form' (ibid.: 257; italics in the original). Although Fox does ask that this be done in 'as educative, least disruptive and least vindictive way as possible', the same criticism could be made of Fox as Eckersley made of Leopold. Who is to say who or what is 'imposing' itself on 'nature'? Who is to judge between the unfolding autonomy of the mollusc and the unfolding autonomy of the millionaire?

Obviously, from a deep ecology perspective humanity is the first candidate for containment, but who is to begin the process of 'terminating the existence of' such an unduly imposing species? As I have argued more fully elsewhere, any discussion of human population reduction – one of the central planks of a deep ecology policy – is necessarily class-based, sexist and racist in a world in which human communities are divided by class, sex and 'race' (1992c: 98 f.). The more powerful will always seek to impose any population limitations on the powerless. It is clear that an ecocentric deep ecology that does not also embrace a radically egalitarian social perspective would play into the hands of dominant classes, 'races', nations and gender. In any event, how do we know that current human development on this planet is not part of its own unfolding destiny? How do we know that humanity, even in its present state of technological development and population reach, is unnatural?

Following Naess, Fox argues that humans will understand nature's cosmology through an expanded sense of the self. This is not the 'egoic, biographical sense of self', nor one that humans attain individually or collectively through ethical or political development. Rather it is a self that comes in from the outside, it is a reaching for an already existing 'big Self': '[A] transpersonal approach to ecology is concerned precisely with *opening* to ecological awareness: with realising one's ecological, wider, or big Self' (1990: 199; italics in the original). Transpersonal ecology's cosmology requires a new way of looking at the world. For Fox this is the image of the cosmos as an unfolding 'tree of life'. We are all leaves on that tree and adopting this new world-view will, Fox argues, lead us to a new psychological orientation:

> For transpersonal ecologists, given a deep enough understanding of the way things are, the response of being inclined to care for the unfolding of the world in all its aspects follows 'naturally' – not as a *logical* consequence but as a *psychological* consequence: as an expression of the spontaneous unfolding (development, maturing) of the self. (quoted in Eckersley 1992: 63; italics in the original)

Other deep ecologists such as Devall follow a similar analysis (1990: 38 f.). Self-realization therefore becomes the goal, a personal transformation in attaining 'ecological awareness'. This is, of course, idealism, reaching for the 'cosmic mind' of nature, a timeless essence revealing itself. From an ecofeminist point of view any discussion of the idea of self is problematic. How is realization of the cosmic self to be separated from the egoic self that feminists have identified as a patriarchal phenomenon? I will expand upon the ecofeminist critique of deep ecology in the next section.

The Naess/Fox/Devall/Eckersley approach to deep ecology claims that if a transpersonal ecological self were achieved, then moral injunctions would not be necessary: 'The cultivation of this expansive sense of self means that compassion and empathy naturally flow as part of an individual's way of being in the world rather than as a duty or obligation that must be performed regardless of one's personal inclination' (Fox, quoted in Eckersley 1992: 62). Human-centredness is avoided by moving from 'selfishness' to 'Selfishness' in Naess's terms so that 'care flows naturally if the "self" is widened and deepened so that protection of free nature is felt and conceived as protection of ourselves' (quoted in Fox 1990: 217). Human interest therefore dissolves into ecocentrism, although realization of the 'big Self' still depends on human action. The idealism of this perspective means that spontaneity of 'unfolding (development, maturing)' is not determined by the materiality of human connectedness to the natural world *per se*, but by an individual appreciation of the *idea* of connectedness. As a result, transpersonal ecology does not escape from human-centredness in the sense of being human-generated. 'Self'-realization is equally as dependent upon human reason and will as are the demands of the moral extensionism of environmental ethics.

Fox offers humanity an 'experiential invitation' (ibid.: 63) to grasp psychologically the significance of this new cosmology, but what will lead people to take it? If such a cosmology is 'naturally' available, coming as it does from the 'outside', what stops humanity exhibiting an ecological awareness already? The individualized psychologism of Fox's deep ecology ignores the need to have a political analysis of anthropocentrism. This is what ecofeminists argue their analysis can provide (Salleh 1992; Plumwood 1994).

Certainly, traditional non-ecological political approaches can and should be criticized for being human-centred, but ecocentric models take us no further forward in terms of a distinctive political theory. In fact, Eckersley's adoption of Fox's work as the basis of her ecocentric approach to political theory leads her to argue not for a distinctive politics of deep ecology, but for a modified ecosocialism that seems to rest on moral extensionism: '[E]cosocialism has the potential to be revised in an ecocentric direction simply by extending its theoretical horizons, that is, by extending its fundamental norm of respect for all persons to encompass respect for all life-forms and ecological entities' (1992: 181). Despite Fox's intention of developing a psychological approach, the outcome in Eckersley's formulation remains ethical/political. The 'norm of respect' is not an expanded self but an ethical injunction. As I will argue in the next chapter, I think a much stronger ground can be made for ecocentrism through an extension of Marx's materialist analysis rather than a utopian appeal to an expanded ethical socialism.

The word ecocentrism is also problematic in that when set in opposition to anthropocentrism it reflects a dualist conception of humanity versus nature. This leads to a tension in the concept of ecocentrism in relation to humanity. In rejecting human-centredness (anthropocentrism), nature-centredness (ecocentricity) cannot really adopt a position of biological/ecological egalitarianism, that is, the right for each entity to its own existence and development. If human society is seen to be problematic and out of step, then ecocentrism must have at its heart a dualist distinction between 'humanity' and 'nature'. Nature is 'right' and humanity is 'wrong'. This must lead to an anti-human position, where humanity is not seen as part of nature, but against nature. Humanity is trangressing 'nature' and must therefore be punished, and certainly restricted.

I would argue that the concept of ecological holism better expresses the interdependence of humanity and nature within one framework than the concept of ecocentrism with its dualistic assumptions. In contrast to the idealist approach taken by most deep ecologists, I would also prefer to see human envelopment in 'nature' as a material relation, an immanent materialism, that is, the historical unfolding of the material reality of human embodiment and embeddedness within its ecological and biological context. However, I would not see this as having any particular direction in the sense of a determined outcome, although plainly some constructions of human–nature relations are more sustainable than others. This conception of human–nature relations makes the development of a politics of ecology (or, more correctly, ecological holism) vital. The tendency towards an anti-human stance inherent in the dualistic notion of ecocentrism is politically very problematic. Placing the blame for the ecological crisis on an undifferentiated 'humanity' puts equal responsibility on the North and the South, rich and poor, Black and white, men and women. An attack on human-centredness that ignores social differ-ence and inequality is both deeply political and depoliticizing.

Ecofeminists have put the sex/gender divisions within humanity at the heart of their analysis, and this puts them into direct conflict with many deep ecologists, despite the fact that both perspectives take a 'deep' approach to human–nature relations.

Deep ecology and ecofeminism

The deep ecology movement, using the generic term *Man*, simultaneously presupposes the differences between the sexes in an uncritical way, and yet overlooks the significance of this difference. (Salleh 1984: 340; italics in the original)

As Sharon Doubiago has observed, 'the deep ecology movement is shockingly sexist' (1989: 40). Many of its most high-profile supporters have stressed the nobility of 'man' confronting 'nature' in hunting (Aldo Leopold) or wilderness trekking (Bill Devall). Writers in this field, male and female, often describe themselves as climbers or backpackers. Although it is not always explicitly stated, human–nature relations are idealized as the lone figure in the open and wild landscape. This figure is not always male, but is unlikely to be ill, infirm, in a wheelchair or holding the hand of a small child. 'He' is very unlikely to be surrounded by a crowd or a squatter camp. The autonomous nature-oriented individual of deep ecology is, of course, the same as that criticized by feminists in Enlightenment thought (Plumwood 1994). The male individualist values that have crept into deep ecology are represented in Bill Devall's rejection of 'the ordered, bordered, fenced, domesticated, patrolled and controlled' aspects of human life in favour of the self-realization of an ecological self, a 'wild' self (1990: 71). The social construction of this 'self' is not questioned. The climber/backpacker needs boots, backpack, cagoule, lightweight hi-tech equipment. 'He' has to be born, nursed and cherished. 'He' needs income or land to live. The freedom to roam for such people is socially and politically constructed. In Britain, given historic patterns of land ownership, the freedom to roam is problematic even for the socially privileged. Where wilderness does exist, particularly in the United States and Australia, it is often the historical product of 'ethnic cleansing' by incoming European colonists. The lone backpacker image also puts the deep ecologists' approach to population reduction in a problematic light. Is 'humanity' getting in the way of nature, or of the lone 'man' in the landscape?

Ariel Salleh, an Australian sociologist and socialist ecofeminist, was one of the earliest critics of deep ecology. In her 1984 article 'Deeper than Deep Ecology', she showed how Naess's original approach criticized the man/nature dualism without seeing the man/woman dualism that lay within it. She saw many of the problems that Naess sought to overcome as male-constructed problems such as pollution and resource depletion, destructive science and centralization. Women's role in reproduction was ignored in the calls for population control. Biological egalitarianism and the principles of diversity and symbiosis did not seem to take account of women's experiences and lives. Deep ecologists were going to great lengths to establish an abstract environmental ethic, when they could start from women as the 'immediate "living" basis' for an alternative consciousness (1984: 340). Although Salleh praised deep ecology for transcending the 'hard headed scientific approach' in favour of a new meta-physics, a more spiritual consciousness, advocacy of voluntary simplicity and a nonexploitative steady-state economy (ibid : 339), her main criticism was that the principles of deep ecology did not take account of exploitative social relations, particularly between men and women.

The title of Salleh's paper 'Deeper than Deep Ecology' indicated that she saw an ecofeminist approach as more than a correction of deep ecology. She reported later that a colleague had urged her to amend the title to 'deepening deep ecology', but she felt that the original title reflected her position. Salleh has been accused of essentialism (Davion 1994), for seeing the dualistic nature of society as a male construction, while identifying women's fertility cycle, pregnancy and childbirth as a 'fact of life'. In her early work she appeared to take the affinity view of women's relationship with nature, where female embodiment 'ground women's consciousness in the knowledge of being coterminus with Nature' (1984: 340). She invokes the 'feminine' in a way that seems to echo the complementary approach taken by Capra and Porritt: 'The suppression of the *feminine* is truly an all-pervasive human universal. It is not just a suppression of real, live, empirical women, but equally the suppression of the feminine aspects of men's own constitution which is the issue here' (ibid.: 344; italics in the original). Failure to see this meant that deep ecology represented 'the self-estranged male reaching for the original androgynous natural unity within himself' (ibid.). Salleh's later work moves away from the affinity view to a more materialist analysis (1994). She became more concerned with the material oppression of real women, rather than the suppression of a feminine universal.

The main criticism raised by ecofeminists is that the deep ecology critique of anthropocentrism (human-centredness) ignores the role of androcentrism (male-centredness). The question of whether humanity as a whole should be held accountable for the ecological crisis, or some aspect of its internal organization such as patriarchy, has given rise to a prolonged debate between ecofeminists and deep ecologists. Jim Cheney, writing in 1987, echoed Salleh's view that deep ecology was reflecting a particularly male (white, middle-class) experience of estrangement from nature:

> What I want to argue is that deep ecological attempts to overcome human (really masculine) alienation from nature fail in the end because they are unable to overcome a masculine sense of the self and the kinds of ethical theory that go along with this sense of self. (1987: 121)

Drawing on Carol Gilligan's notion of a woman's 'different voice' (1982), Cheney argues for a woman-oriented environmental ethic based on responsibility, trust, care and love, rather than the more distant and abstract conception of rights or justice. A holistic approach would not swallow up the 'other' in an expanded self, but accept the relationships of responsibility that 'others' such as nature bring in a 'moral community' (ibid.: 132). A sense of 'deep connectedness' cannot produce universal moral edicts but rather the 'ability to respond in a caring manner, which, in turn, [is] a function of the depth of one's own understanding of the human moral community and the clarity and depth of one's understanding of, and relationship to, the nonhuman world or elements of that world' (ibid.: 144). The importance of recognizing the role of androcentrism in creating ecological destructiveness was also stressed by Marti Kheel: 'Whereas the anthropocentric worldview perceives humans as the center or apex of the natural world, the androcentric analysis suggests that this worldview is unique to men' (1990: 129). Kheel sees the deep ecologist's search for an expanded self as a way of 'transcending the concrete world of particularity in preference for something more enduring and abstract' (ibid.: 136). Warning ecofeminists not to be seduced by transcendent holistic philosophies, Kheel calls for a 'deep holistic awareness of the interconnectedness of all of life . . . a *lived* awareness that we experience in relation to *particular* beings *as well as* to the larger whole' (ibid.: 136–7; italics in the original). Salleh, Cheney and Kheel are all asking for a more grounded approach to human–nature relations, which addresses the issue of sex/gender and the particularity of women's lives.

Warwick Fox replied to these and other criticisms in 1989. He argued that deep ecologists have been misunderstood, and maintains that they are not concerned with a misanthropic blaming of all humanity. Deep ecologists are not against humans *per se*, but against human-centredness, that is, using human interests and needs as a legitimating ideology in exploiting nature. Human-centredness is a 'cultural spell' (1989: 22) which legitimizes all dominant groups. In this context, debates about the causes of inequality are diversionary:

> What the ecofeminist criticism of deep ecology's focus on anthropocentrism overlooks then, is the fact that deep ecologists are not primarily concerned with exposing the *classes of social actors* historically most responsible for social domination and ecological destruction, but rather with the task of sweeping the rug out from under the feet of these classes of social actors by exposing the most fundamental kind of *legitimation* that they have habitually employed in justifying their position. (ibid.: 24)

Fox argues that the ecofeminist idea of embeddedness is too specific and local and that the 'different voice' should not be experiential but cosmological and transpersonal (ibid.: 12). He argues that deep ecology's critique of anthropocentrism is more comprehensive than the ecofeminist critique of androcentrism. In a very telling criticism, he points to the weakness of prioritizing patriarchy rather than racism or imperialism. However, Fox himself goes to the other extreme by denying the culpability of any specific group through an emphasis on 'humanity' or human-centredness as the problem. This ignores the fact that human society is not just 'human-centred', it is also constructed out of racism, sexism, imperialism and class exploitation. For Fox, to point to any one of these oppressions is to be guilty of a 'simplistic' and perhaps witless human-centredness:

> [D]eep ecologists find it particularly frustrating to witness representatives of simplistic social and political perspectives waving the banner of ecology while in fact continuing to promote, whether wittingly or unwittingly, the interhuman and, hence, human-centred agenda of their respective theoretical legacies. (ibid.: 17)

Fox has no basic quarrel with other social movements if they 'revise their perspectives' in line with deep ecology. He points to the dilemma in the fact that a perfectly egalitarian human society could be deeply destructive ecologically. Humanity is urged to 'jump' to a cosmological consciousness, although the motivation for this is unclear. In the absence of a self-interested human-centred material motivation, it appears that, rather tautologically, only an ecological consciousness will motivate people to gain ecological consciousness.

Fox and Eckersley both reject ecofeminism for its particularity, despite seeing some basic similarities to deep ecology:

> Like transpersonal ecology, ecofeminism is concerned with our sense of self and the way in which we experience the world rather than with formal value theory. Like transpersonal ecology, ecofeminism also proceeds from a process oriented, relational image of nature and seeks mutualistic social and ecological relationships based on a recognition of the interconnectedness, interdependence and diversity of all phenomena. (Eckersley 1992: 63–4)

Although Eckersley favours Fox's transpersonal ecology as the basis of her own ecocentrism, she identifies ecofeminism as an ecocentric perspective. Central to this is the critique of hierarchical dualism and 'masculine' culture. She sees the reassertion of the relationship beween women and nature as 'a source of empowerment for women and the basis of a critique of the male domination of women and non-human nature' (ibid.: 64). However, she criticizes ecofeminism for its lack of a cosmology. Whereas transpersonal ecology starts from the assertion of the 'tree of life', ecofeminism starts from the particularized gender experience of women. Ecofeminism does not work towards an appreciation of interconnectedness from the 'outside in', from an awareness of humanity's place in the cosmos, but from the 'inside out', based on the experiences, feelings and particular bodies of women. Against the claims of ecofeminism, Eckersley sees Fox's approach as avoiding partiality, attachment, possessiveness and parochialism, and that 'cosmologically based identification represents a more impartial, inclusive and, hence more egalitarian approach' (ibid.: 65).

Eckersley rejects the 'body-based' arguments for women's superior knowledge of nature on the grounds that men are also embodied. She ascribes the differences in their experience of embodiment to the socially constructed consequences of oppression. Echoing the liberal and socialist feminist critique of ecofeminism, Eckersley sees discussion of women's bodily difference as legitimizing their subordination as 'natural' beings, if not creating it. While arguing that to stress a sex/gendered bodiedness is to maintain the male–female dualism, she does accept, with the standpoint perspective, that women's oppression means that they have a 'vantage point of "critical otherness"'. This is a social position from which women 'can offer a different way of looking at the problems of both patriarchy *and* ecological destruction' (ibid.: 67; italics in the original). A standpoint perspective becomes problematic for Eckersley if women go on to claim that they have the *only* vantage point and ignore the fact that some women are complicit in patterns of behaviour that cause ecological destruction.

Eckersley also wishes to dissociate men *per se* from oppressive masculine stereotypes. Women's special vantage point should not be treated as a privileged perspective: '[P]rivileging – rather than simply rendering visible and *critically* incorporating – the special insights of women can sometimes lead to a lopsided and reductionist analysis of social and ecological problems' (ibid.: 67; italics in the original). She rejects the arguments for a feminist 'ethic of care', as this merely upends the present prioritization of values. A lopsided, universalistic and abstract masculinist ethic would be replaced by an overly particularistic feminist one. Her answer, like that of Ynestra King, is to transcend the dualisms so that gender differences can be overcome. However, the actual mechanism of this transcendence is unclear.

Like Fox, the main plank of Eckersley's objections to ecofeminism is that it gives patriarchy priority over anthropocentrism as the main cause of the ecological crisis. In a reversal of the matriarchal arguments, she points out that patriarchy has existed in societies that did exist harmoniously with the natural world. Women's oppression is therefore not directly connected with the oppression of nature. Eckersley does not wish to deny that anthropocentrism and patriarchy can be mutually reinforcing, but that 'emancipation of women need not necessarily mean the emancipation of nature and vice versa' (ibid.: 68). Like many deep ecologists, she slips from a discussion of ecofeminism to a critique of equal opportunities/equality feminism, a point also noted by Salleh (1992) and Slicer (1995).

Patriarchy, according to Eckersley is part of a wider problem of anthropocentrism that is traced once more to the western philosophical system: '[P]atriarchy may be seen as not the root of the ecological crisis but rather a subset of a more general problem of philosophical dualism that has pervaded Western thought . . . from the time of the classical Greek philosophers' (ibid.: 69). However, like Fox and many of those who draw attention to the 'logic of domination' and the problem of dualism, Eckersley does not theoretically address the material basis of Greek society in patriarchy and slavery. Patriarchy is therefore seen as representing a cultural, rather than a material domination. This means that Eckersley is left with only personal transformation as the basis of political action: 'we need to transcend masculine and feminine stereotypes and cultivate a new kind of *person* (ibid.: 69; italics in the original). Drawing loosely on Habermas, Eckersley calls for a general ecocentric emancipatory framework that would incorporate all oppressions. She anticipates that the 'experiences and perspectives' of all the oppressed groups can be 'harmonized' within such a general theory (ibid.: 70). Inequalities are to be dissolved, not resolved.

Reviewing the debate in 1992, Salleh reflected on how ecofeminists and deep ecologists seemed to have been talking past each other. The main culprit she claims is the defensiveness of male theorists: 'As women begin forging new cultural meanings of their own . . . many men find themselves left behind – which can be a disturbing experience' (ibid.: 198), and she refers to 'men not used to having their ideas tested by women' (ibid.: 199). She does, however, note that some men, notably Jim Cheney, have adopted an ecofeminist perspective (Cheney 1987, 1994).

Ariel Salleh's basic and ongoing criticism of deep ecology and the search for an environmental ethics is that none of the paradigms presented have succeeded in integrating a social analysis into their ethical and philosophical concerns (1992: 196). Without such a social analysis, a new radical movement cannot be built, a point also made by Plumwood (1994). Unlike Eckersley, Salleh sees ecofeminism as a distinct political perspective and not a sub-perspective of ecocentrism, and claims that it is necessary to go 'back to women's lived experiences in a time of global crisis' (1992: 202). Just to subsume ecofeminism under 'deep ecology', as Warwick Fox proposes, would lose a distinctive contribution to radical debate. Ecofeminism presents: 'an urgent feminist political moment embodied in this little word: the need for lessons from a different cultural experience to be aired, listened to, taken seriously, and acted upon' (ibid.). In seeing ecofeminism as being concerned with 'a transvaluation of values, such that the repressed feminine, nuturant side of our culture can be woven into all social institutions and practices' (ibid.: 203), Salleh's position could be seen as essentialist. However, she goes on to argue that: 'it is nonsense to assume that women are any closer to nature than men ... ecofeminists would like to see men give up their attempts to control women and nature and join women in their identity with nature' (ibid.: 208). Salleh supports Ynestra King's view of women as choosing to identify with nature. By confusing ecofeminism with feminism, deep ecologists have criticized women for their aim of equality in an ecologically destructive system, or for moving from a demand for equality with men to a celebration of women's differences and superiority to men (Zimmerman 1987, 1990). For Salleh, this misses the ecofeminist analysis of the ecological impact of the social construction of sex/gender differences under patriarchy. Ecofeminists do not wish to join men in a patriarchal society or celebrate a patriarchally constructed image of 'woman'. They seek to challenge the male–female division without ignoring the importance of the work that women have been made to do under patriarchy: 'Feminism is a catalyst in the ongoing development of human self-consciousness. Ecofeminists are now waiting for men to take the corresponding next step in their emancipation from patriarchy so that together we can "negotiate" a fair and human "contract" with "nature"' (1992: 204).

Salleh agrees with Eckersley that patriarchy has existed 'from the beginning of recorded history' (ibid.) and this is why without a feminist analysis, deep ecology will not escape from the framework of patriarchal culture and power relations. Deep ecology can only go deeper if it looks at reintegration at a material, not a metaphysical level: 'we want reintegration with our natural, material base, not abstract, disembodied, transcendence out of it' (ibid.: 213). In order to explore that material base, deep ecologists need to understand 'how "man's relation to nature" is constructed by means of his relation to woman' (ibid.: 215). Rejection of ecofeminism as 'woman's politics' or 'femocentrism' is to miss the broader analysis that it offers. It is, in fact, reflecting the androcentric dualism of women being the 'Other' to male concerns. Salleh agrees with the aim of deep ecology to break down the 'ontological dualism of humanity versus nature', but warns that 'the movement's unconscious androcentrism continues to be a very real obstacle' (ibid.: 214). The dilemma for ecofeminists is the 'zig-zag course' they have to follow between feminist demands for women's political voice, ecofeminist aims of undermining the patriarchal relation to nature that underpins current political systems, and a need to demonstrate that women can offer an alternative basis for human–nature relations (ibid : 197).

Constructing a politics of nature

To argue that deep ecologists have ignored or marginalized the divisions within humanity is not to underestimate the importance of the radical challenge that they make to western presumptions of human dominance over nature (Murphy 1994). As Carolyn Merchant has shown, western scientific rationality has constructed a view of the non-human natural world as dead and therefore materially, politically and ethically available for exploitation (1983). For deep ecologists and ecofeminists, nature must be seen as alive, as having its own agenda and agency. As McLaughlin has argued, 'both feminism and ecology seek an understanding of all of nature that is relational, holistic and non-hierarchical' (1993: 150). Both see the 'death' of nature as resting in the dualistic thinking that lies at the heart of western society and politics. However, as we have seen, deep ecologists have also adopted a dualist approach in their view of ecocentrism as being opposed to anthropocentrism. While ecocentrism and anthropocentrism can be seen as opposed ideologically (and Fox certainly sees them this way), within the framework of a deep ecology cosmology, ontologically, humanity must be seen in all its manifestations as part of nature in its widest sense. This is a contradiction within deep ecology that I have already pointed out. For most deep ecologists, and many ecofeminists, humanity/'man'/western society seems to exist in a limbo; it was once part of 'nature', but lost its way.

As I have argued, ecological holism is a less confusing term than ecocentrism to express a 'deep' view of humanity as embodied and embedded within the natural world, interconnected and interdependent. To be interconnected and interdependent is not, however, necessarily to be in harmony or in a non-competitive, non-exploitative or non-destructive relationship. The latter are all relations of connection and/or dependence in various ways. I would not see the concept of ecological holism as implying a harmonious, teleological or ordered pattern. It merely makes an ontological statement about the ultimate physicality of all living and non-living matter. Botkin has argued that 'nature moves and changes and involves risks and uncertainties', and 'harmony' may be discordant (1990: 190). Within deep ecology there is, in contrast, a tendency to adopt an idealist metaphysics of cosmological harmony. Nature then becomes not only alive, but a transcendent force that humanity must discover, in a expanded self (Fox) or an ecosophy (Naess).

Deep ecologists are certainly right to argue that western dualism has given far too much credence to human agency. However, it would be wrong to upend this by seeing nature as controlling humanity in some teleological sense. A politics of nature would not see humanity as controlling 'dead' nature, or an alive nature 'unfolding' humanity (once the latter gets back on the right path). The problem once again is motivation: what would lead hu(man)ity back to the path of ecological balance? A dualist concept of ecocentrism cannot allow for any motivation based on human self-interest. However, an awareness of ecological holism, of the immanence of humanity as a material fact, rather than being an idealist notion, I would argue, is a more politically 'workable' approach. Humanity's connection to an ecological 'whole' has a material form and material consequences. A politics of nature would need to see humanity, non-human nature and the interrelated whole as actors in a necessarily uncertain process. This raises fundamental questions about the nature of human subjectivity.

The human self-centredness that deep ecologists rightly condemn (with postmodernism) is the Enlightenment conception of humanity as the rational, self-determining subject of history. Within this perspective all else becomes an object, or even the creation of the human (white, male, middle-class) mind and power, a critique which can also be applied to postmodernism. In contrast, ecofeminists and deep ecologists would want to argue that the natural world is also a subject of history. It has its own creative power and agency (Lovelock 1979), and, some would argue, consciousness (Capra 1983). Both perspectives are right. Humans may change 'nature' but they do not construct its ultimate reality, its aliveness. As McLaughlin argues, knowledge of the natural world is always beyond human grasp. The immanence of human existence is always framed in radical uncertainty about material conditions in their widest and deepest sense. This view shares with postmodernism an assertion of the radical uncertainty of human existence and the hubris of human knowledge systems in claiming that they can control nature, but from a material rather than a cultural perspective. Botkin still sees the necessity for a scientific/technological response in adapting to these uncertainties (1990). For McLaughlin, a political response is also necessary, as scientific knowledge will always be limited (1993), a view that I would share, together with Merchant (1992) and Hayward (1994).

For many deep ecologists and spiritual ecofeminists the first stage must be a deep, even spiritual, awareness of human immanence, a position that Soper rejects (1995). With Gottlieb (1992) and Starhawk (1990), I would argue that a spiritual or 'deep' awareness of immanence is not incompatible with a radical and rational politics or a (modified) scientific approach. A spiritual/deep understanding does not necessarily imply a *mystical* evocation of some transcendent force (nature, a transcendental self or goddess). I see it as representing a deep level of *human* consciousness and ecological awareness. What people have called spirituality is an aspect of human consciousness that 'rational' society has ignored to its cost. However, a spiritual appreciation of immanence does not imply harmony or provide an ecological 'ten commandments'. Ecological awareness, awareness of immanence, however achieved, is just the starting point (motivation) for developing a politics of nature. I would agree with Soper and against the deep ecologists that it is not possible to 'read off' the mind of nature, spiritually, politically, ethically or even scientifically. Far from revealing its unfolding and humanity's particular place in that unfolding, nature as a whole and in its parts is radically uncertain in its direction and outcome. Humanity is in such difficulties because nature is so 'under-determining' of human existence (Soper 1995: 144). Because of this radical uncertainty, much deeper than Beck's concept of risk (1992), a human-generated approach to human–nature relations, a politics of nature, is essential.

A politics of nature is necessary not only to understand and regulate human–nature relations, but to understand human–human relations in this context. While it is important to have a 'deep' orientation to nature, and humanity's place in it, given that humanity is not an undifferentiated whole, it is essential to understand the construction of human–nature relations within the context of human–human relations. Without the certainties of science or the 'unfolding' of nature, I would argue that the most appropriate epistemological approach would be immanent realism. As a species, humanity has material needs within an encompassing natural world that has its own dynamic. The historical construction of the human–nature relationship is therefore a dialectical one between humanity and nature as agents, and within human society itself. Human–nature relations are not realized as an 'idea', but realized materially as a living process.

Failure to address politically the divisions within humanity as it confronts the immanence of human existence means that the material consequences of the human condition fall disproportionately upon women and other oppressed and exploited groups. I would therefore argue that a politics of nature demands a 'deep' materialist analysis not only of human–human social relations, but of human–nature relations. Some ecofeminists are developing such an approach based on an analysis of the sex/gender relations of human embodiment and embeddedness. This approach has been taken in various ways by Ynestra King, Maria Mies, Vandana Shiva, Ariel Salleh and myself. In the next chapter I will look at the way these ideas relate to other social and materialist analyses of human–nature relations: social ecology and eco-Marxism.

7

Social Ecology, Ecosocialism and Social/ist Ecofeminism

It is eminently *natural* for humanity to create a second nature from its evolution in first nature ... The ecological crisis we face today is very much a crisis in the emergence of society out of biology ... The fact that these two natures exist and can never be dualized into 'parallels' or simplistically reduced to each other accounts in great part for my use of the words '*social ecology*'. (Bookchin 1990: 203; italics in the original)

Murray Bookchin's social ecology has been very influential in the development of ecofeminism and the green movement, particularly in the United States. Bookchin expressed a very early and prescient concern about ecological dangers and his Institute of Social Ecology in Vermont has been credited with being one of the original homes of ecofeminism in the mid-1970s (Heller 1990). In his introduction to *The Ecology of Freedom* published in 1982, Bookchin traces the origin of his ideas back to the early 1950s when he first wrote on the danger of chemicals in food. He recalls that from the start he always saw the ecological crisis in a social context, so that 'the very notion of the domination of nature by man stems from the very real domination of human by human' (ibid.: 1). Bookchin's broad conception of the domination of human by human – hierarchy – replaces the more specific Marxist concept of class exploitation, or the feminist concept of patriarchy. The political solution is to have a radical egalitarian society, something that Bookchin has advocated throughout his works (1980, 1982, 1989, 1990, 1995). Like many greens who take an anarchist perspective, Bookchin's vision of the good society would be 'human-scale', decentralized and non-hierarchical. It would be run on a communal basis with face-to-face relationships and decision-making by consensus or participatory democracy. Unlike many greens, however, Bookchin's ideal society is not a self-sufficient rural idyll, but loose federations of self-governing municipalities.

Since Bookchin sees the domination of 'human by human' as the cause of ecological destructiveness, the solution to ecological destruction would be in reformed human relations. The good society would be, by definition, an ecological society. It would not seek to transcend natural conditions or ecological boundaries. People would take what they needed and no more. Lying behind this analysis is a conception of humanity and human–nature relations as ultimately *naturally* harmonious, a view shared by many green thinkers.

Although Bookchin criticizes deep ecology and 'centricity' (1990: 211), he does see humanity as part of nature and therefore as part of the whole evolutionary process. This is why he considers it perfectly natural for humanity to want to create a 'second nature': 'By second nature, I refer to a uniquely human culture, a wide variety of institutionalized human communities, an effective human technics, a richly symbolic language, and a carefully managed source of nutriment' (1990: 201). First nature (the ecosystem) and second nature (human society) are always in a dialectical relationship, neither can determine the other. First nature is always a limiting factor for second nature, but second nature continually mediates (acts upon, interprets) first nature. Both are set upon a non-specific teleological journey from simplicity to complexity. Bookchin argues that the 'natural' process would be for human communities and the embracing ecosystem to develop through the dialectical process of actualizing the immanent potentialities they embody at every stage. First nature is no longer to be seen as something to be manipulated entirely for human ends. What is needed is a radical view of nature that sees it as active and continually developing, together with a radical view of human development in second nature. Although Bookchin's evolutionary model does not prescribe any particular route for development, a basic assumption is that if each part of the whole (human communities individual species, smaller ecosystems) and the whole itself are left to evolve without interference, then the result will be harmony. It will reflect the ideal of 'unity in diversity'. Social ecology is the realization of that 'unity in diversity' by bringing human–human relations back to their most 'natural' and 'original' form – mutuality and symbiosis.

Bookchin describes his philosophical framework as dialectical naturalism. He takes from Kropotkin the concept of mutuality and symbiosis in nature (1955). Mutual aid between people is the 'natural' human condition. Anything else is an aberration, a corruption. The

emergence of hierarchy in human society is an example. One difficulty in such an analysis is to explain why hierarchy should arise.
Bookchin's answer is rather like that of 'matriarchal' cultural feminists. Once, all human societies were 'organic', harmonious, small
scale and egalitarian basing their economic relations on usufruct.
Then, hierarchy 'arose' (1982: 43 f., 62 f.). The breakdown of early
neolithic village society marks a decisive turning-point in the development of humanity: 'In the millennia-long era that separates the
earliest horticultural communities from the "high civilizations"
of antiquity, we witness the emergence of towns, cities, and
finally empires . . . a qualitatively new social arena' (ibid.: 62). In
Remaking Society Bookchin rejects the claim made by some cultural
feminists that hierarchy as represented by patriarchy emerged through
'Kurgan' invasions of the prehistoric matriarchal societies of 'Old
Europe' (6000–4000 BCE). Kurgans were pastoral, warlike people
deemed to come from north of the Black Sea (Gimbutas 1982). Instead,
Bookchin suggests that hierarchy emerges in all societies through the
growth of 'male's civil domain . . . male gerontocracies, warrior
groups, aristocratic elites and the State' (1989: 76). I would certainly
agree with Bookchin that the idea of a Kurgan invasion is not helpful,
as it does not explain how patriarchy emerged in 'Kurgan' society.
The invasion theory is also implicitly racist. It is the 'stranger' who
carries the 'disease' of patriarchy. Bookchin's explanation is much
more plausible – that hierarchy is immanent in all human society.
However, the problem then becomes why hierarchy should be seen
as an aberration. It could be argued that hierarchy and competition
are as 'natural' as mutuality and symbiosis. This is, of course, what
many right-wing theorists have suggested and left-wingers have
long sought to refute. Basing social ethics on the assumed 'natural-
ness' of harmony or competitiveness is always problematic, because
evidence from the natural world shows it to be both symbiotic and
competitive. Right and left can both claim 'natural' evidence.

Bookchin is on much stronger ground when he talks about the
dialectic between first and second nature and the contradictions
between them. Despite his reference to male domination in the
emergence of hierarchy, Bookchin does not pursue the sex/gender
dimensions of those contradictions as society 'emerges' out of first
nature. For ecofeminists these contradictions are represented by the
hierarchical dualisms that appear to have a more deleterious effect on
women than men. Nor does Bookchin explain why these contradictions emerge at one point in history. Are they not a constant in
human–nature relations? Was there ever a Golden Age where Adams

and Eves frolicked together in an egalitarian and ecological Garden of Eden? I use this metaphor advisedly because all initial harmony theories follow the same model of the Fall. Joan Bamberger has argued convincingly that where such stories exist among clan peoples including the 'myth of matriarchy', they are generally used by men to justify the subordination of women, as in the case of the Genesis story (1974). If women once had power and lost it, they must somehow have deserved to lose it. As I have discussed more fully elsewhere, a more feasible explanation is that the creation of social space out of biological/ecological conditions is always problematic. Where men take that social space, as Bookchin suggests, it is not just a perverse, aberrant act, it is a 'stealing' of women's (slaves', younger peoples') time (Mellor 1992: 117 f.). Anthropological evidence from gathering, hunting and early gardening societies shows that, as ever, women do the routine, necessary, constricting work while men do the infrequent and socially prestigious tasks, including hunting and rituals (Sanday 1981).

Although his 1982 work *Ecology of Freedom* seems to imply something of a regret for a Golden Age, Bookchin denies this forcefully in his later works (1990, 1995). He sees first and second nature as being on an evolutionary and potentially harmonious path as humanity emerges from the 'primitive' to the modern. Humanity has somehow strayed from the true path and must reason its way back: 'Only by removing the fetishes that are obscuring our capacity to see reality as it is and as it *should* be, can we re-enchant humanity as a creative and innovative agent in the world and the living potentiality for self-realization as rational beings' (1995: 256; italics in the original). The 'fetishes' that obscure humanity's vision are all those social constructions that fetter human potential, such as: 'deities, ideologies, mystical forces, "angels", myths, magical practices, misanthropies, transcendental value systems, institutions, social relationships, technologies, laboratories – and mundane commodities' (ibid.: 254). All of these constrain human creative potential, which for Bookchin is human reason and its creations, science and technology. By using these abilities constructively, it is humanity, not nature, that is enchanted, in the sense of holding the key to harmony and sustainability: 'Such rational beings can be expected to have ethical responsibility for the welfare of non-human life *precisely* because they are sensible to the pain, suffering and death of all living beings' (ibid.: 256; italics in the original). Advanced science and technology should not be abandoned, as some greens argue, but used to free humanity from the constraints of material existence. Bookchin clearly sees necessity as incompatible with the development of culture. People need space and time in which to re-enchant themselves. Bookchin's ideal human is transcendent not immanent. While Bookchin goes some way towards the green position by seeing humanity and nature in a dialectical relationship, in the end his position is one of a hierarchical dualism, with humanity 'realizing' the cosmological destiny of both itself and nature. 'Dialectical naturalism' is an idealist philosophy of harmonious freedom, as all first and second nature reaches its immanent potential led by the creative consciousness of humanity. As Plumwood has argued, Bookchin's social ecology allows no space for non-human nature to have a voice and does not explore the power dynamic between humans and non-human nature:

> [T]he difference of nature is subtly erased when it comes to establishing that it has no independence of being or interest which could properly impose constraints on human interference . . . The incorporation of nature into the human sphere by defining humanity as 'nature rendered self-conscious' makes a political conception of human-nature relations impossible. (1994: 69)

It is surprising that in developing a theory which he describes as dialectical naturalism, Bookchin does not see all the elements of that dialectic, including non-human nature, as having agency and potential, and in many ways this is what Bookchin seems to imply. However, the evolutionary privilege he gives to humanity undermines such an egalitarian view of human–nature agency. I would agree with Bookchin that only humanity has a conscious awareness, and this does put it in a very special, privileged and responsible position, but I would not agree with his optimism about western rationalism, nor his use of the notion 'primitive' in the context of earlier human societies. As Kovel has pointed out (1996) there is an ambivalence at the heart of Bookchin's theory, as it seems to embrace two different versions of human development. One is progressivist/modernist and evolutionary, which sees human 'reason' as becoming infinitely more aware and complex; the other seems to be an origin and 'fall' theory of lost harmony, as hierarchy destroyed early symbiotic communities. Rudy (1996) also queries Bookchin's assertion that all hierarchy has social rather than natural origins. He argues that Bookchin's claim that the original form of hierarchy was gerontocracy could be seen as resting on the biological phenomenon of ageing, as elderly members of the community used their power to harness the energy of younger people.

Despite these criticisms, Bookchin has been enormously stimulating to green thinkers and many ecofeminists, and his *The Ecology of Freedom* was one of my own sources of inspiration. His dialectical approach certainly takes the analysis of human–nature relations forward, although I would advocate a reformulated dialectical (and historical) materialism rather than his dialectical naturalism. However, given Bookchin's emphasis on the broad-based concept of hierarchy and his espousal of western rationalism, it was perhaps inevitable that social ecology and ecofeminism should eventually part company. This was signalled in the late 1980s when one of Bookchin's closest associates, Janet Biehl, wrote a book renouncing her previous commitment even to 'social ecofeminism' and proclaimed the superiority of social ecology (1991).

Ecofeminism and social ecology

As a woman and a feminist, I deeply value my power of rationality and seek to expand the full range of women's faculties. I do not want to reject the valuable achievements of Western culture on the claim that they have been produced primarily by men. (Biehl 1991: 7)

Janet Biehl claims that social ecofeminism was intended originally to introduce the ideas of social ecology and feminism to left-wing thought (1988: 1). Chiah Heller, who is credited by Biehl with naming social ecofeminism, saw it as more directed at feminism: 'making an appeal to feminists to critically examine the nature philosophies inherent in their own theories, and to consider the value of adopting a radical, ecological perspective' (1990: 154). This quote is taken from a paper originally written in the late 1970s, in which Heller comes close to the cultural ecofeminist position that Biehl now condemns. Criticizing de Beauvoir's approach, Heller urged feminists to make sure they were not adopting a dualist nature-hating outlook in attempting to escape from their association with nature. Instead, feminists should follow social ecology's 'innovative concept of nature as a realm of potential freedom . . . a radical, liberatory view of the natural world, a world not completely bound to the fetters of natural law' (ibid.: 156). At the same time Heller condemns cultural feminists for reintroducing an idea of natural law in claiming that women's values can be discerned from nature, or that women have any 'innate' ability to co-operate or exhibit ecological sensibility. Both liberal and cultural feminists advocate a 'cheap unity', the former with men ignoring patriarchal culture, the latter with all women ignoring their differences.

Rather than ignoring the culture–nature dualism as in the case of liberal feminism, or upending it in favour of cultural feminism's woman–nature dyad, Heller argues for a dialectical acknowledgement of the developmental dialogue between women and between women and nature. Women, like men, are constructors of 'second nature', that is 'a nature which is the realization of the potential for self-consciousness in "first nature"' (ibid.: 162). There is no sense here that the developmental dialogue is a conflictual one between women and men or between women as they construct 'second nature'. The conflict with social ecology's humanism emerges when Heller attempts to explain men's more destructive orientation to the natural world. At this point Heller puts forward the cultural feminist 'difference' argument:

> Woman emerges both individually and historically out of first nature in such a way that allows woman to develop an enhanced, often implicit awareness of our interconnected relationship to the natural world. For many different biological and social reasons, male second nature did not historically fulfil its potential for developing this primary awareness. (ibid.: 163)

In order not to present this as a 'natural' difference in evolutionary outcome, Heller argues that women have made an 'evolutionary choice' at an 'unconscious level'. This seems in many ways to be worse than women's difference being biologically determined. They have chosen their path – effectively the right, but subordinate path – whereas men have chosen the wrong path, but gained power. Why this has happened is not clear. Women's subordinate position does, however, give them a privileged standpoint and political agency.

> Women are to show that natural evolution is a surprisingly free process . . . informed by a *social* ecology, women may develop an ecological standpoint . . . revealing that evolution is in great part a self-determined process . . . to appreciate woman's unique opportunity to become the historical subject of an era which so direly needs an objective, social ethics as well as an ecological, empathetic ethics of care. (ibid.: 165; italics in the original)

Much is expected of women here. They are to develop an 'objective ecological ethics' in revolt against 'hierarchy, patriarchy, the centralization of power, and capitalism . . . all consequences of having lived out the myth of transcendence' (ibid.: 166). At this point, social ecology regains the initiative – women do not act alone, or even on a feminist basis. The 'patricentric' cultures they face do not represent all men. Against patriarchy/hierarchy is set the 'eco-libertarian culture based on social ecology' (ibid : 167). What is not explained is how eco-libertarian men escape the 'unconscious' choice for hierarchy that men must have made. In the dialectical relationship that Heller identifies, difference does not represent power. Individuals and groups are set on evolutionary paths, each developing along its own dynamic 'each woman chooses, responds, and evolves in her own distinct way' (ibid.: 168). Such a disconnected individualist view is more reminiscent of liberal than social/ist feminist thinking.

While Heller identifies with many of the aims of ecofeminism – ecological awareness, challenge to dualism, coalitions between women, opposition to all oppressions, the need for a new earth-centred spirituality – her framework for analysis is continually hampered by the naturalist and degendered assumptions of social ecology: '[A]s we derive from nature the ecological principles of interdependence, complementarity, and spontaneity, we may apply these principles to our personal relationships, our political structures, and into our communities' (ibid.: 172). The tensions between social ecology and ecofeminism inherent in Heller's paper were made increasingly explicit in Janet Biehl's work (1988, 1991). Eventually, a choice had to be made; this particular diversity did not result in unity. Writing in the late 1970s, before ecofeminism had become firmly established as a distinct feminist perspective, Heller claimed that she was 'not interested in nihilistically throwing away any liberal or cultural feminist "babies" with their bathwater' in developing an ecofeminism based in social ecology (ibid.: 156). By 1991 Biehl had found social ecology and ecofeminism to be incompatible, and the babies were being ejected.

Writing in 1988, Biehl saw social ecofeminism as a non-gendered approach: 'social ecofeminism regards all people, both men and women, as capable of an ethic of care'. As an ethic of care is seen to be more prevalent in the private realm of domestic relationships, the fault lies in the commercialization and bureaucratization of society. The answer is a reform of society on anarchist principles:

> Social ecofeminism shares with social ecology the demand that economic life come under the control of the political realm by a municipalization of the economy and the creation of a moral economy, an economy of cooperatives and meaningful local work that addresses local community needs. In a local, municipal economy, where the workplace is located at or near the home, women's full participation in a moral economic life is possible. (1988: 7)

Following Bookchin, Biehl sees the ecological crisis as reflecting a crisis of social relations, caused by hierarchy in all its forms. Patriarchy only exists as one form of hierarchy, it is neither the original, nor the primary oppression. There is nothing special about women, or their relationship to the natural world. There seems little point, then, in continuing to espouse the idea of a social ecofeminism. Writing in 1991, Biehl follows the logic of this position and rejects ecofeminism in all its forms: '[T]he very word *ecofeminism* has by now become so tainted by its various irrationalisms that I no longer consider this a promising project' (1991: 5; italics in the original).

Biehl's main targets are spiritual, cultural and poetic ecofeminism, as represented by Starhawk, Daly, Collard, Griffin and many of the contributors to the anthologies edited by Plant (1989) and Diamond and Orenstein (1990). Biehl objects to what Diamond and Orenstein saw as the strength of their anthology, the many voices and the interweaving of poetic and academic approaches. For Biehl, this merely shows that ecofeminism has no coherence as a movement or a perspective. Her objection is to the 'magic, goddesses, witchcraft, privileged quasi-biological traits, irrationalities, Neolithic atavisms and mysticism . . . this highly disparate body of hazy, poorly formulated notions, metaphors and irrational analogies invites women *to take a step backward* (ibid.: 6; italics in the original). It is what she sees as the predominance of such ideas in ecofeminist thought that has led Biehl to condemn ecofeminism as a whole. However, this would not be a true reflection of ecofeminism. As I have already pointed out, there are many strands to ecofeminism, and more recent work, admittedly published after Biehl wrote her book, is much more measured and academic in tone. A detailed examination of Biehl's critique shows that what has actually happened is that the radical feminism of ecofeminism has threatened to overwhelm social ecology. Hierarchy as a universal human problem is being supplanted by hierarchy as a sex/gender issue. The specific position of women in relation to nature, particularly as represented by affinity ecofeminists, threatens to undermine the whole project of social ecology. If women are essentially closer to nature, the dialectical relationship between humanity and nature is more complex than at first envisaged. Even if a materialist analysis of women's role in the sex/gender division of labour replaces a more essentialist version, the problem of sex/gender divisions in 'humanity' still remains. Social ecology cannot allow this:

As a form of eco-anarchism, social ecology's guiding precept is that we cannot rid ourselves today of the ideology of dominating nature until we rid ourselves of hierarchy and class structures in human society – including not only sexism and homophobia and racism, but also the nation-state, economic exploitation, capitalism, and all the other social oppression of our time. (ibid.: 5)

I do not have a problem with the general idea behind such an assertion, apart from what is meant by 'sexism'. Biehl refers to two particular issues, sexual liberation and women's rights to equal participation in society. She adopts an equality view of humanity: there is no fundamental difference of power or interests between men and women. The aim of feminism is to 'gain the best benefits of the Enlightenment and the most valuable features of civilization for women, on a par with thinking and humane men' (ibid.: 6). Feminists must not follow ecofeminists in 'irrationalism', rather they should use the legacies of democracy, reason and scientific method that the Enlightenment has bequeathed. Such a view ignores the dualistic nature of western society and culture that many feminists as well as ecofeminists have identified (Lloyd 1984). Salleh has argued that, in her commitment to the western conception of reason, Biehl departs even further from a feminist position than Bookchin himself, who described the mutualism as exhibited by women's domestic labour as libertarian reason *par excellence* (Salleh 1996: 261). Following Bookchin, Biehl asserts that if men do dominate women it is as a by-product of men's domination of each other. Men did not 'consciously' intend to dominate women (1988: 6), although it is implied that they consciously intended to dominate each other. If none of it was conscious, then we have emergent social forms of hierarchy for which we have no explanation other than historical contingency or even 'nature'. This is effectively what Biehl is saying: 'historically, based on their biology and on history men have occupied the public realm' (ibid.: 5) as a result of which 'men have been pressed to forget their caring natures and to participate in systems of domination' (ibid.: 4). What has 'pressed' men into hierarchy is left unclear.

Like Bookchin (and Marx and Engels), Biehl sees the original sexual division of labour as unproblematic. In 'tribal societies' two 'realms' existed: '[P]ublic and private, which were really two cultures between men and women, [that] depended on a biological division of labour and culture between the sexes for their very survival' (ibid.: 5). At some point men used their physical strength, or some other source of social power, to subordinate other men and, as a by-product, women. Out of this comes all the hierarchical complexities of human existence. Biehl's naturalistic approach to the sexual division of labour in human history is based on a universalist application of the public/private division in modern industrial society:

> Needless to say, in early organic societies, the domestic realm was the women's realm, and the emerging public realm was the men's realm . . . in its beginnings the public realm did not necessarily exist in a hierarchical relationship with the domestic . . . The two were initially complementary to each other. (ibid.: 145)

There is no sense here of how much productive work women did in pre-industrial societies. The private world appears to be construed in its western sense of the place in which children are socialized into 'second nature'. It is also odd to import the western model of the public and the private together with the sex/gender division of labour, while leaving behind their hierarchical qualities. The public world is seen unproblematically as a free-floating forum. The material base of the 'public' is unclear, although slavery is mentioned, as is the creation of an agricultural surplus. As women have been the major agriculturalists in history, presumably it is they who created the surplus. The example of the Greek city-states is very important for Bookchin's and Biehl's anarchism, as they are seen as the cradle of participatory democracy. The inequalities of Greek society are acknowledged, but Biehl claims that, despite this, 'it must be emphasized that the *potentiality* for including everyone in citizenship was present in the democratic framework that the Athenians devised' (ibid.: 149; italics in the original). This is something that ecofeminists would challenge.

Biehl takes issue with Ynestra King, who also started off in the social ecology movement, for arguing that the domination of women by men is an original and primary oppression and that western culture, including 'democracy' and 'reason', remains patriarchal. Biehl criticizes King for her suggestion that ecofeminists adopt the woman–nature connection as a political expedient. Biehl maintains that women and nature are either connected or they are not. To assert, as King does, that women may 'choose' not to sever the (socially constructed) connection between woman and nature is 'to believe ecofeminist fairy tales'. An ethical system cannot be grounded on a 'consciously manipulated falsehood' (1991: 96). What matters here is what is meant by the woman–nature connection. Biehl is reading it very literally as an essentialist assertion, whereas King is building upon what she identifies as a material and ideological weakness of patriarchy that could be turned against it. For King, in failing to see women as a 'bridge' between culture and nature, social ecology is missing a crucial area of analysis:

> Social ecologists are asking how we might survive on the planet and develop systems of food and energy production, architecture and ways of life that will allow human beings to fulfill our material needs and live in harmony with nonhuman nature . . . this perspective [was] developed by Murray Bookchin to whom I am indebted . . . while this analysis is useful, social ecology without feminism is incomplete. (in Plant 1989: 19)

To bring feminism into social ecology would not mean accepting the proposition that the domination of men over women was the original domination, or to adopt the reductionist position that it is the primary one throughout all history. However, the domination of men over women seems to be *one* of the original forms of domination, and it still persists almost universally. From an ecofeminist perspective it is not possible to accept the social ecologists' assertion of the existence and political potential of a 'universal humanity', which ignores the fundamental problems around the differences between men and women as biologically sexed and socially gendered beings.

Biehl's central concern is that ecofeminism's concentration on women and women's lives means the denial of a public politics. In particular, ecofeminism would not develop a critique of economic and political structures of domination or look to collective political action. This is perhaps true of some ecofeminist spiritualists or metaphysicians like Mary Daly, but even a follower of Wicca like Starhawk advocates political action: 'whatever we do, our spirituality should be grounded in action' (1990: 85). Biehl's social ecology, in turn, denies the politics of the private. Her acceptance of the dualism of the public and the private places the political focus of social ecology entirely upon a sexed and gendered public realm. Within this realm there is to be an ethical and political struggle around the principles of ecological sustainability and egalitarianism which will (hopefully) lead to an ecologically sustainable non-hierarchal society. This is an idealist politics, as it lacks a materialist explanation for the emergence and persistence of hierarchy within human society or the human domination of nature. I would want to argue that a materialist and material analysis of sex/gender relations in the construction of humanity's relation to non-human nature can point a way forward.

Ecofeminism and Ecosocialism

As I have argued throughout this book, despite the influence of cultural and spiritual feminism, ecofeminism is necessarily a materialist theory because of its stress on the immanence (embodiedness and embeddedness) of human existence. Both social and socialist ecofeminists see a dialectical relation between human structures of inequality and the destruction of nature. It would seem, therefore, that ecofeminism would have at least some relationship with Marx's historical materialism, and this has already become clear in the discussion of standpoint theory. Although a growing number of Marxists have been exploring the relationship between red and green and (rarely) feminist perspectives (Bahro 1984; O'Connor, J. 1988; Gottlieb 1992; Pepper 1993; O'Connor, M. 1994; Leff 1995; Benton 1996), Marxist theory generally is not renowned for its sensitivity to either feminist or green issues. While most feminist theory would see itself as both socially egalitarian and ecologically sensitive even if it is not explicitly ecofeminist, green socialists do not necessarily incorporate a feminist or ecofeminist position (Pepper 1993).

Ecofeminists incorporate an implicit or explicit rejection of capitalism in their critique of western society, although very few adopt a socialist analysis in the Marxian sense. Carolyn Merchant has argued the case for a socialist analysis of the ecological crisis couched in terms of socialist feminism: 'Socialist feminism views change as dynamic, interactive and dialectical, rather than as mechanistic, linear and incremental . . . A socialist feminist environmental ethic involves developing sustainable, non-dominating relations with nature and supplying all peoples with a high quality of life' (1990: 105). Merchant points out that 'socialist feminist environmental theory gives both reproduction and production central places', thus denying the centrality of the Marxian analysis of production. In a later book Merchant advocates a 'radical ecology' as the basis of a socialist position in which social movements such as bioregional movements, grassroots struggle and mainstream environmental campaigning have largely replaced social class as political agents (1992).

Socialist ecofeminism is in a difficult position, as it draws on seemingly contradictory frameworks, the social constructionism and economic determinism of socialist analysis and the ecologically holist, nature-oriented approach of ecofeminism. This is not helped by the fact that socialist feminists have been particularly resistant to ecofeminism, identifying it with cultural/spiritual feminism and arguing that it diverts attention from economic struggle and sex/gender inequality (Agarwal 1992; Jackson 1994, 1995). Carolyn Merchant has also made a similar critique, although her position later shifted towards a deeper ecologism as the critical point in human–nature relations: 'Weaving together the many strands of the ecofeminist movement is the concept of reproduction construed in its broadest sense to include the continued biological and social reproduction of human life and the continuance of life on earth' (1992: 209). Given the struggle that socialist feminists have had with Marxism (Barrett 1980; Hartmann 1981) it perhaps seems strange that an ecofeminist should be arguing for a return to a materialist analysis that builds in part on Marx's theories. However, as I have argued elsewhere and will elaborate here, socialist, green and feminist ideas are all necessary for a radical politics that will lead to an ecologically sustainable and socially just society (Mellor 1992a). Marx's framework, critically amended, can provide elements of that analysis (Mellor 1992b, 1993). There is certainly evidence that Marx and Engels were much more aware of ecological issues than were their followers and apostles (Parsons 1977).

One attempt to reinvigorate Marxism from a green and feminist perspective is the journal *Capitalism, Nature, Socialism*, launched in 1988, which called in its 'Prospectus' for 'discourses between feminism, social ecology and Marxism' (p. 5). The editor James O'Connor launched the opening issue with his analysis of the 'second contradiction of capital'. The first contradiction of capital is the classic Marxist analysis of the crisis of production. The second contradiction refers not to the crisis within capitalist production, but the structural conditions within which the production process exists. According to O'Connor, Marx identified three production conditions (1988: 16 ff.), the first of which is the external physical environment. Marx and Engels were well aware of the physical and economic importance of the natural environment, as Parsons has recounted (1977). They saw natural resources as a free gift to capital and were concerned about pollution and waste as people moved into industrial cities. Marx even noted that valuable human excrement was pouring into rivers rather than being spread on to the land. The second condition of production was the mental and physical fitness of 'labour power', and the third, 'the communal general conditions of social production' (O'Connor 1988: 16). O'Connor interprets this as the social infrastructure. The importance of his analysis is his argument that a crisis in the *conditions* of production can lead to a crisis for capital and the possibility of a socialist revolution in the same way that Marx predicted for a crisis in production itself. However in the former case critical agents of change would include social movements. But O'Connor's analysis is still essentially a Marxist one in that the crisis that occurs is still a crisis for capitalism. The second contradiction of capital alleges that capitalism is fouling its own nest. Capitalism cannot guarantee an adequate physical and social environment for its own functioning. When social movements respond to this crisis they are still responding to a crisis of capitalism. O'Connor argues that the ecological crisis of the conditions of production is a contradiction between capital and nature, not humanity and nature. The 'limits of nature' is an ideological concept. It is not nature that is limited, but capitalism.

While O'Connor's analysis of the conditions of production came much closer to the concerns of feminism than orthodox Marxism, the focus is still capitalism, not patriarchy. The conditions of production can be seen as embracing reproductive processes, but this has not been central to O'Connor's analysis or the subsequent debates around the 'second contradiction' in the journal. These debates have been mainly conducted by men on a malestream agenda concerned with the ways in which the ecological crisis has impinged on capitalism. One exception is Martin O'Connor, who sees 'non-commodity domains – the domains of intertwined human, communal and natural activities of repair, renewal, regeneration and reproduction – . . . as furnishing the necessary material and social conditions for commodity production, market exchange and capital accumulation' (1994: 106). He describes capital in this context as being engaged in 'parasitism', a concept which in many ways is more helpful than exploitation, domination or oppression to explain the relationship involved. He argues that it is this parasitism which creates for capital 'a crisis in the reproduction of these conditions of production' (ibid.).

The failure to integrate feminism into malestream ecosocialism has been taken up by ecofeminists. In the third issue of *Capitalism, Nature, Socialism* Lori-Ann Thrupp claimed that ecosocialism was in danger of missing the 'rich theoretical and historical analysis' being developed by ecofeminism (1989: 170). She pointed to the common exploitation that women and nature have received at the hands of patriarchy, and the role that women have played in labour, anti-military and environmental struggles. Drawing on the early work of Carolyn Merchant, Thrupp distinguished between the radical feminist grounding of human nature in human biology with its evocation of ancient rituals and goddess worship, and socialist ecofeminism which sees both 'nature and human nature as historically and socially constructed' (ibid.: 172). Ecofeminism would broaden the base of socialist ecology, Thrupp argued, by giving both production and reproduction a central place in materialist analysis.

In response to Thrupp's criticisms, James O'Connor, together with another eco-Marxist Daniel Faber, maintained that some ecofeminist ideas were unhelpful, such as intuition as opposed to science and technology, the privileging of the human body over 'mind' and 'organic theories emphasizing emotional ties to the community ("caring")' (Faber and O'Connor 1989: 177). It is hard to see how the second contradiction of capital could not take account of ideas around women's relationship to caring and communal relations if it is attempting theoretically to relate reproduction to production. A similar point has been made by Ariel Salleh: ' "caring" however despised . . . is nevertheless the kind of unpaid service/labor that women under capitalist patriarchy are required to put in. While society denigrates the worth of such work, social reproduction would not occur without it' (Salleh et al. 1991: 134). Like Thrupp, Salleh argued that ecosocialism without ecofeminism was incomplete and vice versa (ibid.: 129). It was necessary to understand the dynamics of the mode of production and the social construction of gender. Far from claiming a biological essentialism, Salleh argued, socialist ecofeminists criticize gender as 'reified naturalism'. What ecofeminists are seeking to understand is how such 'patriarchal gender images become enmeshed in social institutions in a hegemonic way' (ibid.: 130). At the same time ecofeminists have to deal with the fact that human beings inhabit sexed bodies that are embedded in the natural world. The ideological constructs of patriarchy and capital ('Mother' Nature, woman as 'feminine', 'human nature', economic value and ownership) also relate to biological and material processes. Salleh calls upon socialists to:

> examine the social, political and economic consequences of biological sex . . . to come to terms with the material conditions of women's lived experience . . . Politicians cannot thrust 'the biological' aside. That is precisely what has brought Western capitalist patriarchy to its present ecological impasse. (ibid.: 131)

This ecological impasse could be overcome if ecofeminists and ecosocialists joined together to dismantle 'the ideological artifice which divides "humanity" from "nature" '. This could not be achieved if ecosocialists continued to hold on to Enlightenment concepts of transcendence over 'bodily embeddedness in place and in relationships', and failed to understand the 'fundamental premise of ecofeminism that in patriarchal cultures, men's assumed right to exploit nature parallels the use/s they make of women' (ibid.).

The arguments of socialist ecofeminists centre around the concepts of production and reproduction and the relationship between
capitalism and patriarchy which have long preoccupied socialist
feminism (Sargent 1981). The core of this argument is whether an
analysis based on sex/gender stands independent of an analysis
based on production relations. Despite the best efforts of many
theorists, a 'marriage' between Marxism and feminism was not
achieved, and Salleh is concerned that the same will happen with
ecosocialism:

> Many women spent the best part of the 1970s and 1980s trying to get brother
> socialists to re-think the gender-blind categories of Marxism to zero effect.
> It would be a shame if dialogue between ecofeminists and ecosocialists in the
> 1990s was simply a repeat of that old history. (Salleh et al. 1991: 134)

If ecosocialism/Marxism is adequately to address the issues raised by
ecofeminism, it is clear that they will have to reject not only the male
and productivist basis of Marxist theory, but also the Enlightenment
conception of transcendence over material necessity (Mellor 1992b).

Ecosocialists like Daniel Faber and James O'Connor, who draw on
a Marxist base, are understandably concerned that the ecofeminist
emphasis on patriarchy will divert attention from the massive and
corrupting power of capitalism. Political answers will be sought in
personal transformation, or claims for new movements, or spiritual
forces that do not directly engage with current structures of power.
Essentialist readings of women and nature will replace a materialist
analysis of economic relations. Feminist and ecological concerns
about the limits and dynamics of nature will ignore those aspects of
human–nature relations that are socially constructed. From the perspective of historical materialism, such a course would trap human
societies in a reified naturalism, whereby social relationships would
be presented as ordained by biology or nature. The green argument
that there are 'natural' limits to growth or that nature contains within
it a 'natural' balance, or claims by some feminists that they are
'naturally' more peace-loving and co-operative, risk presenting constructs of human society as constructs of nature, as many socialist
feminists have pointed out. Like Salleh, I would argue that this
dilemma will not be overcome by denying the material issues at the
basis of the feminist and ecological critique. What is necessary is to
address the central question of how to theorize the finite nature of the
planet and the biological differences between men and women without falling into ecological and biological determinism. To maintain
that there is a biological and ecological limit to human activity and

capacity for social reconstruction is not to revert to essentialism, but to begin to theorize the conditions of humanity's material existence. This endeavour raises the critical issue of the relationship between the seemingly ahistoric universals of biological sex and nature as 'essential' features of human existence, and the historical materialism of class analysis and other relations of oppression and exploitation.

Historical materialism asserts that the constraints on, and potential for, collective human development and creativity are socially constructed and thereby capable of being socially resolved. The dilemma between essentialism and materialism is whether the socially materialist analysis of historical materialism can integrate the physical material reality of humanity (and particularly women) and nature. Can historical materialism bring women in without taking account of their biology, or nature in without confronting the constraint of its 'natural' limits? These problems are inherent in the debate between ecofeminism and ecosocialism.

What is material about historical materialism?

Species-life, both for man and for animals, consists physically in the fact that man, like animals lives from inorganic nature ... Man *lives* from nature, i.e. nature is his *body*, and he must maintain a continuing dialogue with it if he is not to die ... for man is part of nature.

... Estranged labour ... estranges man from his own body, from nature as it exists outside him, from his spiritual essence (*Wesen*), his *human* essence.

... The immediate, natural, necessary relation of human being to human being is the *relationship* of *man* to *woman*.

... Communism as fully developed naturalism, equals humanism, and as fully developed humanism equals naturalism; it is the *genuine* resolution of the conflict between man and nature. (Marx 1955: 327, 329, 347, 348; all italics in the original)

All these statements are drawn from Marx's *Economic and Philosophical Manuscripts* of 1844. They set out many ideas familiar even to deep ecologists: ecological holism; the integration of 'man' with nature; the devastating effects on 'man' if he is separated from a direct relationship with the grounds of his 'means of life'; nature as 'means of life' reflects both subsistence needs and the realization of species-being in the creative act of labour in interaction with the natural world (ibid.: 325); communism, by eliminating private ownership and alienated labour, will bring 'man' back into a direct unalienated relationship with the natural world and his own human nature, which is also a spiritual relationship to 'his' being.

The problem in Marx's theory is the position of women. Throughout his work it is clear that he and Engels see heterosexual relationships and the sexual division of labour as 'natural'. Engels's attempt to address the position of women, although welcome, starts from the clear assumption of a natural division of labour and women's desire for monogamous heterosexual relationships (1884). He also distinguished between the production and reproduction of 'immediate life'. In Marx and Engels's *The German Ideology* the social relations of production refer to 'the production of life, both of one's own labour and of fresh life by procreation' (1970: 50). The fundamental condition of human life, the first 'historical act', is the production of material life described as 'eating and drinking, a habitation, clothing and many other things' (ibid.: 48). Do 'many other things' include new human beings, suckling and nurture? As historical materialism developed, some biologically 'fundamental conditions of human life' were incorporated into production, such as habitation and clothing, while others, such as procreation and personal care, were excluded. As Mary O'Brien has argued, if some means of survival produced definite social relations and particular forms of consciousness, surely the same should apply to other means of survival, such as procreation? Socialist feminists have been faced with the choice of abandoning Marx's project altogether or attempting to reformulate historical materialism from a feminist perspective.

Despite its failure to integrate sex/gender relations, Marx's historical materialism is still relevant for socialist ecofeminism because, like Bookchin's social ecology, it sees a dialectical relationship between human society and nature. The starting point for a feminist historical materialism, like Marx's historical materialism, would be alienated and exploited labour, but broadened to embrace the sex/gender division of labour. As Iris Young points out, the division of labour was as central to Marx's analysis as the category of class, particularly in *The German Ideology*, and it has been later Marxist theorists who have explored the latter at the expense of the former (1981: 51). The division of labour, can, Young argues provide a less gender-blind version of historical materialism:

> Agreeing that the category of class is gender blind and hence incapable of exposing women's situation, we can nevertheless remain within the materialist framework by elevating the category of *division of labour* to a position as fundamental as, if not more fundamental than that of class. (ibid.: 50; italics in the original)

Young refers to the 'gender' rather than the sexual division of labour in order to dissociate herself from the argument that all men oppress all women as a sex class in the sense used by Firestone. However, Young does agree with many ecofeminists that the sex/gender division of labour was the primary one (ibid.: 53). With Engels, Young sees the original sex/gender division of labour subsequently giving way to other divisions of labour such as slavery or class. In making this point Young argues against the idea of there being distinct systems of exploitation and oppression as represented by capitalism and patriarchy: '[T]he situation of women is not conditioned by two distinct systems of social relations which have distinct structures, movements and histories . . . capitalist patriarchy [is] one system in which the oppression of women is a *core* attribute' (ibid.: 44; italics in the original). The importance of a materialist analysis is that it does not rest on psychological or biologically essentialist explanations. Arguments about physical differences (Firestone) or child-rearing practices (Chodorow) are replaced by assertion of the direct interest of patriarchy (and/or capitalism) in the oppression and exploitation of women. The move to a materialist analysis did, however, unleash a search for the nature of patriarchy/capitalism's interest in the control of women's labour. This became known as the domestic labour debate where the primary focus was capitalism (Malos 1980), and materialist feminism where the primary focus was patriarchy (Delphy and Leonard 1992). In general, ecofeminists give priority to patriarchy as the source of women's subordination and ecological degradation, with capitalism as its latest, and most destructive manifestation. However, by paying attention to the particular experience of *western* patriarchy, the question of non-western, non-capitalist patriarchy is left rather unclear.

Young follows Elise Boulding in suggesting that the sex/gender division of labour allowed men to specialize in such a way that men could obtain control over, and access to, resources that women could not. Capitalism is only the latest manifestation of this, hence her use of the term capitalist patriarchy: 'Capitalism does not merely use or adapt to gender hierarchy . . . from the beginning it was *founded on* gender hierarchy which defined men as primary and women as secondary' (1981: 61; italics in the original). In opposing capitalist patriarchy, socialist feminists have tended to resist the cultural feminist approach of revaluing women's work. However, socialist ecofeminists are much closer to cultural feminists in this regard. Maria Mies was one of the first feminists to advocate what could be described as a materialist ecofeminist position (1986). Like Young, she addresses capitalist patriarchy, seeing 'patriarchal civilisation as a system of which capitalism constitutes the most recent and most universal manifestation' (1986: 13). Although her explanation for the male conquest of women – violence – is closer to that of Firestone, Mies's analysis rests very much on the sex/gender division of labour, as capitalist patriarchy exploits women, the natural world and the South. Central to Mies's analysis of the international division of labour is the 'housewification' of women in the North as consumer-housewives and in the South as producer-housewives' (ibid.: 126). To undermine the sex/gender division of labour by attacking the distinction between production and reproduction and to revalue women's work would therefore be to undermine the whole project of capitalist patriarchy:

> [L]abour can only be productive in the sense of producing surplus value as long as it can tap, extract, exploit, and appropriate labour which is spent in the *production of life* or *subsistence production* which is largely non-wage labour mainly done by women . . . this *production of life* is the perennial precondition of all other historical forms. (ibid.: 47; italics in the original)

Mies attacks Marx and Engels's distinction between production and reproduction, and argues that women's work is essential to reproducing the conditions of production, anticipating some of the arguments made by James O'Connor (1988). She maintains that the production of children and domestic labour is work like any other, and more essential than most. Women's work, even childbirth, is not any more 'natural' than any other form of work. All represent activities of species-being, that is, humanity in interaction with nature: 'It is of crucial importance . . . that women's activity in producing children and milk is understood as truly *human* that is, *conscious, social activity*' (ibid.: 53; italics in the original).

For Mies, women are epistemologically privileged because in their birth-giving and suckling activities, they 'can experience their *whole* body as productive, not just their hands or their heads' (ibid.). From her analysis Mies develops a 'feminist concept of labour'. Work would be defined as the 'direct production of life', which would entail a different concept of work time. The sex/gender segregation of paid work and non-paid work would need to be broken down, as would the distinction between labour and leisure (ibid.: 216 ff.). Although in this book Mies is already clearly sympathetic to ecofeminism and aspects of cultural feminism, she asks that 'New Age feminists, the eco-feminists and others open their eyes and minds to the real colonies whose exploitation . . . guarantees them the luxury of indulging in "Eastern spirituality" and "therapy"' (ibid.: 35), pointing out that capitalism can as easily deliver therapy and spirituality as it can cars or refrigerators. This is a warning well worth remembering. Although Mies's main aim was to show how the exploitation of women is central to global capital accumulation, her analysis also incorporates the basic elements of an ecofeminist analysis that would be developed in later works (1993). With Vandana Shiva, she has pointed to the importance of women's labour in basic subsistence work, particularly in the South. The invisibility of women's work and its position as an 'externality' outside formal patriarchal capitalist economic structures is gradually creeping on to the international political agenda under pressure from feminist analyses (Boserup 1970; Sen and Grown 1987; Waring 1989; Lewenhak 1992; Mellor 1992a, 1997). As Mies has argued, the failure to address the position of women means that capitalism can build upon pre-existing patriarchal structures to produce appalling hardship, where women are exploited as workers and as women, sometimes to the point of 'super-exploitation' when even their basic subsistence is denied (1986: 48).

In women's lives, particularly in subsistence economies, it is impossible to separate productive and reproductive work. It is this work of producing the means of life and of survival that ecofeminists such as Vandana Shiva argue establishes the close relations between women and the natural world. A similar point regarding motherhood is made by the Finnish feminist Hilkka Pietilä:

> Because of the way it mediates beween the biology of procreation and historical institutionalization, motherhood provides a prime site for exploring and constructing boundaries between nature and culture. Historically, the division in Western thought has been dichotomous and drawn in such a way as to exclude women from the social and the historical. (1987: 26)

It is not just that women's work is exploited by patriarchal capitalism by being unrecognized and largely unrewarded or poorly rewarded, but the nature of the work is important in understanding its relationship to humanity's immanence (Mellor 1992a, 1996a, 1997). As Sanday has argued from anthropological evidence, throughout history women have been responsible for the kind of repetitive but vital work that takes large amounts of time, thus freeing men for less essential, more intermittent, and often social, activities (1981).

In modern industrial society a great deal of this work is done by machine energy or by 'cheap' labour based on class, 'race' or sex. Women in industrialized (western) economies do not weed fields, pound grain, collect water and firewood or grow food for their families. There is still, however, a distinct body of work that is associated with women, which I have described as being associated with 'biological time' (1992a: 249 f.). Biological time represents the cycles of the human body, not only the daily needs (sleep, hygiene, food, excretion, shelter, clothing) but the cycles of health and the life-cycle itself. Human embodiment means that these cycles must be addressed. Much of this may be done by social institutions – factories, canteens, health service, educational system – but a great deal remains. One of the main crises for the older industrial economies is the care of the elderly and, ironically, a collapse in the birth rate. Women's work that lies outside 'productive' economic relations is both socially and biologically essential, meeting the immediate needs of family and community. This work is much more wide-ranging in the South than the North, although the critique of women's marginalized position in the 'private' domestic world is more sustained in the North. Charlotte Perkins Gilman has described women's domestic work as 'immediate altruism' (1915: 523). It is immediate in the sense that it responds to the basic recurring needs, for food, personal care, hygiene of close family members. It is altruistic in that it is done on the basis of love or duty. However, as I have argued elsewhere, women's 'altruism' has been imposed on them by patriarchy through 'love', duty or even fear (1992a: 252).

While Marx has analysed the social materialism of capitalist economic relations and class systems, he has not adequately addressed the physical material relations of human immanence. In women's lives the relationship between social materialism and physical (ecological/biological) materialism is represented in the under-labouring work that women do that is not incorporated into the 'material' world of men as represented in the theoretical framework of historical materialism. Equally, the under-labouring work of non-human nature is ignored. By that token, overthrowing capital will not resolve the 'second contradiction' of the conditions of production for either women or nature. The ecological catastrophes of the command economies of Eastern Europe are evidence of this, together with their domestic exploitation of women.

Women and nature: a matter of time

The rhythms of the environment and the body are inseparable from human being, from well-being and from everyday social life. (Adam 1995: 45)

Ignoring women's role in meeting the needs of biological time produces a public world that can compartmentalize human existence. As a result, decisions can be made which do not take account of the complexities of human existence, which are based on transcendence not immanence. The fiction of 'economic man' (or for that matter (male) class warrior) ignores the realities of human existence as embodied beings, and the way that social space and time is constructed (Mellor 1997). Failure to take account of human embodiment in all its facets enables 'economic man' or 'class warrior' to ignore the wider implications of human biological and ecological embeddedness. Failure to recognize women's work means that male-dominated capitalism (and socialism) is constructed on a false premise, of the independently functioning individual. This individual is reflected in economic terms as 'free' labour or as 'economic man' and in political terms as the (private) citizen. Only a small minority of men, and an even smaller minority of women, actually achieve sufficient power to function independently, socially, politically or economically, but that does not prevent the public world from being constructed on that basis. It is this idea of the abstract, autonomous individual that ecofeminists see as represented in the hierarchical dualisms of western culture. As I have described elsewhere, the world of capitalist and socialist patriarchy is based on an idealized male–experience–reality (ME-reality) as against the tangible and actualized women's–experience–reality (WE-reality) (Mellor 1992a: 258). In this sense a feminist analysis that focuses upon women's experience is a more firmly grounded materialism than the Marxist emphasis on the predominantly 'male experience' of the public world of production. By separating production from 'reproduction' and from nature, capitalist (and socialist) patriarchy has created a sphere of 'false' freedom that ignores biological and ecological parameters. For most people the experience of ME-reality is not, however, a good one. They do not feel 'free' in their labour or able to exercise their preferences as 'economic man'. The social and economic relations of ME-reality are as exploitative and unstable as Marx predicted. Materialist ecofeminism would broaden Marx's analysis to show how ME-reality is constructed.

The integration of ecofeminism with ecosocialism cannot be achieved by trying to add women to a male-dominated productivist socialism; that has been tried many times and failed lamentably. Marxian socialism must be reconstructed to take account of the way in which the capitalist patriarchal sphere of production is materially dependent upon women, nature and other exploited groups. Ariel

Salleh, in addressing the problem of 'embodied materialism' (1994: 106), sees women's 'labor experiences' as grounds for an 'ecopolitical critique' of capitalism and as the model of a sustainable alternative. She sees women as 'mediators' of nature in four ways: giving birth and suckling, carrying out caring and maintenance chores that 'bridge' men and nature, making goods as farmers, weavers, herbalists, etc. and as a symbolic representation of nature. Salleh, like Mies (1986) and Hartsock (1983), sees these activities as giving women epistemic privilege: 'Through this constellation of labors, women are organically and discursively implicated in life-affirming activities, and they develop gender-specific knowledges grounded in this material base' (1994: 107). Like Mies, Salleh sees women's work as underpinning capitalism but also that this introduces a contradiction in what Mies and O'Connor have called the conditions of production and what Salleh refers to as the conditions of existence: 'Women's traditional positioning between men and nature is a primary contradiction of capitalism, and may well be the deepest, most fundamental contradiction of all' (ibid.: 112). According to Salleh, women as human subjects are being treated by capitalism as objects both of nature and of capital. This puts them in a position of non-identity that allows them to break out of the framework of capitalist patriarchy. Their marginal position makes them 'not quite labor' and, although they are not 'nature', they are in a position where they are able to identify with nature. In Collins's terms, women are outsiders-within (1990) in the construction of society-against-nature. Salleh sees the struggles of women on environmental issues as evidence of the political efficacy of their contradictory and marginal status.

To focus on women's work and reproductive role is not essentialist, but materialist (Mellor 1992b), as it exposes the construction of a social world which has its material base in women's time and work. Women's articulation of a perspective that reflects their social condition is not essentialist, nor does it detract from the 'primary' economic struggle with capital. In fact, as Salleh, Mies and others have argued, women's socio-economic position provides the basis of a more fundamental critique of capitalism. Women's lives are caught in a network of interconnected relationships, not as an essentialist ideal, but as a material reality. Their embodiment is also a material reality. An ecofeminist historical materialism would explore the connection between the biological differences between men and women and the social construction that is put upon them. This is not to say that biology determines the power relationships between men and women, but it does constrain them. To resolve those power relations will not mean that biological differences between the sexes will wither or be 'willed away'. As Pat and Hugh Armstrong have argued, to ignore biological differences is more likely to lead to the subordination of women than a radical politics that takes account of them (1988: 252). However, it is equally important not to overstress the importance of biological differences to the exclusion of other patterns of exploitation and domination. Many women do not carry out work that supports biological time, although they do tend to employ other women to do it for them. Patterns of inequality between women cut across this analysis. What is important about the work that women primarily do is that it illustrates the material dilemma of human embodiment. The impact of human embodiment is, however, equally illustrated by class, 'race' and colonial exploitation. To start from women's experiences is not to claim centrality or priority over other oppressions.

Conclusion

A synthesis of ecosocialism and ecofeminism would need to put sex/gender differences in bearing the burden of human immanence at the heart of historical materialism. The division of labour between men and women is neither purely biological nor purely social. It is based on sex/gender, which means that social and biological questions need to be addressed. Historical materialism must address 'embodied materialism', in Salleh's terms. In meeting human needs, as Marx pointed out, humanity is part of nature, and 'man' should have a 'continuing dialogue' with his 'inorganic' body. Marx's epithet that '[men] make history, albeit not under conditions of their own choosing' can be seen as applying as much to physical as to social constraints. Human biological differences and ecological limits are not determinant any more than are social relations; humanity can respond to them in many ways. It is also true that much of those differences and limits are themselves socially constructed. As Hartsock argued, it is necessary to identify what is social in order to be able to address the natural politically (1983: 233). I would want to argue that the converse is equally the case.

Despite Marx's early assertion of the importance of the relationship between humanity and nature, Marxist historical materialism has developed with a conception of economic relations that is concerned with social (class, property) relations at the expense of physical (biological, ecological) relations. In defining historical materialism as social materialism around production relations, and ignoring women's work and the physical materialism of human embodiment, Marx and Marxism have based their theory on economic relations as defined by capitalist patriarchy. By reifying economic relations in this way, Marxist socialism has been theoretically limited by the boundaries of the capitalist patriarchal mode of production. A similar point has been made by Maria Mies:

> by focussing . . . on this capitalist concept of productive labour . . . Marx himself has theoretically contributed to the removal of all 'non-productive' labour . . . from public visibility . . . I consider this narrow capitalist concept of 'productive labour' the most formidable hurdle in our struggle to come to an understanding of women's labour. (1986: 48)

An ecofeminist historical materialism (materialist ecofeminism) would insist that the capitalist patriarchal concept of economic relations is not seen as the sole determinant of 'material reality'. Materialist ecofeminism starts from the fact that the boundaries of women's lives are not defined by capitalist patriarchal economic relations. Women cross and re-cross the boundaries of the so-called public–private world and the society–nature dyad. At present Marxist theory reflects the historically specific structure of western capitalist patriarchy, which prioritizes the interests of some men (and a few women) against the remaining men, exploited and oppressed by 'race' and class, the vast majority of women and non-human nature. This is not to deny the exploitative reality or global dominance of capitalist economic relations or class politics, but to see them as one aspect of a much wider set of material relations and political agency. Nor is it to claim that theory or practice based on women's experience – WE-reality – will of itself confront multinational companies, end the nuclear arms race or prevent the exploitation of workers. An ecofeminism that does not embrace class or 'race' analysis would be as theoretically and politically limited as an ecosocialism that does not embrace a feminist analysis.

What cannot be assumed is that human society is so exclusively determined by its mode of production that all other social/biological/ecological structures will 'fall into line' if that mode of production is changed. Quite rightly, socialists have waged a fierce battle against all forms of naturalism and essentialism that would claim that certain aspects of human *social* existence are beyond social control. However, in defence of political action around the social it is important not overly to socialize the natural, a point I made earlier in the context of postmodernism. To do so obscures the ecological framework of human existence and leads to a mystification of the material conditions of human life. While there is no predetermined destiny in biology or ecology, it is necessary to respond politically to their reality. Not to do so would fail to confront the material reality of those who do the work of embodiment and the ecological limitations to human activity. What is needed is a deep materialist socialism that addresses immanence and the material relations that construct transcendence. Such a socialism would need to challenge not only the divisions of class society, but all the other dualisms that ecofeminists (and others) have identified.

8

Feminism and Ecology: A Material Connection

In bringing together ecology and feminism, ecofeminists see women and nature as subject to the destructive socio-economic and technological systems of modern male-dominated society. Sex/gender is put at the heart of this analysis, but this is not to exclude other cross-cutting dimensions of oppression and exploitation. To start with one oppression is not to claim that it has precedence, but to see if elements of the analysis may be useful in looking at other oppressions. It is also important that the debate about difference does not deny the possibility of undertaking a critique from *any* social perspective.

The specific focus of ecofeminism is the role of sex/gender inequality in the construction of human–nature relations. This focus does not mean that ecofeminism collapses the social into the biological/ecological, but it does not seek radically to separate them. Ecofeminism sees all humanity as embodied, and those bodies are sexed. Gender does not map directly on to sex, and sex itself is heavily socially circumscribed. 'Man' and 'woman' are the product of the interaction of biological and social factors. There is no essential or universal type of man or women, but 'men' and 'women' do exist with enough commonality to make such concepts practically and theoretically useful. For ecofeminists there are aspects of women's bodies and social experience that can usefully be explored to help understand the current imbalance in human–nature relations. This imbalance has occurred within the context of a global system that is male-dominated, specifically by men from economically dominant societies with a history of war, militarism and imperialism, nationalism, racism and colonialism.

Although ecofeminists often make generalized statements that seem to refer to all men and all women, their specific focus is the pattern of dominance that arose in European society associated with the historical development of science, technology, industrialism and capitalism. This is not to ignore the fact that earlier societies have been ecologically destructive (Ponting 1991) or that ecologically benign societies can be patriarchal. It could be argued that male-domination and women's oppression have been more ubiquitous in history than ecological destruction. The interesting question for ecofeminists is the way in which the two have come together in the present era. Ecofeminists see the origins of the present ecological crisis as lying in the specific material and cultural developments of the North/West as reflected in socio-economic structures, science and technology, philosophy and religion. Judaeo-Christianity, with its assertion of God's gift to 'Man' of domination over the natural world, has morally justified ecological exploitation. Woman's subordination has also been justified through her historical blame for the 'fall' of man from ecological and social grace in the plentiful and peaceful Garden of Eden. The emphasis on human-centredness and individualism in western philosophy has laid the moral basis for consumerism, private ownership and profit-seeking, which drives both ecological and human exploitation. Western religion and philosophy have underpinned the interventionist, reductionist and amoral approach to the natural world in western science and technology that services economic and military expansion. All these developments have been dominated by white men, usually from middle- or upper-class backgrounds. 'Race', class and sex/gender are therefore inextricably intertwined.

What is distinctive about ecofeminism is that it sees the subordination of women and ecological destruction as linked. The nature of this link has been central to this book. If, as affinity ecofeminists suggest, this link is between all women and nature, the specificity of western society is problematic. However, as we have seen very few ecofeminists ultimately rest their case on biological determinism. Even where a universalized notion of patriarchy is proposed, the political focus is upon the western form. This would lead to a more socially and historically contingent view of the relation between women's subordination and ecological destruction. They have come together at a particular historical point and in a particular socio-cultural formation. Ecofeminists disagree about where, historically, this point comes. Some suggest that the dawn of (European) history came with the invasion of 'matriarchal' Old Europe by patriarchal 'Kurgans', others with (western) male-dominated religion, philosophy or science, and yet others with the emergence of hierarchy, private property or industrial capitalism.

Whatever the historical location or explanation given, ecofeminists have a strong, not a weak, notion of contingency. As Plumwood argues, the connection between women and nature points to 'structure not coincidence' (1994: 64). For many ecofeminists, particularly those with a theological or a philosophical background, this structure resides in the forms of knowledge and belief that justify and sustain western patriarchy. In particular, the Christian and rationalist rejection of the body and the prioritization of mind or soul (Ruether 1975). Women are essentialized, naturalized and condemned by their association with the body. I have argued that a purely cultural explanation for the oppression of women and exploitation of nature lacks any material or historical explanation of why this should occur. It is an idealist perspective whose only political solution is a struggle around ideas. Instead, I have argued for a materialist perspective on the woman–nature connection. However, the dualism at the heart of western patriarchy is both material and cultural, based on a sharp distinction between body and mind/soul, society/culture and nature, and between men and women. From Plato's prioritization of abstract thought to Descartes' distinction between mind and body; from Aristotle's sphere of freedom in the life of the *polis* as against the sphere of necessity in the world of the *oikos*, to the Western liberal distinction between the public and the private, the hu(man) world has been constructed over and against the world of nature and the world of women. For ecofeminists it is these dualisms that have led to the 'mastery' and thereby the destruction of nature by western rationalistic, scientific and industrial cultures (Plumwood 1993).

In setting out a materialist ecofeminism, with Salleh (1994) and Ynestra King (1990), I have argued that the sex/gender division of labour around human embodiment is the crucial factor. Women are materially associated with, and largely responsible for, human embodiment, whether as paid or unpaid work. While feminists have traditionally opposed women's association with the 'natural' work of mothering, nurturing and caring, ecofeminists have followed cultural feminists in revaluing women's work. Ecofeminists have embraced immanence and not sought transcendence. The dilemma for ecofeminism is that its two elements are in contradiction to each other. While feminism has historically sought to explain and overcome women's association with the natural, ecology is attempting to re-embed humanity in its natural framework. The relationship between woman and nature is not an easy one for feminists schooled in European cultures and their offshoots. Throughout the nineteenth and twentieth centuries feminists struggled to break out of the excluded half of these dualisms. Mary Wollstonecraft in 1792 argued for the right of women to take their place in public life, both politically and economically. Similarly Simone de Beauvoir heralded second-wave feminism by railing against the limitations of a woman's body. Second-wave feminism realized that liberal notions of women's rights and opportunities in the public world could not be achieved without radical attacks on the construction of the private (family, sexuality) and the ability of women to control their own bodies and labour.

Feminists and ecofeminists have responded in various ways to the use of women's association with nature/biology as a justification for the dualist power structure that separates 'public man' from 'private woman'. The first is to attempt to transcend or 'jump' the barrier by denying its claims about women's difference. This is what liberal 'equal opportunities' feminism and Marxist feminism have tried to do. The association of women with biology/nature/the domestic world is seen as an error that can be put right through equal opportunities policies or social change through class struggle. Male/female equality is humanity's 'natural' condition. There is no fundamental or material conflict around sex/gender. Conflicts of interest that do exist are imposed by external factors such as ignorance, tradition, religion or capitalism. Through appropriate social policies these will be overcome. This position is not compatible with ecofeminism, as it does not challenge existing human–nature relations.

A second response is to attempt to dissolve the dualism by confronting and challenging the assumptions about woman/nature that it represents and the sex/gendered divisions of labour that result. Such a solution acknowledges the unequal sex/gender power relations in dualist structures, but maintains the ultimate common interest and equality of men and women. This is the solution offered by the various androgyny or gynandry (Ferguson 1989) feminisms including socialist feminism and some radical feminisms.

A third response is to see the masculine–feminine dualism as potentially complementary, although not in its current destructive form. Destructive behaviour occurs because masculine values are currently too dominant; more emphasis on feminine values are needed to restore the balance. This approach is taken by some feminist green thinkers who adopt the idea of yin and yang, the feminine and masculine spirit as complementary (Henderson 1983).

Cosmologically, the masculine and the feminine are seen as the two complementary sides of a common humanity that need to be re-combined into one whole. Bits of the human 'whole' have got disaggregated in ways that are socially and ecologically dangerous. What is needed is to put them back together. I have described this as an ecofeminine rather than an ecofeminist perspective (Mellor 1992c).

A fourth approach is to see masculine/patriarchal values as inher-ently damaging and destructive. One half of the dualism must be destroyed. This is the position taken by most affinity ecofeminists. However, despite their strong links with radical/cultural feminism and emphasis on women's embodiment, most affinity ecofeminists do not see *men* and *women* as in fundamental conflict. Despite the initial impression given by their rhetorical language and condemna-tion of man/male and praise for women/the female, most do not see men as a lost cause. The problem arises with patriarchal structures which 'emerge' as cultural forms. When these structures are con-fronted and defeated men and women can adopt a suitably earth-centred approach. Unlike the ecofeminine approach, this perspective would prioritize women-centred values and see male-centred values as destructive rather than complementary.

A radical difference perspective, on the other hand, would see sex/ gendered dualist structures as representing a fundamental and en-during difference and/or conflict of interest between men and women. This is the approach taken by some radical cultural feminists, some postmodern feminists, lesbian separatists, radical materialist femin-ists and some affinity ecofeminists. The problem for such a position is that there is no political solution. Men are, and will always remain, the enemy. While women's subordination could be solved if all women withdrew from all men, this could not resolve the problem of ecological destruction if resources remained in male control. Wrest-ing natural resources from men would require a physical rather than a cultural struggle, in which women are unlikely to wish to engage. Changing words and reclaiming meanings is not enough. (Some) ecofeminist spiritualists claim that they can call upon the power of supernatural forces, in particular the goddess. As with all mystical claims, belief in such assertions is an act of faith. I, personally, do not have such a faith. I do believe that human beings have a spiritual dimension to their consciousness but this is a *humanist* spirituality. It rests on human feelings, emotions and awareness. I do not doubt its power for individuals, but such feelings are equally available to the racist or the nationalist.

I want to argue for an approach that sees the sex/gender dualism as resting on the dilemma of human embodiment. The difference/ conflict based on sex/gender and the other dualisms associated with it cannot be transcended, dissolved or resolved before the whole question of the relationship between humanity and the natural world is addressed. The position I am advocating is a deep materialist ecofeminism that analyses the material relations of sex/gender in terms of the confrontation of human immanence, physical embodiment and ecological embeddedness. Like Ynestra King (and Marx) I would take the living human body as the point of departure. This is not to assume that sex/gender relations encompass the whole dilemma of the physical materiality of humanity. I see ecofeminism as contributing to a wider debate about the material relations into which humans enter when confronting their embodiment and embeddedness. Marx's historical materialism addressed the social relations of class in this context. Later analyses have seen racism and imperialism/colonialism as equally, if not more, important. These dimensions are not in a hierarchy of oppressions, but rather a matrix that cut across each other (Collins 1990).

In order to explore materialist ecofeminism as a perspective, it is necessary to bring together the green perspective on human–nature relations and a materialist feminist perspective on sex/gender relations. In this sense materialist ecofeminism is more sympathetic to deep ecology than other radical ecological perspectives such as social ecology or ecosocialism. Getting the relations between humans right will not resolve the ecological imbalance because the source of much of the conflict between humans is the unacknowledged problem of immanence. Both Bookchin and Marx have identified the dialectical nature of the relationship between humanity and the natural world. However, other aspects of their work have prioritized humanity at the expense of non-human nature. Bookchin has called for the 're-enchanting of humanity' as the focus of social and natural agency, and the later Marx and Marxism have focused upon the social construction of nature. As I have argued, historical materialism needs to be ecologically deepened back to Marx's position in his early works. Social materialism as class relations are socially constructed on the basis of the physical needs of the human species: physical materialism. No matter how sophisticated the mode of production becomes, the demands of physical materialism are never lost.

This is the insight of ecofeminism, and is common to both affinity and contingency/social constructionist ecofeminism. The needs of human embodiment are shared by all humanity but are disproportionately borne in the bodies and lives of women. In bringing together the domination of women with the domination of nature eco-feminism brought into sharp focus the central dilemma of feminism: how could women's association with nature be asserted without falling into an essentialist and naturalist trap? Ecofeminism seemed to be facing feminism with two choices: either women's affinity with nature was 'natural', or some social explanation had to be found for the domination of both women and nature. The problem with the first was that it falsely universalized the idea of 'women'. The woman who drove a Cadillac or dined at the Ritz was as much in tune with the earth (at least potentially) as the woman who washed her clothes in a river or collected wood from the forest. The problem with the second was that it could find no social explanation that was 'universal' enough to explain the way in which women were dominated across history and cultures. The domination of women preceded capitalism and industrialism, it was pre-Christian/Judaism/Islam. It existed in the more nature-oriented cultures of the East and the South. As Salleh has argued: 'this debate over the universality of feminine oppression is pure scholasticsm. Looking at the real world, can one name a single modern society not governed by men or by a token woman operating within patriarchal values?' (1992: 209).

Like Salleh, I do not see the universality of women's oppression as lying in their 'natural' affiliation with the natural world, but the connectedness of all humanity with nature. Women do have particular bodies which do particular things, but what matters is how society takes account of sexual differences and the whole question of the materiality of human existence. Women are not closer to nature because of some elemental physiological or spiritual affinity, but because of the social circumstances in which they find themselves – that is, their material conditions. Women's disproportionate responsibility for human embodiment is partly expressed in the work that women do, but also in their availability for biological needs – what I have called biological time. Whatever social lives people construct they are always delimited by bodily existence. Equally, social lives are delimited by the ecosystem.

Immanent realism: the dynamics of ecological holism

The insight of green thinkers has been to return to a conception of the natural world as having its *own* ontological status. Non-human nature is not a dead nature that transcendent humans can manipulate at will and without consequences. It is an alive nature that enfolds human beings. The ecological criticism of western culture is that its dualistic social structures and forms of knowledge ignore the fact that humanity is part of the natural world. Humanity is always immanent. Transcendence is socially constructed against 'nature'. All the theologies, philosophies and social theories that have proclaimed the ontological and epistemological superiority of humanity stand condemned for a human-centredness that amounts to hubris. The natural world is not dead or dumb or a product of the human mind. It is material, real, dynamic and always beyond human knowing.

The concept used by deep ecologists to express a nature-centred approach is ecocentrism. As I have pointed out, this can be a confusing term, as it implies a dualist divide between humanity and nature. Ecocentrism is often expressed in a way that sees humanity as outside of 'nature', particularly in the emphasis on wilderness. 'Untouched' nature is seen as more 'natural' than when peopled by human beings. Unless human beings were created by God or came from Mars they have evolved out of the physical materials of this planet, and their intelligence is part of that natural process. This point is well made by Bookchin. Humans are inside, not outside of the processes of life. They are part of the dynamics of the ecological whole. For this reason the concept I would prefer is ecological holism. Ecological holism sees humanity as part of a dynamic interactive ecological process where the whole is always more than the sum of its parts.

As immanent beings, humanity has no Archimedean point from which to assess its own conditions, let alone the complex interrelations of all the material forces in the natural world. The dynamics of the natural world exist in their own right with or without conscious human intervention or knowledge. I would agree with Stephanie Lahar that an ontology of nature is needed which sees it as *'fundamentally material and subjective'* (1991: 37; italics in the original). Lahar also calls for a 'foundational characterisation of reality' (ibid.: 36). In postmodern parlance any demand for a foundation is held suspect, demanding a humanist 'grand narrative'. I would agree that humanity cannot have a 'grand narrative' to explain its own position, as ultimately the physical conditions of human existence are beyond knowing. Ecologically, humanity exists in a condition of radical uncertainty. However, a postmodern perspective is not appropriate to ecological holism, as it still ontologically prioritizes humanity. All agency remains with human language/culture, if not with the Enlightenment 'subject'. I would concur with the thrust of Lahar's desire for a 'characterisation of reality', but would see this as a *grounding* for humanity's awareness of the radical uncertainty about its ecological and biological potential/limitations, rather than as a foundational base for certain human knowledge.

The natural world is ultimately an intransitive object of knowledge, in Bhaskar's term (1978: 21). He argues for a transcendental realism that sees the structures and mechanisms of the natural world as generating phenomena which are turned into knowledge through the social activity of science. This means that 'science is not an epiphenomenon of nature, nor is nature a product of man [*sic*] (1978: 25). Like Marx and Bookchin, Bhaskar is advocating a dialectical relation between humanity and the natural world. However, as we have seen, a dialectical view can often hide dualist assumptions. What is important is that the dialectical relationship between humanity and non-human nature is always within the framework of the wider whole. A concept like transcendental realism is misleading in this context, as it implies that humanity can 'transcend' its natural condition if only in its patterns of knowledge. In the dialectical relation between humanity and nature, the notion of transcendence gives the impression of 'outsideness'. For this reason I would prefer the concept 'immanent realism' to describe the dialectical relation between humanity and nature. The concept 'transcendental realism' does not clearly indicate a non-dualist approach to humanity and nature; 'immanent realism' indicates a much more holistic view of humanity as part of nature.

What Bhaskar argues for is a critical realism, and this is echoed by other writers in the green and ecofeminist field (Plumwood 1993; Hayward 1994; Dickens 1996). Critical realism would challenge positivist, scientific knowledge in terms of the social relations that are contained within them. As Hayward argues, 'sound critical social theory is as important as natural knowledge and ecological goodwill' (1994: 86). To this I would add the need for an immanent critical realism that would check the human-centredness of critical social theorists. Hayward, like Bookchin, sees no contradiction between an ecological approach and the continuation of the creative and critical processes of the Enlightenment. Largely, I would agree, except that I do not share their optimism about the potential ultimately to resolve the contradictions of human immanence. Critical realism, based on a purely social critical theory, will not provide a solution. From the perspective of ecological holism it remains human-centred.

Humanity's immanence will always mean that any knowledge about the natural world is bound to be partial. Even if a knowledge of all the components of the natural world was assembled, this would never reveal the dynamics of the whole. The interconnectedness of all existence means that the ultimate consequences of any particular act can never be known. Immanent realism demands, first of all, a profound awareness of the ecological whole. There are many ways in which immanence could be 'realized'. It may be possible to achieve this through a scientific understanding, but it could also be achieved through the 'spiritual' awareness that many people feel when confronted by natural forces. Equally, the physiological experience of embodiment, embracing the realities of life, love and death, could be another channel of awareness. Ecofeminist spiritualists are perfectly logical in saying that it is possible to think through the body, or experience holism as a spiritual force. It may be that ecological holism can *only* be experienced as a 'revelation', which could be described as wisdom.

Awareness of the radical uncertainty of human immanence should be the starting point of all other knowledge. This requires recognition of the *essentially* dialectical and non-dualist nature of the relation between humanity and the dynamic ecological whole. It would also recognize the independent agency of the interconnected whole. This does not deny human agency, but human agency would always need to show ecological reflexivity and humility. Such an approach does not take moral or political agency, or even scientific knowledge from humanity, in fact it makes them all more vital. The loss of the positivist scientific assumptions that the machinery of nature will be revealed cannot be replaced by an equivalent assumption of a revelation of the holistic 'meaning' of nature. If the dynamic whole is unknowable by traditional scientific methods, why should it be any more 'knowable' through an ecological metaphysics? I have criticized the latter approach as idealism. Holism has historically given rise to a number of classical cosmologies that seek to place humanity within the 'whole', such as the chain of being. Similar idealist assumptions are present in many modern ecological thinkers who share the implicit or explicit notion of harmony in nature. Even Bookchin's dialectical naturalism comes much too close to idealism with its implication of a teleology that will lead to human freedom. Why should the evolution of nature have been designed to benefit humanity? Why not rats or bacteria?

I see no reason why humanity should be in harmony with a holistic nature. Many species have evolved and collapsed again (for example, I understand that a sabre-toothed mammal has evolved and disappeared several times). What is special about humanity is that it can grasp the tenacious nature of its existence. I do not think that for humanity there is an original harmony that has been lost or a teleological harmony to come. If anything, humanity is *essentially* in conflict with non-human nature in using human consciousness and reflexivity to create a special and privileged niche. In doing this humanity is neither natural or unnatural. Therefore deep ecologists cannot say 'nature' would be better off without humanity. However, humanity cannot exist without 'nature' and as there is no 'natural' way for humanity to relate to it, human existence in nature becomes a material, political and moral question. How can we live? How ought we to live? This is human-centred in orientation and motivation but the political conclusions would need at least to recognize the ecological framework of human activity. This would not satisfy deep ecologists, but it would go much further towards balancing human–nature relations than current political theory and practice. If, as I have argued, there is no natural balance in 'nature', and as humanity cannot transcend its ecological connectedness, a sustainable connectedness for humanity would need to be created through human reason and political action – in short, a politics of human–nature relations. Such a politics would start from an analysis of the structures that have created the present pattern of malconnectedness between the dominant structures within humanity and non-human nature. For ecofeminism, the subordination of women, particularly as represented in western dualist social structures and patterns of thought, is central to understanding the destructiveness of current human–nature relations.

Materialist ecofeminism: mediating society

It is as if women were entrusted with and have kept the dirty little secret that humanity emerges from non-human nature into society in the life of the species and the person. The process of nurturing an unsocialised, undifferentiated human infant into an adult person – the socialisation of the organic – is the bridge between nature and culture. The western male bourgeois then extracts himself from the realm of the organic to become a public citizen, as if born from the head of Zeus. He puts away childish things. He disempowers and sentimentalises his mother, sacrificing her to nature. But the key to the historic agency of women with respect to the nature/culture dualism lies in the fact that the traditional activities of women – mothering, cooking, healing, farming, foraging – are as social as they are natural. (King 1990: 116)

The basic argument of materialist ecofeminism is that western society has created itself against nature. That is, power is defined by the ability of certain individuals and groups to free themselves (temporarily) from embodiedness and embeddedness, from ecological time and biological time (Mellor 1992a). Ecological time is the pace of ecological sustainability for non-human nature. Biological time represents the life-cycle and pace of bodily replenishment for human beings. It appears that throughout history women have carried the burden of biological time, and, as Shiva has argued, in subsistence economies operated within ecological time (1989). As Bookchin has pointed out (without exploring the gendered and ecological implications), this left social space and time largely in the hands of men. While men may have exploited their 'free' time in traditional society to make war, trade and politics, the position is much more dangerous in modern industrialized and militarized societies. The hallmark of modern capitalist patriarchy is its 'autonomy' in biological and ecological terms. The sex/gender and ecological consequences of economic activities are cast aside as 'externalities' (Mellor 1997). Western social and economic structures are based upon an idealized image of individuality. Western 'man' is young, fit, ambitious, mobile and unencumbered by obligations. This is not the world that most women know. Their world is circumscribed by obligated labour performed on the basis of duty, love, violence or fear of loss of economic support. To take their place in the western public world, women have to present themselves as autonomous individuals, 'honorary men', avoiding domestic obligations, undertaking them in their 'free' time, or paying someone else to carry out that work.

A materialist ecofeminist identification of women and nature is not based on an essential affinity, but reflects women's role as mediators of hu(man) society. It is not women's identity with 'nature' either as biology or ecology that should form the basis of ecofeminism, but a material analysis of the way in which male domination is created and sustained. As Mies has argued, women are one of the 'colonies' of capitalist patriarchy (Mies et al. 1988); they are 'paying the price' (Dalla Costa and Dalla Costa 1995). Women's identification with the 'natural' is not evidence of some timeless unchanging essence, but of the material exploitation of women's work, often without reward (Waring 1989). It is not even always just the work that women do, but their availability. Someone has got to live in biological time, to be available for the crisis, the unexpected as well as the routine. While materialist ecofeminism points to the particular dynamic represented in the sex/gender dualism, this is only one pattern of mediation.

Mediation involves both exploitation and exclusion; it means making time, space or resources for someone else. Mediation is not only carried out by women. In fact, many women are themselves the beneficiaries of mediation. White western women may mediate biological time for their family, but exploit the labour of others, the resources of the South and the sustainability of the earth. The world is not clearly divided into mediators and the mediated: many people stand in complex networks of mediation, on the basis of 'race', class, gender or ethnicity. The most destructive, however, are the industrialized societies of capitalist patriarchy, which rest on a huge network of mediation through exploitation and exclusion: of women, of workers exploited or excluded on the basis of class, 'race' or gender, through the expropriation of colonized lands and the exclusion of colonized peoples (Shiva 1989). In order to sustain these bloated societies, the majority of people on the earth are excluded from the benefits of its resources. The earth and most of its population are sustaining the billion or so people of 'high modernity' who represent the top two-thirds of the richer societies and the elite of poorer ones.

The word that Martin O'Connor suggests for this situation is parasitism, which seems very appropriate (1994). A minority of the human race is able to live as if it were not embodied or embedded, as if it had no limits, because those limits are borne by others, including the earth itself. Physical resources, social time and space are claimed by those who can transcend embodiment. It is lost by those who have to meet the needs of others, whether through love or obligation as wives, mothers, carers, through exploitation as slaves and workers, or through patterns of exclusion on the basis of sex, class, 'race', caste or ethnicity. In this hierarchy of parasitism no one is able to embrace immanence. All the beneficiaries and the mediators are locked into mechanisms that aim at transcendence, if only for the few. The political framework of ecofeminism is to reject transcendence as a goal in favour of embracing immanence. This would necessarily mean confronting all the hierarchical relationships that sustain transcendence. In terms of sex/gender relations, immanence is based not only on the revaluing of women's domestic 'private' work, but also on the necessity to accept the embodied nature of human lives. In this way sex/gender relations can be seen as entwined with human–nature relations. From a materialist ecofeminist perspective it is transcendence that creates patterns of exploitation, oppression and ecological degradation. These negative patterns are created by patterns of dependence that are not acknowledged. Embracing immanence means taking political responsibility for the social and ecological consequences of bodily existence.

Political agency: the standpoint of the mediator

As I have pointed out, most deep green theorists and many ecofeminists take an idealist approach to the politics of nature. This can be represented as a metaphysics of nature, recognizing or embracing the cosmological 'truth' about natural processes, or as a moral/political debate about the appropriate way to 'treat' non-human nature. Set against these approaches is the shallow environmental model of positivist scientific knowledge applying sustainable technologies in response to human self-interest. In contrast to these idealist and positivist approaches, materialist ecofeminism adopts, as its name implies, a critical materialist/structuralist analysis. The politics of nature requires a theoretical analysis of the structural dynamics of human–nature relations and a politics of practice that identifies points of structural weakness and potential political agency. The first element of both is the dynamics of the ecosystem itself. For the political suzerainty of transcendent humanity it is a point of struc-tural weakness. The radical uncertainty of ecological holism gives agency in the politics of nature to nature itself. If human activities outstrip the ability of the ecosystem to sustain them, in a paraphrase of James O'Connor's term, a crisis in the conditions of transcendence will have been reached. The agency of the ecosystem is, however, not sufficient in itself to achieve radical social change. A transcendent elite could exist quite easily within the limits of ecological sustainability if it could hold all other mechanisms of mediation in place. Capitalist patriarchy as a world-dominant system is, however, not in that position.

Capitalist patriarchy justifies its transcendence through the prom-ise of (eventually) extending transcendence to all, including those who are now locked into the hierarchical mechanisms of mediation/ parasitism. Universal transcendence is a promise that in ecological terms capitalist patriarchy cannot achieve. If it attempts to extend the patterns of consumption already achieved in the most parasitical economies, capitalist patriarchy will at some point run up against ecological limits. If capitalist patriarchy does not continue to extend its economic reach, it will fall victim to the classic Marxian problem of failure to realize profits and the inability to control ideologically those it exploits, excludes and oppresses (Mellor 1993). The limitation of Marxist theory is that it only takes account of one form of media-tion: class exploitation. Materialist ecofeminism would extend his-torical materialist analysis to all mechanisms of mediation. Political agency would rest with any peoples or groups who were exploited, marginalized or excluded by transcendent structures of parasitism: people who have lost their land, economic migrants, bonded labourers, underpaid or unemployed workers, those suffering from biological and ecological hazards, floods, drought, pollution, industrial injury, ill health, people subordinated, oppressed and exploited on the basis of ethnicity, 'race' or gender. I would not want to make the case that all or any of these groups hold the answer to ecological sustainability, or that they are likely to be more ecologically benign given the chance. The point is that their chances are limited socially or ecologically to a greater or lesser extent and this unites all these struggles. The political agency that all these groups hold is disadvantage in terms of patterns of transcendence. As with class struggle, it may be possible for the male-dominated structures of transcendence to maintain power through divide and rule; a small concession here and there, a little green trimming. This is why building coalitions and co-ordinated political action is essential. Collective power will come from networks of people and groups all over the world making these connections, building coalitions of struggle not just around ideas, but material conditions. The rather comfortable green concerns of middle Europe or the United States are not so indulgent if they are connected and identify with the campaigns of indigenous peoples for their land and cultural heritage, the position of the landless and the workless, ecologically and economically threatened communities, as well as campaigns around species and habitat.

In analysing the structures of transcendence and the points of potential struggle, materialist ecofeminism adopts a standpoint perspective. Standpoint theory argues that dominant groups can only have a partial view of real relations in society and, in fact, it is in their interest to do so. It is only from the perspective of those who are subjugated, excluded and exploited that a picture of the real situation can emerge. Although standpoint theory has been subject to much criticism, particularly from a postmodern perspective, I have defended it in this book. In terms of the arguments for a feminist epistemology I have made a distinction between claiming a privileged standpoint for all women as *women*, the claim that women gain privileged knowledge through their *particular* experience and arguing for a perspective based on 'women's experience' as an analytical concept. I argue for a critical realist standpoint based on the latter. The structures of mediation in sex/gender systems produce definite social relations for (most) women. It is not being women or having particular experiences that produces a critical perspective, but an analysis of the position of women in sex/gender systems. This analysis may be carried out by women based on their particular experience or by those who identify with that experience. What matters is that political analysis addresses and reflects structural power relations. Political agency emerges from a combination of particular experiences and structural analysis.

Patriarchy or filiarchy?

Central to ecofeminism is the fact that the majority of those who benefit from the exploitation of the planet and its peoples are men. Male domination has been almost universally dubbed 'patriarchy' (Walby 1990), often with the caveat that this does not mean 'rule by the father', but 'rule by men'. Why, then, use the word patriarchy, a word that in a traditional image of family structure implies authority, responsibility, control? A word that better captures the lack of re-sponsibility and awareness of structures of mediation in male-domi-nated societies would be 'filiarchy', the autonomy of the child/son. The son is able to 'play' because his 'mother' is sustaining him. The 'mother' here is any structure of mediation, not just the sex/gender division of labour. The 'filiarch' is a much better analogy than the 'patriarch' for the treatment of the earth and its peoples at the hands of male-dominated society. Whereas the patriarch implies authority and responsibility, the filiarch implies no such thing. He is like the child who claims his autonomy by covering his eyes and saying 'you can't see me'. Filiarchal society has covered its eyes and said 'you can't touch me, I am invincible'. Dominant groups do not 'see' subordinated peoples or the degradation of the planet. As with a child, an appeal to their sense of responsibility is unlikely to succeed. Lack of responsibility is the essence of being a child. It is necessary to pull the filiarch's hands away from his eyes and make him see. This is why a standpoint perspective is vital.

I use the male pronoun here because childhood is also gendered. For girl children throughout history, childhood barely exists as they are caught up in the daily routine of sustenance. Male children, on the other hand, have to be elaborately socialized into (male) cultural life (Cheater 1989). These son-children are, of course, not without talent; in fact they are very precocious. They develop vast edifices and intricate forms of knowledge and cultural productions. There is nothing new in this. Historically, son-children of many cultures have played their games and destroyed their environment – most notably, the people of Easter Island, who destroyed their tree cover in the competitive production of huge ceremonial heads (Ponting 1991). For this reason I am not convinced that the ecological question can be resolved by some form of 'going back'. The filiarch exists in all times and cultures. He absorbs resources, social time and space to avoid the reality of immanence and 'play' in the world of transcendence.

Avoiding reality means remaining unaware. The 'son' is, by definition, not as aware as the 'mother'. In fact, it is his very lack of awareness that allows him to exploit and exclude without engaging with the social or ecological consequences. Raising awareness must mean politically articulating the voice of the 'mother', by which is meant any mediating structure from the planet itself to colonized peoples who make the life of the 'son' possible. The voice of the mother can be heard in any structure of mediation: in the bonded labourer, the woman who has lost her access to common land, the economically and socially excluded people in the rich economies, the exploited worker, the planet itself as it creaks and groans, as well as the domestic and reproductive work of women. In this context it is not essentialist to say that women can 'speak' for nature in their role as mediators of biological time, as exploited workers or excluded peoples. Sons, of course, do not readily listen to the voice of the mother, as Lahar points out in the case of 'mother earth':

> [U]nderstanding the earth as a fundamentally feminine parent is to reduce our sense of the vast and varied subjectivities of the planet and all its life to our projections of human consciousness and to blur the diversified forms of the natural world with our own associations to human bodies, or even the particular bodies of our own mothers. (1991: 38)

The son will not listen to the 'mother' as the feminine. For this reason, claims for androgyny and complementarity will fall upon deaf ears. Non-transcendent males will hear, but they are not filiarchs. Filiarchs are defined by their lack of awareness and responsibility. They will only pay attention to the 'mother' as a structure of mediation when that structure rebels or fails. The importance in bringing together feminism and ecology is that it exposes the mediations of both the earth and women by asking the sons to acknowledge their embodiment and embeddiness and what that means for their claims for autonomy and transcendence.

Taking responsibility

Helga Moss, a Norwegian sociologist and environmentalist, has attempted to think through the patterns of mediation that sustain her as the citizen of an industrialized society (1994). Taking her inspiration from Maria Mies (1986), DAWN and Dorothy Smith (1987), Moss starts from her everyday life. She sees herself as being part of a 'global household' in that she is a consumer of things she has not produced. Someone else, somewhere else is producing the things she consumes. She does not know who or where. Her starting point of responsible consumption is to know the history of every product she buys 'from its beginnings to the point it reaches me' (1994: 240). Moss acknowledges, but does not address, the logical next step of what happens when the product leaves her. Awareness of immanence makes the concrete relations of any product virtually infinite. Who grew/extracted the raw materials? Who made the components? Who made the transport that brought it here? Who drove it? What energy was involved? How do all those people live? What do they consume to support their work? What emissions or elements will the object and the processes that created it break down into? Where will they go and with what effects? For Moss, the life history of a product destroys the liberal notion of the independent consumer and the autonomy of economic processes: 'Considering the possible, indeed probable, link between my consumption-based life-sustaining work at home and the life-destroying production at the other side of the market place opens my eyes to the fact that buying is a political act' (ibid.: 241–2). Moss therefore links all the processes of mediation in making her western lifestyle possible, based on sexism, class, racism, colonialism and ecological damage.

What must follow from such a level of awareness is the need to take responsibility for the 'costs' of transcendence, which means attempting to reduce dependence on mediation to the minimum possible, given that everyone is locked into a mesh of mediating relationships. Even basic survival makes some demands on natural resources and social relations. Merchant has argued that an appropriate response is consciously to reciprocate in structures of mediation (although she does not use this terminology) so that a partnership is created:

[J]ust as human partners, regardless of sex, race, or class must give each other space, time and care, allowing each other to grow and develop individually within supportive nondominating relationships, so humans must give nonhuman nature space, time and care, allowing it to reproduce, evolve, and respond to human actions. (1992: 188)

Structures of responsibility and reciprocity would need to replace the present dualist structures of mediation. Filiarchs would have to learn to live within their own biological and ecological space and time. This does not necessarily mean individualized self-sufficiency. Co-operative work and a division of labour would be more likely to create social space and time that could be shared. Ideally, of course, mediating activities co-operatively shared would be synonymous with social space and time. Labour in Marx's terms would cease to be alienated. Work and life would be one.

Responsibility and reciprocity would mean that in a limited world no one has any right to more than they need, and all provisioning would be as direct and responsible as possible (labour to consumption to disposal). Egalitarian and ecologically sustaining principles would apply. These are the principles of a feminist, green socialism (Mellor 1992a, 1992b, 1993). I have given the sequence of these words much thought. Should it be socialist ecofeminism? Or feminist socialist ecology? I would not want to see socialism as the adjective here – I do not want feminism or ecology defined by transcendent humanist conceptions of socialism. Feminism and ecology, on the other hand, are partial terms, addressing only particular (but vitally important) structures of mediation. I therefore think the core concept should be socialism, meaning the analysis and politics of the social relationships within which humanity organizes itself in terms of human–human relations and human–nature relations. I would want these relationships to be co-operative, egalitarian and ecologically sustainable. I see a materialist ecofeminist analysis as being one of the perspectives that can open up the path to attain that end.

At last a cheer

As I have been writing this book, some core concepts have emerged. Holism, representing the immanence of humanity in its enfolding ecosystem. Uncertainty, as the condition of human biological/ecological existence. Responsibility and Reciprocity as replacements for exploitative structures of mediation/parasitism. Awareness, at both a deep and/or spiritual level and at a practical everyday level in order to begin to live within social and ecological means. Humility, reflecting the need for humanity to learn to live without delusions of transcendence. One day it occurred to me that these spell HURRAH.

Bibliography

Abramovitz, Janet M. (1994): Biodiversity and Gender Issues: Recognising Common Ground. In Wendy Harcourt (ed.), *Feminist Perspectives on Sustainable Development*, Zed Press, London.

Adam, Barbara (1995): *Timewatch: The Social Analysis of Time*, Polity, Cambridge.

Afshar, Haleh (1985): *Women, Work and Ideology in the Third World*, Tavistock, London.

Agarwal, Bina (1992): The Gender and Environment Debate: Lessons from India, *Feminist Studies* 18, no. 1, pp. 119–58.

Alcoff, Linda and Elizabeth Potter (eds) (1993): *Feminist Epistemologies*, Routledge, London.

Alic, Margaret (1986): *Hypatia's Heritage*, Women's Press, London.

Amos, Valerie and Pratibha Parmar (1984): Challenging Imperial Feminism, *Feminist Review* 17, pp. 3–19.

Anand, Anita (1983): Saving Trees, Saving Lives: Third World Women and the Issue of Survival. In Leonie Caldecott and Stephanie Leland (eds), *Reclaim the Earth*, The Women's Press, London.

Apffel-Marglin, Frederique and Suzanne L. Simon (1994): Feminist Orientalism and Development. In Wendy Harcourt (ed.), *Feminist Perspectives on Sustainable Development*, Zed Press, London.

Armstrong, Pat and Hugh Armstrong (1988): Taking Women into Account. In Jane Jenson et al. (eds), *Feminization of the Labour Force*, Polity, Cambridge.

Asian and Pacific Development Centre (1989): *Asian and Pacific Women's Resource and Action Series: Health*, Kuala Lumpur.

Asian and Pacific Development Centre (1992): *Asian and Pacific Women's Resource and Action Series: Environment*, Kuala Lumpur.

Bagby, Rachel L. (1990): Daughters of Growing Things. In Irene Diamond and Gloria Feman Orenstein (eds), *Reweaving the World*, Sierra Club Books, San Francisco.

Bahro, Rudolf (1984): *From Red to Green: Interviews with New Left Review*, Verso, London.

Bamberger, Joan (1974): The Myth of Matriarchy. In Michelle Z. Rosaldo and

Louise Lamphere (eds), *Woman, Culture and Society*, Stanford University Press, Stanford, CA.

Barrett, Michèle (1980): *Women's Oppression Today: Problems in Marxist Feminist Analysis*, Verso, London. Revised edition 1988.

Barrett, Michèle and Mary McIntosh (1982): *The Anti-Social Family*, Verso, London.

Barrett, Michèle and Anne Phillips (1992): *Destabilizing Theory*, Polity, Cambridge.

de Beauvoir, Simone (1968): *The Second Sex*, Jonathan Cape, London.

Beck, Ulrich (1992): *Risk Society*, Sage, London.

Benton, Ted (1993): *Natural Relations*, Verso, London.

Benton, Ted (ed.) (1996): *The Greening of Marxism*, The Guilford Press, New York.

Bhaskar, Roy (1978): *A Realist Theory of Science*, Harvester Press, Sussex.

Biehl, Janet (1988): What is Social Ecofeminism? *Green Perspectives*, no. 11, pp. 1–8.

Biehl, Janet (1991): *Finding Our Way: Rethinking Ecofeminist Politics*, Black Rose Books, Montreal.

Birke, Lynda (1986): *Women, Feminism and Biology*, Harvester, Brighton.

Bock, Gisela and Susan James (1992): *Beyond Equality and Difference*, Routledge, London.

Bookchin, Murray (1980): *Toward an Ecological Society*, Black Rose Books, Montreal.

Bookchin, Murray (1982): *The Ecology of Freedom*, Cheshire Books, California.

Bookchin, Murray (1989): *Remaking Society*, Black Rose Books, Montreal.

Bookchin, Murray (1990): Ecologizing the Dialectic. In John Clark (ed.), *Renewing the Earth*, Green Print, London.

Bookchin, Murray (1995): *Re-Enchanting Humanity*, Cassell, London.

Bordo, Susan (1987): *The Flight to Objectivity: Essays on Cartesianism and Culture*, SUNY Press, Albany.

Boserup, Ester (1970): *Women's Role in Economic Development*, St Martins Press, New York.

Boston Women's Health Collective (1978): *Our Bodies Our Selves*, Penguin, Harmondsworth.

Botkin, Daniel B. (1990): *Discordant Harmonies: A New Ecology for the Twenty-first Century*, Oxford University Press, Oxford.

Braidotti, Rosi, Ewa Charkiewicz, Sabine Häusler and Saskia Wieringa (1994): *Women, the Environment and Sustainable Development*, Zed Press, London.

Bramwell, Anna (1989): *Ecology in the Twentieth Century*, Yale University Press, London.

Brown, Wilmette (1984): *Black Women and the Peace Movement*, Falling Wall Press, Bristol.

Bullard, Robert D. (1990): *Dumping in Dixie: Race, Class and Environmental Quality*, Westview Press, Boulder, Colorado.

Bullard, Robert, D. (1993): The Anatomy of Environmental Racism. In Richard Hofrichter (ed.), *Toxic Struggles*, New Society Publishers, Philadelphia.

Butler, Judith (1990): *Gender Trouble*, Routledge, London.

Button, John (ed.) (1990): *The Green Fuse*, Quartet, London.

Caldecott, Leonie and Stephanie Leland (eds) (1983): *Reclaim the Earth*, The Women's Press, London.

Capra, Fritjof (1976): *Tao of the New Physics*, Flamingo, London.

Capra, Fritjof (1983): *The Turning Point*, Flamingo, London.

Carlassare, Elizabeth (1994): Destabilizing the Criticism of Essentialism in Ecofeminist Discourse, *Capitalism, Nature, Socialism* vol. 5 (3), issue 19, pp. 50–66.

Carson, Rachel (1985): *The Silent Spring*, Penguin edition first published 1962.

Cheater, Angela (1989): *Social Anthropology*, Unwin Hyman, London.

Cheney, Jim (1987): Ecofeminism and Deep Ecology, *Environmental Ethics* vol. 9, pp. 115–45.

Cheney, Jim (1989): Postmodern Environmental Ethics: Ethics as Bioregional Narrative, *Environmental Ethics* vol. 11, pp. 117–34.

Cheney, Jim (1994): Nature/Theory/Difference. Ecofeminism and the Reconstruction of Environmental Ethics. In Karen Warren (ed.), *Ecological Feminism*, Routledge, London.

Chodorow, Nancy (1974): Family Structure and Feminine Personality. In Michelle Z. Rosaldo and Louise Lamphere (eds), *Woman, Culture and Society*, Stanford University Press, Stanford, CA.

Chodorow, Nancy (1978): *The Reproduction of Mothering*, University of California Press.

Christ, Carol P. (1992a): Why Women Need the Goddess: Phenomenological, Psychological and Political Reflection. In Carol P. Christ and Judith Plaskow (eds), *Womanspirit Rising*, HarperCollins, New York.

Christ, Carol P. (1992b): Spiritual Quest and Women's Experience. In Carol P. Christ and Judith Plaskow (eds), *Womanspirit Rising*, HarperCollins, New York.

Christ, Carol P. and Judith Plaskow (eds) (1992): *Womanspirit Rising*, Harper Collins, New York; 1992 edition.

Clark, John (ed.), (1990): *Renewing the Earth*, Green Print, London.

Clarke, Robert (1973): *Ellen Swallow: The Woman Who Founded Ecology*, Follett Co., Chicago.

Collard, Andrée with Joyce Contrucci (1988): *Rape of the Wild*, The Women's Press, London.

Collins, Patricia Hill (1990): *Black Feminist Thought*, Unwin Hyman, London.

Coote, Anna and Beatrix Campbell (1982): *Sweet Freedom*, Picador, London.

Corea, Gena (1985): *The Mother Machine: Reproductive Technologies from Artificial Insemination to Artificial Wombs*, The Women's Press, London; 1988 edition.

Costello, Alison, Bernadette Vallely and Josa Young (1989): *The Sanitary Protection Scandal*, Women's Environmental Network, London.

Dalla Costa, Mariarosa and Giovanna F. Dalla Costa (eds) (1995): *Paying the Price*, Zed Press, London.

Daly, Mary (1973): *Beyond God The Father*, The Women's Press, London; 1986 edition.

Daly, Mary (1978): *Gyn/Ecology: The metaethics of Radical Feminism*, The Women's Press, London; 1991 edition.

Dankelman, Irene and Joan Davidson (1988): *Women and Environment in the Third World*, Earthscan, London.

Davion, Victoria (1994): Is Ecofeminism Feminist? In Karen Warren (ed.), *Ecological Feminism*, Routledge, London.

Davis, Angela (1990): *Women, Culture and Politics*, The Women's Press, London.

Davis, Elizabeth Gould (1971): *The First Sex*, G. P. Putnam Sons, New York.

Delphy, Christine (1993): Rethinking Sex and Gender, *Women's Studies International Forum* vol. 16, no. 1, pp. 1–9.

Delphy, Christine and Diana Leonard (1992): *Familiar Exploitation*, Polity, Cambridge.

Devall, Bill (1990): *Simple in Means, Rich in Ends,* Green Print, London.

Devall, Bill and George Sessions (1985): *Deep Ecology,* Peregrine Smith Books, Layton UT.

Diamond, Irene and Gloria Feman Orenstein (eds) (1990): *Reweaving the World,* Sierra Club Books, San Francisco.

Dickens, Peter (1996): *Reconstructing Nature,* Routledge, London.

Dinnerstein, Dorothy (1987): *The Rocking of the Cradle and the Ruling of the World;* The Women's Press, London. First published in 1976 as *The Mermaid and the Minotaur,* Harper and Row, New York.

Dinnerstein, Dorothy (1989): Survival on Earth: The Meaning of Feminism. In Judith Plant (ed.), *Healing the Wounds: The Promise of Ecofeminism,* Green Print, London.

Dobson, Andrew (ed.) (1991): *The Green Reader,* André Deutsch, London.

Dobson, Andrew (1995): *Green Political Thought,* Routledge, London.

Doubiago, Sharon (1989): Mama Coyote Talks to the Boys. In Judith Plant (ed.), *Healing the Wounds: The Promise of Ecofeminism,* Green Print, London.

Douthwaite, Richard (1992): *The Growth Illusion,* Green Books, Hartland.

Easlea, Brian (1983): *Fathering the Unthinkable: Masculinity, Scientists and the Nuclear Arms Race,* Pluto Press, London.

d'Eaubonne, Françoise (1980): Le Feminisme ou la mort. In Elaine Marks and Isabelle de Courtivron (eds), *New French Feminisms: An Anthology,* University of Massachusetts Press, Amherst.

Eckersley, Robyn (1992): *Environmentalism and Political Theory,* UCL Press, London.

Ecologist, The (1993): *Whose Common Future?* Earthscan, London.

Ehrenreich, Barbara and Deirdre English (1979): *For Her Own Good,* Pluto, London.

Eisenstein, Hester (1984): *Contemporary Feminist Thought,* Unwin, London.

Eisler, Riane (1987): *The Chalice and the Blade,* Unwin, London; 1990 edition.

Ekins, Paul (1992): *A New World Order: Grassroots Movements for Global Change,* Routledge, London.

Engels, Friedrich (1884): The Origin of the Family Private Property and the State. In Marx and Engels (1970): *Selected Works,* Lawrence and Wishart, London.

Epstein, Barbara (1993): Ecofeminism and Grassroots Environmentalism in the United States. In Richard Hofrichter (ed.), *Toxic Struggles,* New Society Publishers, Philadelphia.

Erlich, Paul (1972): *The Population Bomb,* Ballantine, London.

Evans, Judy (1993): Ecofeminism and the Politics of the Gendered Self. In Andrew Dobson and Paul Lucardie (eds), *The Politics of Nature,* Routledge, London.

Evans, Mary (ed.), (1982): *The Woman Question: Readings on the Subordination of Women,* Fontana, London.

Evans, Mary (1985): *Simone de Beauvoir: A Feminist Mandarin,* Tavistock, London.

Faber, Daniel and James O'Connor (1989): The Struggle for Nature: Replies, *Capitalism, Nature, Socialism* vol. 1, no. 3, pp. 174–8.

Ferguson, Ann (1989): *Blood at the Roots,* Pandora, London.

Ferguson, Kathy (1993): *The Man Question,* University of California Press, Berkeley.

Finger, Matthais (1993): Politics of the UNCED Process. In Wolfgang Sachs (ed.), *Global Ecology,* Zed Press, London.

Firestone, Shulamith (1970): *The Dialectic of Sex,* The Women's Press, London; 1979 edition.

Flax, Jane (1990): Postmodernism and Gender Relations in Feminist Theory. In Linda Nicholson (ed.), *Feminism/Postmodernism*, Routledge, London.

Forum Against Sex Determination and Sex Preselection Group (1994): Using Technology, Choosing Sex: The Campaign Against Sex Determination and the Question of Choice. In Vandana Shiva (ed.), *Close to Home*, New Society Publishers, Philadelphia.

Fox, Warwick (1989): The Deep Ecology – Ecofeminism Debate and its Parallels, *Environmental Ethics* vol. 11, pp. 5–25.

Fox, Warwick (1990): *Toward a Transpersonal Ecology*, Shambhala, Boston.

Friedan, Betty (1963): *The Feminine Mystique*, Penguin, Harmondsworth; 1985 edition.

Fuss, Diana (1989): *Essentially Speaking*, Routledge, London.

Gatens, Moira (1991a): *Feminism and Philosophy: Perspectives on Difference and Equality*, Polity Press, Cambridge.

Gatens, Moira (1991b): A Critique of the Sex/Gender Distinction. In Sneja Gunew (ed.), *A Reader in Feminist Knowledge*, Routledge, London.

Gibbs, Lois (1993): Foreword to Richard Hofrichter (ed.), *Toxic Struggles*, New Society Publishers, Philadelphia.

Gilligan, Carol (1982): *In a Different Voice: Psychological Theory and Women's Development*, Harvard University Press, Cambridge, Mass.

Gilman, Charlotte Perkins (1915): *Women and Economics*, G. P. Putnam and Sons, London.

Gimbutas, Marija (1982): *The Goddesses and Gods of Old Europe*, University of California Press, Berkeley.

Goldsmith, Edward (1992): *The Way*, Random Century, London.

Gottlieb, Roger S (1992): *Marxism 1844–1990: Origins, Betrayal, Rebirth*, Routledge, London.

Griffin, Susan (1978): *Women and Nature: The Roaring Inside Her*, Harper and Row, New York.

Griffin, Susan (1989): Split Culture. In Judith Plant (ed.), *Healing the Wounds: The Promise of Ecofeminism*, Green Print, London.

Griffin, Susan (1990): Curves Along the Road. In Irene Diamond and Gloria Feman Orenstein (eds), *Reweaving the World*, Sierra Club Books, San Francisco.

Gruen, Lori (1994): Toward an Ecofeminist Moral Epistemology. In Karen Warren (ed.), *Ecological Feminism*, Routledge, London.

Gunn Allen, Paula (1990): The Woman I Love is a Planet; The Planet I Love is a Tree. In Irene Diamond and Gloria Feman Orenstein (eds.), *Reweaving the World*, Sierra Club Books, San Francisco.

Haraway, Donna (1991): *Simians, Cyborgs, and Women*, Free Association Books, London.

Harcourt Wendy (ed.) (1994): *Feminist Perspectives on Sustainable Development*, Zed Press, London.

Hardin, Garrett (1968): The Tragedy of the Commons, *Science* vol. 162, pp. 1243–8.

Harding, Sandra (1991): *Whose Science? Whose Knowledge?* Open University Press, Milton Keynes.

Harding, Sandra (1993): Rethinking Standpoint Epistemology: "What is Strong Objectivity"? In Linda Alcoff and Elisabeth Potter (eds), *Feminist Epistemologies*, Routledge, London.

Hartmann, Heidi (1981): The Unhappy Marriage of Marxism and Feminism: Towards a More Progressive Union. In Lydia Sargent (ed.), *The Unhappy*

Marriage of Marxism and Feminism, Pluto, London.

Hartsock, Nancy (1983): *Money, Sex and Power*, Northeastern University Press, Boston.

Hartsock, Nancy (1987): The Feminist Standpoint: Developing the Ground for a Specifically Feminist Historical Materialism. In Sandra Harding (ed), *Feminism and Methodology*, Open University Press, Milton Keynes.

Häusler, Sabine (1994): Women and the Politics of Sustainable Development. In Wendy Harcourt (ed.), *Feminist Perspectives on Sustainable Development*, Zed Press, London.

Hayward, Tim (1994): *Ecological Thought*, Polity, Cambridge.

Hekman, Susan J. (1990): *Gender and Knowledge*, Polity, Cambridge.

Heller, Chiah (1990): Toward a Radical Eco-feminism. In John Clark (ed.), *Renewing the Earth*, Green Print, London.

Henderson, Hazel (1978): *Creating Alternative Futures*, Perigree Books, New York.

Henderson, Hazel (1980): *The Politics of the Solar Age*, Knowledge Systems Inc., New York; 1988 edition.

Henderson, Hazel (1983): The Warp and the Weft: The Coming Synthesis of Eco-Philosophy and Eco-Feminism. In Leonie Caldecott and Stephanie Leland (eds), *Reclaim the Earth*, The Women's Press, London.

Hofrichter, Richard (ed.) (1993): *Toxic Struggles*, New Society Publishers, Philadelphia.

hooks, bell (1981): *Aint I a Woman: Black Women and Feminism*, South End Press, Boston.

hooks, bell (1984): *Feminist Theory: From Margin to Center*, South End Press, Boston.

Hülsberg, W. (1988): *The German Greens*, Verso, London.

Hynes, Patricia (1985): Ellen Swallow, Lois Gibbs and Rachel Carson: Catalysts of the American Environmental Movement, *Women's Studies International Forum* vol. 8, no. 4, pp. 291–8.

Hynes, Patricia (1993): *Taking Population Out of the Equation*, Institute on Women and Technology, Amherst.

Irigaray, Luce (1985): *Speculum of the Other Woman*, Cornell University Press, Ithaca.

Irvine, Sandy and Alec Ponton (1988): *A Green Manifesto*, Optima, London.

IUCN/UNEP/WWF (1991): *Caring for the Earth: A Strategy for Sustainable Living*, Gland, Switzerland.

Jackson, Cecile (1994): Gender Analysis and Environmentalisms. In Michael Redclift and Ted Benton (eds), *Social Theory and the Global Environment*, Routledge, London.

Jackson, Cecile (1995): Radical Environmental Myths: A Gender Perspective, *New Left Review* no. 210, March/April, pp. 124–40.

Jaggar, Alison M. and Susan Bordo (eds), (1989): *Gender/Body/Knowledge*, Rutgers University Press, New Jersey.

Jain, Shobita (1991): Standing Up for Trees: Women's Role in the Chipko Movement. In Sally Sontheimer (ed.), *Women and the Environment: A Reader*, Earthscan, London.

Jayaweera, Swarna, Malsei Dias and Nedra W. Goonewardene (1994): Women and Poverty: The Experience of the Accelerated Mahaweli Development Programme in Sri Lanka. In Noeleen Heyzer and Gita Sen (eds), *Gender, Economic Growth and Poverty*, Kali for Women, New Dehli, with International Books, Utrecht, with Asian and Pacific Development Centre, Kuala Lumpur.

Jones, Maggie and Wangari Maathai (1983): Greening the Desert: Women of Kenya Reclaim the Land. In Leonie Caldecott and Stephanie Leland (eds), *Reclaim the Earth*, The Women's Press, London.

Kabeer, Naila (1994): *Reversed Realities*, Verso, London.

Keller, Evelyn Fox (1983): *A Feeling for the Organism: The Life and Work of Barbara McClintock*, Freeman, San Francisco.

Keller, Evelyn Fox (1985): *Reflections on Gender and Science*, Yale University Press, New Haven.

Keller, Evelyn Fox (1992): *Secrets of Life, Secrets of Death*, Routledge, London.

Kelly, Petra (1984): *Fighting for Hope*, Chatto and Windus, London.

Kelly, Petra (1988): Towards a Green Europe and a Green World. In Felix Dodds (ed.), *Into the 21st Century*, Green Print, London.

Kheel, Marti (1990): Ecofeminism and Deep Ecology: Reflections on Identity and Difference. In Irene Diamond and Gloria Feman Orenstein (eds), *Reweaving the World*, Sierra Club Books, San Francisco.

King, Ynestra (1981): Feminism and the Revolt of Nature, *Heresies* 13, Fall, pp. 12–16.

King, Ynestra (1983a): The Ecofeminist Imperative. In Leonie Caldecott and Stephanie Leland (eds), *Reclaim the Earth*, The Women's Press, London.

King, Ynestra (1983b): Toward an Ecological Feminism and a Feminist Ecology. In Joan Rothschild (ed.), *Machina Ex Dea*, Pergamon, Oxford. Reproduced in Judith Plant (ed.), *Healing the Wounds: The Promise of Ecofeminism*, Green Print, London.

King, Ynestra (1990): Healing the Wounds: Feminism, Ecology and Nature/Culture Dualism. In Irene Diamond and Gloria Feman Orenstein (eds), *Reweaving the World*, Sierra Club Books, San Francisco. Also in Alison M. Jaggar and Susan R. Bordo (eds), *Gender/Body/Knowledge*, Rutgers University Press, New Jersey.

King, Ynestra (1993): Feminism and Ecology. In Richard Hofrichter (ed.), *Toxic Struggles*, New Society Publishers, Philadelphia.

Kovel, Joel (1996): Negating Bookchin. In *Murray Bookchin: Nature's Prophet*, Center for Political Ecology/Capitalism, Nature, Socialism Pamphlet 5, Santa Cruz, CA.

Krauss, Celene (1993): Blue-Collar Women and Toxic-Waste Protests: The Process of Politicization. In Richard Hofrichter (ed.), *Toxic Struggles*, New Society Publishers, Philadelphia.

Kropotkin, Peter (1955): *Mutual Aid*, Extending Horizon Books, New York.

Kuletz, Valerie (1992): Interview with Barbara Holland-Cunz, *Capitalism, Nature, Socialism* vol. 3 (2), pp 11–16.

LaDuke, Winona (1993): A Society Based on Conquest Cannot Be Sustained: Native Peoples and the Environmental Crisis. In Richard Hofrichter (ed.), *Toxic Struggles*, New Society Publishers, Philadelphia.

Lahar, Stephanie (1991): Ecofeminist Theory and Grassroots Politics, *Hypatia* vol. 6, no. 1, pp. 28–45.

Leff, Enrique (1995): *Green Production: Toward an Environmental Rationality*, The Guilford Press, New York.

Leland, Stephanie (1983): Feminism and Ecology: Theoretical Considerations. In Leonie Caldecott and Stephanie Leland (eds), *Reclaim the Earth*, The Women's Press, London.

Lewenhak, Sheila (1992): *The Revaluation of Women's Work*, Earthscan, London.

Liddington, Jill (1989): *The Long Road to Greenham*, Virago, London.

Lloyd, Genevieve (1984): *The Man of Reason. 'Male' and 'Female' in Western Philosophy*, Methuen, London.

Lorde, Audre (1980): An Open Letter to Mary Daly. In Audre Lorde (1984): *Sister Outsider*, The Crossing Press, Trumansburg, New York.

Lovelock, James (1979): *Gaia*, Oxford University Press, Oxford.

MacCormack, Carol P. (1980): Nature, Culture and Gender: A Critique. In Carol P. MacCormack and Marilyn Strathern (eds), *Nature, Culture and Gender*, Cambridge University Press, Cambridge.

McKibben, Bill (1990): *The End of Nature*, Penguin, Harmondsworth.

McLaughlin, Andrew (1993): *Regarding Nature: Industrialism and Deep Ecology*, SUNY, New York.

McLennan, Gregor (1995): Feminism, Epistemology and Postmodernism: Reflections on Current Ambivalence, *Sociology* vol. 29, no. 3, pp. 391–409.

Malos, Ellen (ed.) (1980): *The Politics of Housework*, Allison and Busby, London.

Manes, Christopher (1990): *Green Rage*, Little Brown, Boston.

Marx, Karl and Friedrich Engels (1970): *The German Ideology*, Lawrence and Wishart, London.

Maynard, Mary (1994): Methods, Practice and Epistemology; The Debate about Feminism and Research. In Mary Maynard and June Purvis (eds), *Researching Women's Lives from a Feminist Perspective*, Taylor and Francis, London.

Meadows, D., H. J. Randers, and W. W. Behrens (1972): *The Limits to Growth*, Universe Books, New York.

Mellor, Mary (1992a): *Breaking the Boundaries: Towards a Feminist Green Socialism*, Virago, London.

Mellor, Mary (1992b): Ecofeminism and Ecosocialism: Dilemmas of Essentialism and Materialism, *Capitalism, Nature, Socialism*, vol. 3 (2), pp. 1–20.

Mellor, Mary (1992c): Green Politics: Ecofeminist, Ecofeminine or Ecomasculine? *Environmental Politics*, vol. 1 (2), pp. 229–51.

Mellor, Mary (1993): Building a New Vision: Feminist Green Socialism. In Richard Hofrichter (ed.), *Toxic Struggles*, New Society Publishers, Philadelphia.

Mellor, Mary (1996a): Myths and Realities: A Reply to Cecile Jackson, *New Left Review* no. 217, pp. 132–7.

Mellor, Mary (1996b): The Politics of Women and Nature: Affinity, Contingency or Material Relation? *Journal of Political Ideologies* vol. 1, no. 2, pp. 147–64.

Mellor, Mary (1997): Women, Nature and the Social Construction of 'Economic Man', *International Journal of Ecological Economics*, vol. 20, no. 2, pp. 129–140.

Merchant, Carolyn (1983): *The Death of Nature*, Harper and Row, New York, first published 1980.

Merchant, Carolyn (1990): Ecofeminism and Feminist Theory. In Irene Diamond and Gloria Feman Orenstein (eds), *Reweaving the World*, Sierra Club Books, San Francisco.

Merchant, Carolyn (1992): *Radical Ecology*, Routledge, London.

Mies, Maria (1986): *Patriarchy and Accumulation on a World Scale*, Zed Press, London.

Mies, Maria, Veronika Bennholdt-Thompson and Claudia von Werlhof (1988): *Women: The Last Colony*, Zed Press, London.

Mies, Maria and Vandana Shiva (1993): *Ecofeminism*, Zed Press, London.

Miles, Rosalind (1988): *The Women's History of the World*, Penguin, Harmondsworth.

Millet, Kate (1970): *Sexual Politics*, Avon Books, New York.

Mitter, Swasti (1986): *Common Fate, Common Bond*, Pluto, London.

Moss, Helga (1994): Consumption and Fertility. In Wendy Harcourt (ed.), *Feminist Perspectives on Sustainable Development*, Zed Press, London.

Murphy, Raymond (1994): *Rationality and Nature*, Westview, Oxford.

Naess, Arne (1973): The Shallow and the Deep, Long Range Ecology Movement, *Inquiry* vol. 16, pp. 95–9.

Naess, Arne (1988): Deep Ecology and Ultimate Premises, *The Ecologist* vol. 18, nos. 4/5, pp. 128–32.

Naess, Arne (1990): Deep Ecology. In Andrew Dobson (ed.), *The Green Reader*, André Deutsch, London.

Narayan, Uma (1989): The Project of Feminist Epistemology: Perspectives from a Non-Western Feminist. In Alison M. Jaggar and Susan R. Bordo (eds), *Gender/ Body/Knowledge*, Rutgers University Press, New Jersey.

Newman, Penny (1994): Killing Legally with Toxic Waste: Women and the Environment in the United States. In Vandana Shiva (ed.), *Close to Home*, New Society Publishers, Philadelphia.

Nicholson, Linda (ed.) (1990): *Feminism/Postmodernism*, Routledge, London.

Noddings, Nel (1984): *Caring*, University of California Press, Berkeley.

O'Brien, Mary (1981): *The Politics of Reproduction*, Routledge and Kegan Paul, London.

O'Connor, James (1988): Capitalism, Nature, Socialism: A Theoretical Introduction, *Capitalism, Nature, Socialism* Issue 1, pp. 11–38.

O'Connor, Martin (1994): On the Misadventures of Capitalist Nature. In Martin O'Connor (ed.), *Is Capitalism Sustainable?* The Guilford Press, New York.

Oakley, Ann (1972): *Sex, Gender and Society*, Temple Smith, London.

Omvedt, Gail (1989): India's Movements for Democracy: Peasant, 'Greens', Women's and People's Power, *Race and Class* vol. 31 (2), pp. 37–46.

Omvedt, Gail (1994): 'Green Earth, Women's Power, Human Liberation': Women in Peasant Movements in India. In Vandana Shiva (ed.), *Close to Home*, New Society Publishers, Philadelphia.

Ortner, Sherry (1974): Is Female to Male as Nature is to Culture. In Michelle Z. Rosaldo and Louise Lamphere (eds), *Woman, Culture, Society*, Stanford Univeristy Press, Stanford; reproduced in Mary Evans (ed.), *The Woman Question*, Fontana, London.

Ostergaard, Lise (ed.), (1992): *Gender and Development*, Routledge, London.

Paehlke, Robert (1989): *Environmentalism and the Future of Progressive Politics*, Yale University Press, New Haven.

Parkin, Sara (1989): *Green Parties*, Heretic Books, London.

Parsons, Howard L. (1977): *Marx and Engels on Ecology*, Greenwood, London.

Pepper, David (1993): *Ecosocialism*, Routledge, London.

Pietilä, Hilkka (1987): Alternative Development with Women in the North. Paper given to Third International Interdisciplinary Congress of Women Dublin, 6–10 July, also published in Johan Galtung and Mars Friberg (eds.), Alternativen Akademilitteratur, Stockholm 1986.

Pietilä, Hilkka and Jeanne Vickers (1990): *Making Women Matter*, Zed Books, London.

Plant, Judith (ed.) (1989): *Healing the Wounds: The Promise of Ecofeminism*, Green Print, London.

Plumwood, Val (1986): Ecofeminism: An Overview and Discussion of Positions and Arguments, *Australasian Journal of Philosophy*, Supplement to vol. 64, June, pp. 120–38.

Plumwood, Val (1990): Women, Humanity and Nature. In Sean Sayers and Peter

Osborne (eds), *Socialism, Feminism and Philosophy*, Routledge, London (originally published in Radical Philosophy, Spring 1988).

Plumwood, Val (1993): *Feminism and the Mastery of Nature*, Routledge, London.

Plumwood, Val (1994): The Ecopolitics Debate and the Politics of Nature. In Karen Warren (ed.), *Ecological Feminism*, Routledge, London.

Ponting, Clive (1991): *A Green History of the World*, Penguin, London.

Porritt, Jonathon (1984): *Seeing Green*, Blackwell, Oxford.

Programme of the German Green Party (1983): Heretic Books, London.

Rao, Brinda (1989): Struggling for Production Conditions and Producing Conditions of Emancipation: Women and Water in Rural Maharashtra, *Capitalism, Nature, Socialism* Issue 2, pp. 65–82.

Reed, Evelyn (1975): *Women and Evolution: From Matriarchal Clan to Patriarchal Family*, Pathfinder, New York.

Rich, Adrienne (1976): *Of Woman Born*, W. W. Norton, New York; re-issued 1991, Virago, London.

Riley, Denise (1988): *Am I that Name? Feminism and the Category of 'Woman' in History*, Macmillan, London.

Rose, Hilary (1986): 'Beyond Masculinist Realities: A Feminist Epistemology for the Sciences'. In Ruth Bleier (ed.), *Feminist Approaches to Science*, Pergamon, London.

Rose, Hilary (1994): *Love, Power and Knowledge*, Polity, Cambridge.

Roseneil, Sasha (1995): *Disarming Patriarchy: Feminism and Action at Greenham*, Open University Press, Buckingham.

Rowbotham, Sheila (1973): *Hidden from History*, Pluto, London.

Rubin, Gayle (1974): The Traffic in Women: Notes on the 'Political Economy' of Sex. In Michelle Z. Rosaldo and Louise Lamphere (eds), *Woman, Culture, Society*, Stanford University Press, Stanford.

Ruddick, Sara (1989): *Maternal Thinking*, The Women's Press, London.

Rudig, Wolfgang (1990): *Green Politics One*, Edinburgh University Press, Edinburgh.

Rudy, Alan (1996): Ecology and Anthropology in the Works of Murray Bookchin. In *Murray Bookchin: Nature's Prophet*, Center for Political Ecology/Capitalism, Nature, Socialism Pamphlet 5, Santa Cruz, CA.

Ruether, Rosemary Radford (1975): *New Woman, New Earth*, The Seabury Press, New York.

Ruether, Rosemary Radford (1979): Motherearth and the Megamachine. In Carol P. Christ and Judith Plaskow (eds), *Womanspirit Rising*, HarperCollins, New York; 1992 edition.

Ruether, Rosemary Radford (1989): Toward an Ecological-Feminist Theory of Nature. In Judith Plant (ed.), *Healing the Wounds: The Promise of Ecofeminism*, Green Print, London.

Sachs, Wolfgang (1993): *Global Ecology*, Zed Press, London.

Salleh, Ariel (1984): Deeper than Deep Ecology, *Environmental Ethics* vol. 6, pp. 335–41.

Salleh, Ariel (1992): The Ecofeminism/Deep Ecology Debate: A Reply to Patriarchal Reason, *Environmental Ethics* vol. 14, Fall, pp. 195–216.

Salleh, Ariel (1994): Nature, Woman, Labour, Capital: Living the Deepest Contradiction. In Martin O'Connor (ed.), *Is Capitalism Sustainable?* Guilford, New York.

Salleh, Ariel (1996): Social Ecology and the 'The Man Question', *Environmental Politics* vol. 5, no. 2, pp. 258–73.

Salleh, Ariel, Martin O'Connor, James O'Connor, and Daniel Faber (1991): Discussion: Eco-Socialism/Eco-feminism, *Capitalism, Nature, Socialism* vol. 2 (1), issue 6, pp. 129–40.

Sanday, Peggy (1981): *Female Power and Male Dominance*, Cambridge University Press, Cambridge.

Sargent Lydia (ed.) (1981): *The Unhappy Marriage of Marxism and Feminism*, Pluto, London.

Sayers, Janet (1982): *Biological Politics: Feminist and Anti-Feminist Perspectives*, Tavistock Publications, London.

Schumacher, E. F. (1973): *Small is Beautiful*, Blond and Briggs, London.

Scott, Joan W. (1991): Deconstructing Equality-versus-Difference: or the Uses of Poststructuralist Theory for Feminism. In Marianne Hirsch and Evelyn Fox Keller (eds), *Conflicts in Feminism*, Routledge, London.

Seager, Joni (1993): *Earth Follies Feminism, politics and the environment*, Earthscan, London.

Segal, Lynne (1987): *Is the Future Female?* Virago, London.

Sen, Gita (1994): Women, Poverty and Population: Issues for the Concerned Environmentalist. In Wendy Harcourt (ed.), *Feminist Perspectives on Sustainable Development*, Zed Press, London.

Sen, Gita and Caren Grown (1987): *Development, Crises and Alternative Visions*, Monthly Review, New York.

Shiva, Vandana (1989): *Staying Alive*, Zed Press, London.

Shiva, Vandana (1993): *Monocultures of the Mind*, Zed Press, London.

Shiva, Vandana (ed.) (1994): *Close to Home*, New Society Publishers, Philadelphia.

Shiva, Vandana (1994): The Seed and the Earth: Biotechnology and the Colonisation of Regeneration. In Vandana Shiva (ed.), *Close to Home*, New Society Publishers, Philadelphia.

Simons, Margaret and S. Benjamin (1979): Simone de Beauvoir: An Interview, *Feminist Studies* 5, pp. 330–45.

Singer, Peter (1976): *Animal Liberation: A New Ethic for Our Treatment of Animals*, Jonathan Cape, London.

Smith, Dorothy (1987): *The Everyday World as Problematic: A Feminist Sociology*, Open University Press, Milton Keynes.

Snitow, Ann (1992): Feminism and Motherhood: An American Reading, *Feminist Review* 40, pp. 32–51.

Sontheimer, Sally (ed.), (1991): *Women and the Environment: A Reader*, Earthscan Publications, London.

Soper, Kate (1995): *What is Nature?* Blackwell, Oxford.

Spelman, Elizabeth V. (1988): *Inessential Woman*, The Women's Press, London.

Spretnak, Charlene (1982): *The Politics of Women's Spirituality*, Doubleday, New York.

Spretnak, Charlene (1985): The Spiritual Dimension of Green Politics. In Charlene Spretnak and Fritjof Capra, *Green Politics*, Paladin, Glasgow.

Spretnak, Charlene (1990): Ecofeminism: Our Roots and Flowering. In Irene Diamond and Gloria Feman Orenstein (eds), *Reweaving the World*, Sierra Club Books, San Francisco.

Spretnak, Charlene (1991): *States of Grace*, HarperCollins, New York.

Spretnak, Charlene and Fritjof Capra (1985): *Green Politics*, Paladin, Glasgow.

Starhawk (1982): *Dreaming the Dark: Magic, Sex and Politics*, Beacon Press, Boston.

Starhawk (1987): *Truth or Dare: Encounters with Power, Authority and Mystery*, Harper and Row, San Francisco.

Starhawk (1990): Power, Authority and Mystery: Ecofeminism and Earth-based Spirituality. In Irene Diamond and Gloria Feman Orenstein (eds), *Reweaving the World*, Sierra Club Books, San Francisco.

Stone, Merlin (1976): *When God was a Woman*, Harcourt Brace, New York.

Swimme, Brian (1990): How to Heal a Lobotomy. In Irene Diamond and Gloria Feman Orenstein (eds), *Reweaving the World*, Sierra Club Books, San Francisco.

Teverson, Rosemary (1991): *Survival of the Fairest. Can Women Make it to the Top in the Conservation Movement?* British Association of Nature Conservationists, Newbury, Berks.

Thrupp, Lori-Ann (1989): Discussion: The Struggle for Nature: Replies, *Capitalism, Nature, Socialism* vol. 3, pp. 169–74.

Tokar, Brian (1987): *The Green Alternative*, R. and E. Miles, San Pedro, CA.

Tokar, Brian (1990): Eco-Apocalypse, *New Internationalist* no. 210, pp. 14–15.

Wainwright, Hilary (1994): *Arguments for a New Left*, Blackwell, Oxford.

Walby, Sylvia (1990): *Theorizing Patriarchy*, Blackwell, Oxford.

Ward, Barbara (1966): *Spaceship Earth*, Penguin, Harmondsworth.

Ward, Barbara and René Dubos (1972): *Only One Earth*, Penguin, Harmondsworth.

Waring, Marilyn (1989): *If Women Counted*, Macmillan, London.

Warren, Karen J. (1987): Feminism and Ecology: Making Connections, *Environmental Ethics* 9 (1), pp. 3–20.

Warren, Karen J. (1990): The Power and Promise of Ecological Feminism, *Environmental Ethics* 12 (2), pp. 121–46.

Warren, Karen J. (ed.) (1994): *Ecological Feminism*, Routledge, London.

Warren, Karen J. (ed.) (1996): *Ecological Feminist Philosophies*, Indiana University Press, Bloomington.

Weizsacker, Christine von (1993): Competing Notions of Biodiversity in Wolfgang Sachs (ed.), *Global Ecology*, Zed Press, London.

Women's Environmental Network (WEN) (1989): *Women, Environment, Development*, Seminar Report WEN, London.

World Commission on Environment and Development (1987): *Our Common Future*, Oxford University Press, Oxford.

Young, Iris Marion (1981): Beyond the Unhappy Marriage: A Critique of Dual Systems Theory. In L Sargent (ed.), *The Unhappy Marriage of Marxism and Feminism*, Pluto, London.

Young, Iris Marion (1985): Humanism, Gynocentrism and Feminist Politics, *Women's Studies International Forum* vol. 8, no. 3, pp. 173–83.

Young, Iris Marion (1990): *Throwing Like a Girl*, Indiana University Press, Bloomington.

Zimmerman, Michael E. (1987): Feminism, Deep Ecology and Environmental Ethics, *Environmental Ethics* vol. 9, pp. 21–44.

Zimmerman, Michael E. (1990): Deep Ecology and Ecofeminism: The Emerging Dialogue. In Irene Diamond and Gloria Feman Orenstein (eds), *Reweaving the World*, Sierra Club Books, San Francisco.

Index